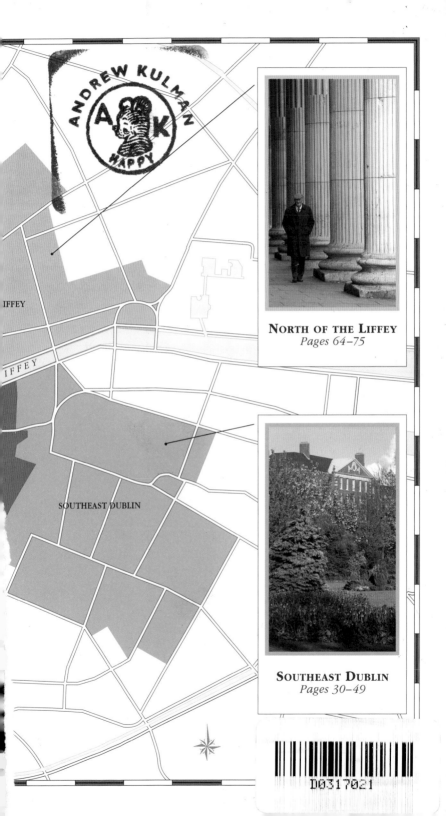

IFFEY

IFFEY

NORTH OF THE LIFFEY
Pages 64–75

SOUTHEAST DUBLIN

SOUTHEAST DUBLIN
Pages 30–49

John Short

003531 284/252.

EYEWITNESS *Travel Guides*

DUBLIN

EYEWITNESS *TRAVEL GUIDES*

DUBLIN

Main Contributor: TIM PERRY

DORLING KINDERSLEY

LONDON • NEW YORK • SYDNEY • MOSCOW

www.dk.com

A DORLING KINDERSLEY BOOK

www.dk.com

PROJECT EDITOR Claire Folkard
ART EDITOR Jo Doran
EDITOR Freddy Hamilton
DESIGNERS Paul Jackson, Nicola Rodway
MAP CO-ORDINATOR David Pugh

MANAGING EDITOR Fay Franklin
MANAGING ART EDITOR Annette Jacobs
SENIOR MANAGING EDITOR Vivien Crump
DEPUTY ART DIRECTOR Gillian Allan
EDITORIAL DIRECTOR Douglas Amrine

PRODUCTION Jo Blackmore
PICTURE RESEARCH Victoria Peel
DTP DESIGNERS Rachel Symons, Lee Redmond

MAPS
Richie Toomey (ERA-Maptec Ltd, Dublin, Ireland)

PHOTOGRAPHERS
Joe Cornish, Tim Daly, Magnus Rew, Antony Souter, Alan Williams

ILLUSTRATORS
Stephen Conlin, Gary Cross, Claire Littlejohn,
Maltings Partnership, Robbie Polley, John Woodcock

Film output by Graphical Innovations, London
Reproduced in Singapore by Colourscan
Printed and bound by L. Rex Printing Company Limited, China

First published in Great Britain in 1999
by Dorling Kindersley Limited
9 Henrietta Street, London WC2E 8PS

Copyright 1999 © Dorling Kindersley Limited, London

ISBN 0 7513 1151 0

◁ **Government Buildings at dusk**

Façade of St Teresa's Church

CONTENTS

INTRODUCING DUBLIN

**View across the tombstones of
Glasnevin Cemetery**

Bookcases of rare books in Marsh's Library

Traditional Dublin dish of oysters, often consumed with Guinness

Interior of Avondale House, the home of Charles Stewart Parnell

Sheep on the farm at Newbridge Demesne, west of Dublin

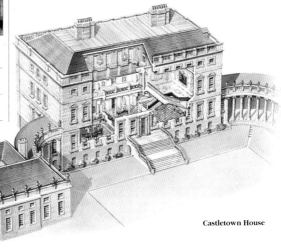

Castletown House

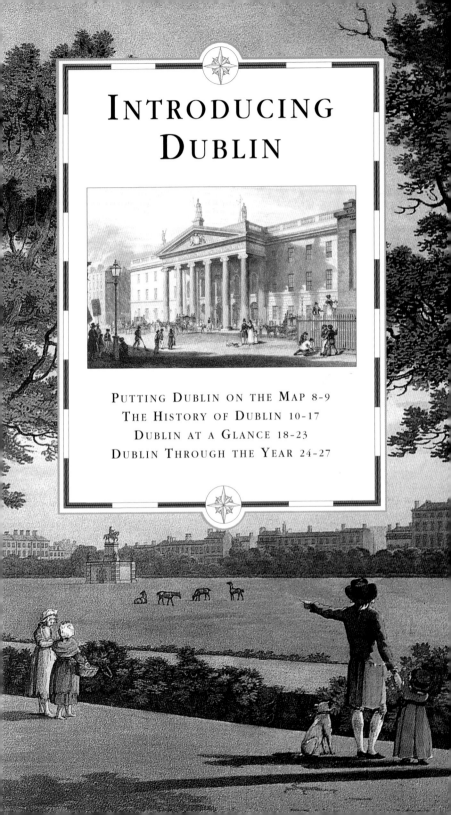

INTRODUCING DUBLIN

Putting Dublin on the Map

D UBLIN IS THE CAPITAL of the Republic of Ireland,
which takes up 85 per cent of Ireland, an island
that lies in the far northwest of Europe. Dublin sits
on the eastern coast of Ireland, on the Irish Sea, which
separates Ireland from Great Britain. The Liffey is the
main river running through the city. Dublin and its
surrounding county have a population of just over
one million, and good international communications.

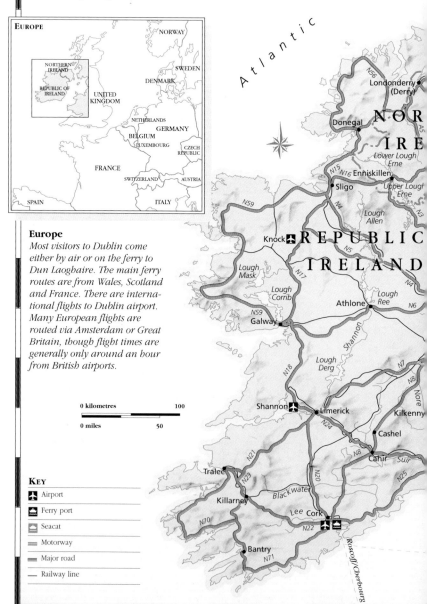

EUROPE

NORWAY

NORTHERN
IRELAND

SWEDEN

DENMARK

REPUBLIC OF
IRELAND

UNITED
KINGDOM

NETHERLANDS

GERMANY

BELGIUM

LUXEMBOURG

CZECH
REPUBLIC

FRANCE

SWITZERLAND

AUSTRIA

SPAIN

ITALY

Europe

*Most visitors to Dublin come
either by air or on the ferry to
Dun Laoghaire. The main ferry
routes are from Wales, Scotland
and France. There are international flights to Dublin airport.
Many European flights are
routed via Amsterdam or Great
Britain, though flight times are
generally only around an hour
from British airports.*

0 kilometres   100

0 miles   50

KEY

✈ Airport

⛴ Ferry port

🚢 Seacat

━ Motorway

━ Major road

— Railway line

Atlantic Ocean

N56

Londonderry
(Derry)

Donegal

N O R

I R E

Lower Lough
Erne

N15 N16 Enniskillen

Sligo

Upper Lough
Erne

N59

Lough
Allen

N4

Knock ✈ R E P U B L I C

N5

I R E L A N D

N4

Lough
Mask

N17

Lough
Corrib

Athlone

Lough
Ree

N6

N59

Galway

Shannon

Lough
Derg

N7

N18

N8

Nore

Shannon ✈

Limerick

Kilkenny

N24

Cashel

Tralee

N21

N8

Cahir

Suir

N23

Blackwater

N20

N25

Killarney

Lee

Cork ✈⛴🚢

N70

N22

Bantry

N71

Roscoff/Cherbourg

GREATER DUBLIN

Swords

Malahide

N3

Dublin
Airport

N2

Finglas

M50

Royal Canal

Glasnevin

Marino

Howth

Liffey

N4

Lucan

Kilmainham

Dublin

Grand Canal

Ballsbridge

Dublin Bay

Clondalkin

Rathmines

N81

Blackrock

M50

Dundrum

N11

Dun
Laoghaire

0 km   5

0 miles   5

Greater Dublin

Nearly one third of the Republic's population lives in Dublin. Nevertheless the city is relatively uncongested and access to the centre from the ports and airport is easy.

SCOTLAND

Islay

Arran

Glasgow

A83

A83

A7

North Channel

Coleraine

Cairnryan

A2

A37

A26

A6

A36

Larne

Stranraer

A75

THERN

M2

Lough Neagh

Belfast

ENGLAND

A595

LAND

A4

M1

Armagh

M1

Newry

A1

A5

M2

A3

Dundalk

N1

Isle of Man

Douglas

A63

M6

OF

Drogheda

Irish Sea

Boyne

N4

Manchester

M62

DUBLIN

Liverpool

M62

Liffey

M50

Dun Laoghaire

M56

M6

Holyhead

A5

A55

A5

Carlow

A487

A470

M54

Barrow

Slaney

N11

Severn

N25

Wexford

M50

Waterford

Rosslare

WALES

Channel

Fishguard

George's

A487

M4

St

A40

A41

Pembroke

M4

M5

Le Havre/Cherbourg

Swansea

M4

CARDIFF

Bristol

Bristol Channel

M5

ADDRESS TO
Chas S. Parnell, Esq.
President of the Irish National Land League.

Sir,

a hearty Cead Mile Failte home again to the country you have so nobly served during your brief sojourn in the United States. Short as your stay has been in that mighty Western Republic it has nevertheless been signalised by the most splendid and opportune services to the present wants of our starving people, while being at the same time pregnant with encouraging hope for the future welfare of our fatherland. While thousands of families, pauperised through the operation of an infamous land system have been saved by your wondrous and indefatigable exertions from the fate which befel our famine-slaughtered kindred in '47 and '48, the heart of Ireland has followed in the wake of your triumphal progress among a generous and sympathetic people, and throbbed with expectant joy as they pledged you the moral support of America in our struggle against felonious landlordism.

As the representative of the Irish People and delegate of the National Land League, you and your colleague Mr. John Dillon, have had extended to you honours and manifestations of encouragement outpassing any yet conferred by the land of Washington Franklin and Carroll upon the champions of oppressed nationalities; and your country felt proudly raised once more to the dignity of a recognised nation when the House of Representatives bestowed upon you the proud privilege of advocating the cause of Ireland before the most representative assembly of the greatest Government in the world. From the St. Lawrence to the Potomac - from the Atlantic seaboard to the plains of Minnesota - the landlord-banished portion of our people have pledged anew their fidelity to Ireland and their vows for her deliverance, when by those enthusiastic greetings immense demonstrations and military parades they welcomed you as the ambassador of their resurgent Ireland while their munificent contributions and promised continued cooperation infuses a spirit of sanguine expectation into our impoverished people that the full cause of their poverty and humiliation will soon fall beneath the united efforts of our entire race.

You are landing in Ireland at a time which may be deemed a momentous period in the history of that coercive and infamous Union which has been such a political scourge to our country and when the spirit of Irish nationality is endangered by the virulent attacks of a truculent and unscrupulous Government. We sincerely hope that you have oped across the waters like another Perseus to save the Andromeda of nations from the political monster now threatening her with national destruction and that her deliverance from immediate danger achieved you will return to the assistance of your colleagues to complete the mission you were sent on by the body of which you are the honoured and trusted head.

Signed.

Patrick Egan	J. F. Grehan	Thomas Sexton
A. J. Kettle	R. J. Donnelly	Michael Davitt

THE HISTORY OF DUBLIN

HE CITY OF DUBLIN *first took form in the early 9th century when Vikings founded one of their largest settlements outside Scandinavia on the site of the present city. Since then, it has suffered wars and conflict over many centuries. In the 20th century Dublin has established its own identity and today it is a thriving, modern city, rich in history and proud of its past.*

Archaeological digs show evidence of civilization in the Dublin area as early as 7500 BC. The 4th millennium BC saw the influx of Neolithic farmers and herdsmen who built monumental tombs such as those found at Newgrange *(see pp112–13)*.

The Celts arrived around 700 BC and things changed little for 1,000 years. When St Patrick arrived in AD 432 bringing Christianity with him to Ireland, the Celts were quick to embrace the religion. During the golden age of Celtic Christianity the Dublin area was home to several churches and it is said that the present-day St Patrick's Cathedral (built in 1192) is where the saint baptized converts around AD 450. This era produced high levels of Christian scholarship, resulting in such treasures as the elaborately decorated Book of Kells *(see p38)*.

The city's modern Gaelic name of "Baile Atha Cliath" derives from a Celtic settlement on the north bank of the River Liffey. Known then as Ath Cliathe ("the ford over the hurdles") it was the only crossing over the river and lay at the junction of four major

Engraving showing St Patrick banishing snakes from Ireland

roads. It was the community at Ath Cliathe that bore the brunt of the island's first planned naval invasion by the Vikings.

THE VIKINGS

Norse Vikings established their first harbour in Dublin in AD 841 and left in AD 902, under pressure from local chieftains. They returned 15 years later and built a stronghold situated between the present location of Dublin Castle and Wood Quay. It was here that the rivers Liffey and Poddle converged in a body of dark, still water which the Vikings called *Dyfflin* or *Dubh Linn* (or "black pool").

In 919 at the Battle of Dublin the Vikings fended off the King of Tara and by the mid-1100s they started to intermarry with the Celts. The Vikings were then defeated at the Battle of Clontarf in 1014 by Brian Boru, the Irish High King. Under King Sitric the Silkbeard, Dublin became a Christian vassal state. He oversaw the construction of a wooden cathedral (later rebuilt as Christ Church). By this time Dublin's population was around 5,000.

TIMELINE

5000–3000	600 First	AD 80 Roman	Viking silver brooch	1096 St
Ireland covered by dense woodland dominated by oak and elm	wave of Celtic invaders	general Agricola considers invasion of Ireland from Britain	795 First Viking invasion of coastal monasteries	Michan's Church (see p74) built

7500 BC	5000	2500	0 AD	200	400	600	800	1000	1200

2500 Building of Newgrange passage tomb *(see pp112–3)*	841 A large Viking fleet passes winter in Dublin	1147 St
c. 7500 BC First inhabitants of Ireland	*Extinct giant deer or "Irish Elk"*	432 Start of St Patrick's mission to Ireland	1014 High King Brian Boru of Munster defeats joint army of Vikings and the King of Leinster at Clontarf	Mary's Abbey *(see p74)* built

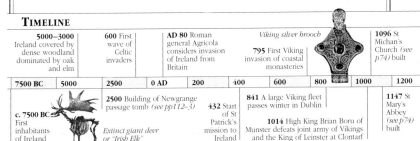

◁ **Address to Charles Stewart Parnell by the Land League**

ANGLO-NORMAN CONQUEST

Feuds in Ireland led to Dermot Mac-Murrough, the King of Leinster, asking Henry II of England to send an army to aid him. This resulted in the appearance of Richard de Clare, better known as Strongbow, in 1169. Within a year he had taken control of Dublin and married MacMurrough's daughter. He was also the instigator of the construction of Christ Church Cathedral (see pp62–3).

The Marriage of Strongbow and Aoife, by Daniel Maclise (1854)

When MacMurrough died in 1171, Strongbow was in line to succeed him. Henry II sent an army to Ireland to check his ambitions, in part by recognizing Strongbow's suzerainty over the province of Leinster. Henry then spent four months in Dublin establishing control.

Under Anglo-Norman control, the structure and size of the city grew. Fortified walls and watchtowers were built, and in 1205 construction on Dublin Castle started. St Patrick's was made a cathedral in 1220 and underwent massive expansion while, in its shadows, the Liberties, the city's earliest suburbs, were growing in strength. The city became overcrowded and in 1348 was struck by the terrifying plague known as the Black Death.

TUDOR AND STUART RULE

Like the Vikings before them, the Anglo-Normans had entwined themselves in Irish society through marriage and religion. Some of them, such as the Fitzgeralds, the Butlers and the Burkes, effectively controlled dynasties. One of them, "Silken" Thomas Fitzgerald, son of the 9th Earl of Kildare, staged a revolt against London in 1534. This was easily defeated by King Henry VIII who then, in 1541, passed the Act of Supremacy that made him King of Ireland and the head of the church which, under the English Reformation, broke from Rome. All land was the property of the English crown and, by dissolving the monasteries and sentencing to death all adult males of the Fitzgerald family, he indicated the start of a strongarm rule over Ireland and the introduction of Protestantism to the island. The reign of Elizabeth I witnessed the development of the island into a British colony, with plantations set up throughout Ireland. She made her mark in Dublin with the creation of Trinity College in 1592 as a seat of Protestant learning, a status it

Henry VIII with Bishop Sherbourne by Lambert Barnard (1519)

TIMELINE

retained well into the 20th century. The college was built on the site of a dissolved monastery. London's grip over Ireland intensified when the Catholic ex-king of England, James II, was defeated by the Dutch Protestant William Prince of Orange (King William III) at the Battle of the Boyne, north of Dublin in 1690.

The Rotunda Hospital in 1795, Dublin's first maternity hospital

THE PENAL LAWS

Five years after his victory at the Battle of the Boyne, William III introduced the first set of Penal laws in 1695. Although this legislation did not outlaw Roman Catholicism, Catholics were prohibited from holding state office, standing for elected office, joining the armed forces or practising law.

THE PROTESTANT ASCENDANCY

While William III's Penal laws were spelling hard times for the Catholic population in the rest of Ireland, Dublin's middle classes and aristocrats (many of them absentee landlords who came to Ireland during the entertaining season) enjoyed a very comfortable existence.

William of Orange at the Battle of the Boyne

Throughout the 18th century they commissioned ostentatious homes such as Leinster House and Powerscourt House. The owners of the grand town houses employed master craftsmen from around the world, such as the German-English architect Richard Castle and the Swiss-Italian stuccodores Paolo and Filippo Francini.

Among the desirable addresses at the time were St Stephen's Green, Marlborough Street to the north of the Liffey and Ely Place on the southside. If they were ill, the Royal Hospital at Kilmainham attended their needs. Dublin also boasted the Rotunda Lying-In Hospital, the first maternity hospital in the British Isles. Much of the funding for this venture came from the adjacent and ornate Rotunda Gardens (no longer in existence), where members of high society frequently met and attended concerts. In Georgian times the privileged Protestants were able to patronize the arts: Handel premiered the *Messiah* in the city in 1742. Eleven years earlier, the still extant Royal Dublin Society was founded to promote the arts, science and agriculture. Many great academics and novelists also emerged from Trinity College, including the philosopher Edmund Burke, and Jonathan Swift, author of *Gulliver's Travels* and the Dean of St Patrick's Cathedral *(see p59)* from 1713 to 1745.

1500	1550	1600	1650	1700	1750

Trinity College (1592)
1592 Trinity College *(see pp36–7)* founded
1690 William of Orange defeats James II at Battle of the Boyne
1695 Penal code severely reduces rights of Roman Catholics
1713 Jonathan Swift appointed Dean of St Patrick's Cathedral
1541 Henry VIII declared King of Ireland by the Irish Parliament
1585 Ireland is mapped and divided into 32 counties
1649 Cromwell lands in Dublin; razes Drogheda and Wexford; Catholic landowners transplanted to far west
Plasterwork from Newman House, built in 1765
1742 First performance of Handel's *Messiah* in Dublin
1731 Royal Dublin Society founded to encourage agriculture, arts and crafts

PUBLIC WORKS IN THE 18TH CENTURY

Many of the most impressive sights in Dublin today were built during the Protestant Ascendancy, in the Georgian era.

Among the most splendid structures of this period are Castletown House (1722–32), the Custom House (1791) and the Four Courts (1786–1802). The two latter buildings were both designed by James Gandon. Dublin was also one of the first cities in the world to enjoy planned development with the inauguration of the Wide Streets Commission in 1751. Further improvements came with the National Botanic Gardens in 1789.

Commerce also helped shape the city. In the 1760s the Grand Canal was built and Ireland's most famous company began in 1759 when Arthur Guinness opened his brewery.

Lacquer cabinet, Castletown House

CATHOLIC EMANCIPATION AND RESISTANCE

Despite lengthy protests by pamphleteers and orators, the first real hint of relaxation of the penal laws came in 1782 when the Irish Parliament, led by Henry Grattan, passed a Declaration of Rights which, as well as pressing for independence for Ireland, also allowed Catholics to practise law. The unsuccessful 1798 revolt by the United Irishmen, led by Dublin Protestant Wolfe Tone, may have been instrumental in convincing the Westminster government to impose the 1800 Act of Union. This dissolved the Irish Parliament and saw the introduction of direct rule from England.

The first 19th-century revolt against British rule was led by Robert Emmet in 1803, who attempted to seize Dublin Castle. The most effective protest of the early part of the century was led by Daniel O'Connell, a Catholic lawyer, who later became known as "The Liberator" as a result of his efforts on behalf of the people who shared his religious beliefs. He supported mass peaceful protests and was elected an MP in 1828 but, as a Catholic, was unable to take his seat. In response to O'Connell's mass rallies and protests, the Emancipation Act of 1829 was passed. O'Connell was the first Catholic to be elected Mayor of Dublin in 1841 but, when he later called for a repeal of the Act of Union, he was jailed.

James Gandon's impressive Custom House, on the north bank of the Liffey

TIMELINE

1751 The Rotunda Lying-In Hospital *(see p70)* is first maternity hospital in the British Isles

1759 Arthur Guinness buys the St James' Gate Brewery *(see pp80–81)*

Guinness Brewery Gate

1791 James Gandon's Custom House *(see p68)* is built

1800 Act of Union: Ireland legally becomes part of Britain

1817 The Royal Canal *(see p83)* is completed

1828 After a five-year campaign by Daniel O'Connell, Catholic Emancipation Act is passed, giving a limited number of Catholics the right to vote

1838 Father Mathew founds temperance crusade – whiskey production is reduced by half

1845 Start of Great Famine, which lasts for four years

| 1750 | 1775 | 1800 | 1825 |

THE GREAT FAMINE AND FURTHER REBELLIONS

The history of 19th century Ireland is dominated by the Great Famine of 1845–48, which was caused by the total failure of the potato crop. Although Irish grain was still being exported to England, around one million people died from hunger or dis-

O'Connell Street shortly after the Easter Rising

ease. By 1900, the pre-famine population of eight million had fallen by

Ration card from Famine period

half. Many of the poor moved into Dublin and the middle class Dubliners moved out to the suburbs. Rural hardship fuelled a campaign for tenants' rights that evolved into demands for independence from Britain. Great strides towards "Home Rule" were made in Parliament by the charismatic politician, Charles Stewart Parnell.

SUPPORT FOR HOME RULE GROWS

In 1902 Arthur Griffin founded the Sinn Fein newspaper; its name, meaning "Ourselves Alone", expressed their central policy thrust and it soon gave rise to a political party of the same name. In 1913 the Irish Volunteers (the forerunners of the Irish Republican Army) were formed. Political freedom was increasingly important at this time of stark poverty and violent clashes between workers and employers. One of the leaders of the workers' side, James Connolly, would soon broaden his political agenda to Republicanism.

WORLD WAR I AND THE EASTER RISING

Although the Home Rule Bill made its final passage through the British parliament, its implementation was suspended due to the outbreak of war. A small contingent felt that the best time to launch an attack on British rule was when Britain was at its weakest. Hence, on Easter Monday 1916, Patrick Pearse and other members of a provisional government proclaimed the Declaration of Independence from the General Post Office *(see p69)* in O'Connell Street. Under the leadership of Countess Constance Markievicz, the band of rebels occupied several buildings.

The Easter Rising was put down within a few days but only after 300 citizens were killed and much of the city centre razed to the ground. The British forces lost patience with the Irish cause and the main rebels were shot for treason at Kilmainham Gaol. This over-reaction made the leaders into martyrs.

Daniel O'Connell, "The Liberator"

1850	1875	1900	1925
1853 Dublin Exhibition is opened by Queen Victoria	**1877** Charles Stewart Parnell becomes leader of the new Home Rule Party	**1907** JM Synge's *Playboy of the Western World* opens	*Despatch bag carried by Constance Markievicz during the Easter Rising*
	1881 Parnell is jailed in Kilmainham Gaol		**1916** The historic but unsuccessful Easter Rising is quashed by the British
Main entrance to Kilmainham Gaol (see p79)	**1884** Founding of Gaelic Athletic Association, first group to promote Irish traditions		**1913** Irish Volunteers founded

View of O'Donovan Bridge which links the north and south sides of modern Dublin

THE IRISH CIVIL WAR

The years after World War I were some of the busiest and bloodiest in Dublin's history. The resentment over the treatment of the Rising leaders, and a plan to bring in conscription in Ireland, helped the cause of the Sinn Fein party, which won three-quarters of Irish seats in the 1918 election. These new MPs refused to take up their seats and instead met at a newly-formed Dáil Éireann (Parliament of Ireland) at the Mansion House (see p39). The Dáil's Minister of Finance was Michael Collins, who was also head of the Irish Volunteers' campaign of urban guerrilla warfare. On the morning of 21 November 1920, Collins ordered the assassination of 14 undercover British officers in Dublin. That afternoon British forces retaliated in what became known as Bloody Sunday, when they shot 12 spectators at a big Gaelic football game at Croke Park stadium. Other small skirmishes continued throughout

the city, including the burning of the Custom House (see p68) in May 1921. Soon after this the British government instigated a truce and both sides signed the Anglo-Irish Treaty.

The treaty gave limited independence to what was to be called the Irish Free State, but six Ulster counties were to be excluded and members of the Free State parliament (the Dáil) would have to swear allegiance to the British monarch. A faction of the Dáil led by Eamon De Valera opposed the treaty and in June 1922 Civil War broke out. Anti-treaty forces occupied the Four Courts building (see p74) but this was bombed (as was much of O'Connell Street) by the army under Collins. The Free State government proved ruthless in its imprisonment and later execution of anti-treaty rebels, but Collins himself finally became a victim when he was ambushed and shot. In May 1923 De Valera ordered an end

Eamon De Valera, a major figure in modern Irish politics

TIMELINE

1918 Sinn Fein sweeps election; Countess Constance Markievicz elected first woman MP

1920 First "Bloody Sunday" at Croke Park

1947 A statue of Queen Victoria is removed from the front courtyard of the Irish parliament buildings

The Irish Flag

1920	1930	1940	1950	1960

1921 Anglo-Irish treaty signed; leads to Civil War

1922 Execution of Michael Collins

Michael Collins, the leader of the Irish Volunteers

1941 German air raid on Dublin

1954 Brendan Behan's The Quare Fellow is published

1963 John F Kennedy, the first US President of Irish descent, visits Dublin

THE HISTORY OF DUBLIN

to the fighting by violent anti-treaty methods and left Sinn Fein.

RECENT HISTORY

Within three years De Valera had formed a new party called Fianna Fáil, which translates as "Warriors of Ireland". By 1932, his party had acquired power after claiming the majority of votes. With only two short periods of time out of office, De Valera held the post of Taoiseach

Young Irish dancers

(prime minister) until 1959, when he became President for a further 14 years. His policies were largely insular and mirrored the Catholic Church on social issues. During World War II De Valera kept Ireland neutral and as a result Dublin only experienced one major bombing incursion from the Luftwaffe.

European City of Culture doorway

After the war, Fianna Fáil were beaten in the election by Fine Gael. Though they were the descendants of the pro-treaty side, it was Fine Gael who oversaw the creation of the Republic of Ireland in 1949, which severed all ties with Britain by leaving the Commonwealth.

Dublin remained relatively immune from the political situation in Northern Ireland, as it does today, though in 1966 the IRA bombed the huge Nelson Column (even larger than the one in London's Trafalgar Square). Its only remaining piece, the massive head, is now on display in Dublin's Civic Museum *(see p58)*. Then in 1972, the British Embassy in Dublin was petrol-bombed, in retaliation for the shooting of 13 civilians on a protest march in Londonderry, in Northern Ireland, on what became known as Ireland's second Bloody Sunday.

DUBLIN IN THE 1990S

In 1991 Dublin was named European City of Culture and this spurred the rejuvenation of Temple Bar *(see pp56–7)* into a world-class cultural quarter. The majority of new development has been south of the river, which exacerbates the divide between north and south. Crime and drugs have also increased in recent years. But despite these problems, Dublin is now a thriving, lively city. Socially it has become more modern and cosmopolitan, which is thanks largely to the progress made under the forward-thinking presidency of Mary Robinson.

Grafton Street in modernized southwest Dublin

1972 Ireland joins European Community

1988 Dublin engages in millennium celebrations to boost its image although most historians trace its founding to an even earlier date

1991 Dublin is the European City of Culture

1998 Peace talks between the British Government and Northern Ireland minister Bertie Aherne result in the Good Friday Agreement

1970	1980	1990	2000

1976 British ambassador assassinated in Dublin

1979 Pope John Paul II celebrates mass in front of more than one million people

President Mary Robinson (1990–97)

1996 Anti-drug campaigner and investigative journalist Veronica Guerin murdered

1990 Mary Robinson is the first woman elected as President of Ireland

DUBLIN AT A GLANCE

ALTHOUGH IT IS a fairly small city, Dublin offers a wealth of different attractions which draw in millions of visitors each year. Those in the city centre or a short way outside Dublin are covered in the *Area by Area* section of this book. Sights further out of the city include the elegant stately homes of Castletown House and Powerscourt. In central Dublin, Temple Bar offers shopping, eating and drinking and the arts in a trendy, relaxed environment. Alternatively the glittering treasures of the National Museum or the liquid treasures of the Guinness Hop Store may lure you inside. A selection of Dublin's most popular sights is given below.

DUBLIN'S TOP TEN ATTRACTIONS

National Museum
See pp42–3

Guinness Hop Store
See pp80–81

Trinity College
See pp36–7

Castletown House
See pp98–9

St Patrick's Cathedral
See p59

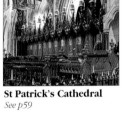

Powerscourt
See pp106–7

National Gallery
See pp46–9

Temple Bar
See pp56–7

Custom House
See p68

Christ Church Cathedral
See pp62–3

◁ The bell tower in Trinity College

Celebrated Visitors and Residents

FOR MANY CENTURIES Dublin has produced some of the greatest literary names in history. However, Dubliners are also famous for music, philosophy and politics. Edmund Burke, widely considered to be the father of British Conservatism, was born to the north of the Liffey. Writers such as Yeats, Beckett and Wilde lived in the city intermittently, having been born in Ireland. Jonathan Swift began the tradition of brilliant Irish writing at around the beginning of the 18th century. Great Irish writing continues to this day, with such prize-winning novels as *Paddy Clarke Ha, Ha, Ha*, written by Roddy Doyle.

The Duke of Wellington
Wellington was born in Dublin, close to what is now Wellington Quay, in 1769. He became one of the most successful generals and politicians in British history.

GF Handel
The German-born composer decided to première his most famous oratorio, the Messiah, in the new Music Hall in Fishamble Street in 1741.

NORTH OF THE LIFFEY

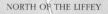

SOUTHWEST DUBLIN

Jonathan Swift
Famous as the author of many literary works, including Gulliver's Travels, *Swift became Dean of St Patrick's Cathedral in 1713.*

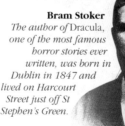

Bram Stoker
The author of Dracula, *one of the most famous horror stories ever written, was born in Dublin in 1847 and lived on Harcourt Street just off St Stephen's Green.*

James Joyce
Quite possibly Dublin's most famous author. Two of his greatest works, Ulysses *and* The Dubliners *are set in Dublin. Many of the characters and places in* Ulysses *are based on reality.*

William Butler Yeats
Born in Sligo, in northwest Ireland, Yeats was one of the founders of the Abbey Theatre. The poet spent much of his adult life in London but returned to Ireland frequently.

Samuel Beckett
The playwright was born south of Dublin and studied at Trinity College (see pp36–7). One of his most famous and enigmatic works is Waiting for Godot.

SOUTHEAST
DUBLIN

Oscar Wilde
This flamboyant author and playwright was born in Dublin – his family home can still be seen on the corner of Merrion Square. He enjoyed great success with such plays as The Importance of Being Earnest.

0 metres   200

0 yards   200

Dublin's Best: Pubs

E VERYONE KNOWS that Dublin is famous for its vast number of drinking establishments but, on arrival in the city, the choice can seem overwhelming. All the pubs are different – they range from vibrant, trendy bars to smoky traditional pubs. Whatever your choice of environment and beverage, you can be guaranteed to find it in Dublin. These pages offer just a taster of the most popular pubs in the city and what they are famous for, but for a more complete listing, turn to pages 132–3.

Slattery's
A very traditional Dublin pub. North of the Liffey, Slattery's attracts fewer tourists than the Temple Bar and Grafton Street pubs. It is considered to be the best pub in the city for live music.

NORTH OF THE LIFFEY

The Stag's Head
This gorgeous Victorian pub has a long mahogany bar and has retained its original mirrors and stained glass. Located down an alley off Dame Street, this atmospheric pub is well worth seeking out.

SOUTHWEST DUBLIN

The Brazen Head
Reputedly the oldest pub in Dublin. The present building, still with its courtyard for coach and horses, dates back to 1750. The interior is full of dark wood panelling and old photographs of Dublin.

Hogan's
A café bar rather than a pub, Hogan's is a stylish establishment serving excellent drinks, and is popular with a young, trendy crowd. It is centrally situated on George's Street.

Oliver St John Gogarty

This famous old pub in the heart of Temple Bar is renowned for its live music throughout the day, and good food. It is named after the poet and friend of James Joyce. The atmosphere is relaxed and it is popular with visitors keen to sample a part of traditional Dublin.

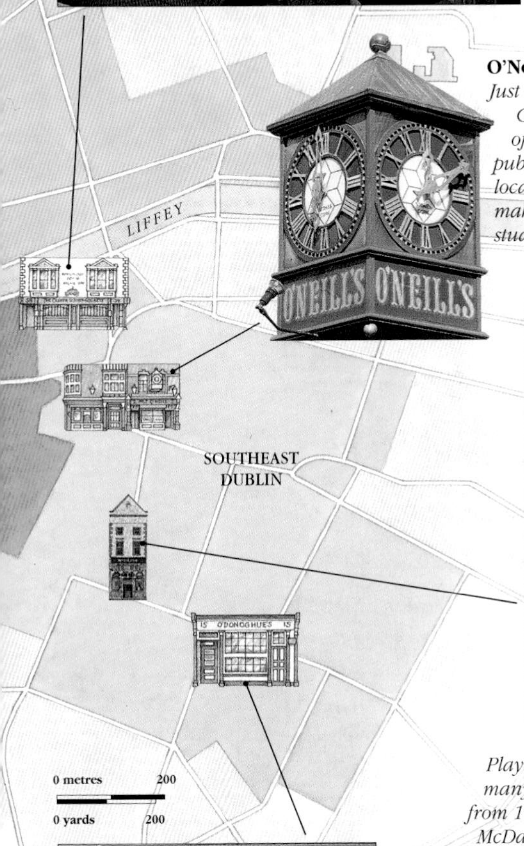
LIFFEY
SOUTHEAST DUBLIN
0 metres 200
0 yards 200
O'NEILL'S O'NEILL'S

O'Neill's

Just round the corner from Grafton Street, O'Neill's is one of the best places in the city for pub food. Its cosy atmosphere and location close to Trinity College make it a favourite with Dublin's student population.

McDAIDS
GUINNESS

McDaid's

Playwright Brendan Behan downed many a pint in this pub, which dates from 1779. Though on the tourist trail, McDaid's retains a bohemian charm, and bars upstairs and downstairs provide space for a leisurely drink.

O'DONOGHUE'S

O'Donoghue's

A good mix of locals and tourists, young and old, frequent this pub in the heart of Georgian Dublin which has been a city favourite for years. Famous as the pub where the Dubliners folk group began in the 1960s, it is known today for its live traditional music.

DUBLIN THROUGH THE YEAR

THE MOST popular months for visiting Dublin are July and August, and this is when the city is busiest. June and September can be pleasant but don't count on the weather, for Ireland's lush beauty is the product of a wet climate. Most Dublin sights are open all year round but, in the low season (generally November to March), some of them have limited opening hours or close completely. In summer, events are held in honour of anything from gardens to James Joyce, but a common thread is music, and few festivals are complete without it. Dublin is at its best when celebrating and is thus a treat at Christmas or New Year. Look out for the word *fleadh* (festival) in the city, but remember, too, that the Irish are a spontaneous people: festivities can spring from the air, or from a tune on a fiddle.

Revellers at the St Patrick's Day parade

Trinity College rowers competing on the Liffey (April)

SPRING

AFTER THE QUIET winter, spring sees a flurry of festivals and events. St Patrick's Day is often said to mark the beginning of the tourist season. This national holiday is celebrated with music and carnival-style abandon throughout the city. Accommodation is often in short supply around this time so do book in advance.

Annual parade through the streets of Dublin to celebrate St Patrick's Day (March)

MARCH

Celtic Flame *(14–17 Mar).* A national festival of contemporary and traditional music, song and dance culminates at various Dublin venues.
St Patrick's Day Festival *(around 17 Mar).* Numerous street theatre acts fill the city during colourful celebrations that centre on a parade on St Patrick's Day itself (17 March).
Temple Bar Fleadh *(around 17 Mar).* Three-day festival of traditional music in honour of St Patrick in the lively Temple Bar area *(see pp56–7).*
Irish Kennel Club Show *(16–17 Mar),* Cloghran, Co Dublin. Annual championship dog show.
Feis Ceoil *(last two weeks),* RDS Ballsbridge *(see p83).* One of Europe's oldest and most prestigious classical music festivals.

APRIL

Colours Boat Race *(first weekend).* A rowing race along the Liffey between University College Dublin and Trinity College.
Howth Music Festival *(Easter weekend).* This pretty fishing village on the outskirts of the city *(see p88)* plays host to three days of popular music.
Dublin Film Festival *(third week).* Festival of new and classic films held at various Dublin cinemas, including the Irish Film Centre *(see p56).*

May Day Parade in central Dublin

MAY

May Day Parade *(1 May).* Celebrations and colourful parades through the city streets on this national holiday.
Dublin Garden Festival *(late May or early Jun),* RDS Ballsbridge. Large, four-day horticultural show.
Laytown Beach Races *(late May or early Jun).* Horse races on a beach north of Dublin.

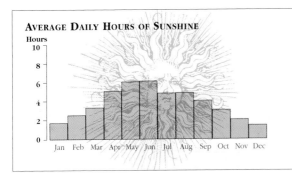

AVERAGE DAILY HOURS OF SUNSHINE

Hours

Sunshine Chart
Hours of sunshine in rainy Dublin are few and far between for most of the year. In summer, however, the days are often long, hot and very sunny. As in the rest of the country, the weather is notoriously unpredictable, so skies can cloud over in minutes.

SUMMER

Summer represents the height of the festive calendar for the visitor and the Dubliner alike and is the city's busiest time of year. There is a succession of outdoor music, arts and community festivals of all kinds, culminating in the city's top social event, the annual Dublin Horse Show.

JUNE

Music in the Park *(Jun–Aug)*
Various city parks hold free open-air concerts at lunchtime on weekdays, and on Sundays.
Photography Exhibitions *(Jun–Sep)*, Dublin Photographic Centre *(see p57)*. Changing exhibitions on different themes during the summer months.
County Wicklow Gardens Festival *(all month)*. Held at private and public gardens south of Dublin, including Powerscourt *(see pp106–7)*.
Bloomsday *(16 Jun)*. Walks, lectures and pub talks across

Bluesman Eric Bibb performing at Temple Bar Blues Festival (July)

the city to celebrate James Joyce's greatest novel, *Ulysses*.
Maracycle *(mid-Jun)*. Thousands of cyclists race each other from Dublin to Belfast and back again.
Scurlogstown Olympiad Celtic Festival *(mid-Jun)*, Trim *(see p114)*. Traditional Irish music, dance, fair and selection of a festival queen.
Music in Great Irish Houses *(second and third weeks)*. Classical music recitals in grand settings at various venues.

JULY

Dun Laoghaire American Week *(first week, see p88)*. US-themed jamboree with bluegrass music, a barn dance and Fourth of July fireworks.
South Docks Festival *(third week)*. A community festival that centres on Pearse Street and City Quay, with shows and activities for all ages.
Temple Bar Blues Festival *(third weekend, see pp56–7)*. Three days of live blues music featuring international stars.

The Dublin Horse Show (August)

AUGUST

Summer Music Festival *(all month)*, St Stephen's Green *(see p39)*. Free lunchtime concerts of both popular and traditional music, as well as sporadic Shakespeare performances in the open air.
Dublin Horse Show *(second week)*, RDS Ballsbridge *(see p83)*. The premier sporting and social event of the Dublin calendar includes dressage, showjumping competitions and a chance to show off your hat on Ladies' Day.
People's Photographic Exhibition *(last weekend)*, St Stephen's Green *(see p39)*. Displays of local amateur photographers' work on the railings around the green.

Powerscourt Gardens, part of the County Wicklow Gardens Festival (June)

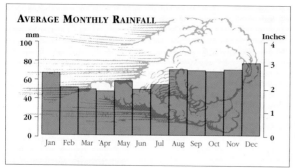

AVERAGE MONTHLY RAINFALL

Rainfall Chart
*Ireland is one of the
wettest countries in
Europe, with rainfall
distributed evenly
throughout the year.
Fortunately, Dublin is
situated in the drier
eastern half of the
country, but visitors
should still be pre-
pared for rain at any
time of year.*

Revellers on Hallowe'en (October)

AUTUMN

AUTUMN KICKS OFF with the
Liffey Swim, a race along
Dublin's river attempted only
by the strong hearted. Later
the traditional sports of Gaelic
football and hurling, the latter
a kind of aerial hockey, hold
their popular national finals in
the city. The theatre festival
held in October is world class.

SEPTEMBER

The Liffey Swim *(first Sat)*.
Since 1920, Dubliners have
turned out to watch swimmers
brave the Liffey's murky waters
from Watling Street Bridge to
the Custom House *(see p68)*.
**Motorcycle Union Of
Ireland Killalane Road Races**
(second weekend), Skerries.
Road-racing final on the streets
of this resort north of Dublin.
All-Ireland Hurling Final
(second Sun), Croke Park.
All-Ireland Football Final
(fourth Sun), Croke Park.
Popular Gaelic football final.

Carpets at the annual Irish
Antique Dealers' Fair (September)

Irish Antique Dealers' Fair
(last week), RDS Ballsbridge
(see p83). The country's most
important antiques fair.

OCTOBER

Dublin Theatre Festival
(first two weeks). Features new
works by Irish playwrights,
plus many foreign productions.
Dublin City Marathon *(last
Mon)*. Starting and finishing
on O'Connell Street, the route
takes in many Dublin landmarks, including Phoenix Park
and Trinity College. Every year
several thousands participate.
Hallowe'en (Samhain)
(31 Oct). On the night when
spirits rise, children wear fancy
dress and celebrations include
a parade and fireworks.

NOVEMBER

Opera Ireland *(a week in
Nov)*. Autumn run at the Gaiety
Theatre. Another short season
is put on in April.
**Toy and Train Collectors'
Fair** *(last Sun)*, Rochestown
Lodge Hotel, Dun Laoghaire
(see p88). Model cars, dolls,
comics and teddy bears. Other
fairs in April and September.

Large field of runners competing in the Dublin City Marathon (October)

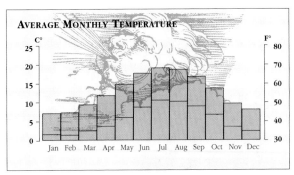

AVERAGE MONTHLY TEMPERATURE

Temperature Chart
This chart gives the average minimum and maximum temperatures for the city. Extremes of temperature are rare: the winter is mild, with the mercury seldom falling below zero. In summer, however, the occasional day can be very warm.

WINTER

ALTHOUGH WINTER is a quiet time for festivals, there is a range of entertainment on offer, including sporting and theatrical events. Christmas is the busiest social period and there are plenty of informal celebrations. There is also a wide choice of National Hunt (steeplechase) race meetings, especially at Leopardstown, south of the city centre.

Glendalough *(see p102)* in the snow

Christmas scene at Mansion House

DECEMBER

Pantomime Season *(Dec–Jan)*. Traditional pantomime performed at theatres in Dublin and throughout Ireland.
Christmas *(24–25 Dec)*. Christian celebrations include going to midnight mass on Christmas Eve.
St Stephen's Day *(26 Dec)*. On the day after Christmas, Catholic boys dress up as Wren boys (chimney sweeps with blackened faces) and sing hymns to raise money for charitable causes.

Leopardstown Races *(26–29 Dec)*. This four-day meeting is the biggest in the country at this traditional time for horse racing.
New Year's Eve *(31 Dec)*. Celebrations around the city to welcome in the New Year.

JANUARY

Salmon and Sea Trout Season *(1 Jan–Sep)*. Start of the season for one of the most popular pastimes in Ireland.
Irish Champion Hurdle *(late Jan)*. Major horse race at Leopardstown *(see p97)*.

Steeplechasers at Leopardstown (January)

FEBRUARY

Five Nations Rugby Tournament *(varying Saturdays Feb–Apr)*, Lansdowne Road. Ireland against England, Wales, Scotland and France, two out of four played in Dublin.
Malahide Food and Drink Affair *(late Feb, see p87)*. A festival of Irish food and drink, plus cultural activities.

PUBLIC HOLIDAYS

New Year's Day (1 Jan)
St Patrick's Day (17 Mar)
Good Friday
Easter Monday
May Day (1 May)
June Bank Holiday (first Mon in Jun)
August Bank Holiday (first Mon in Aug)
October Bank Holiday (last Mon in Oct)
Christmas Day (25 Dec)
St Stephen's Day (26 Dec)

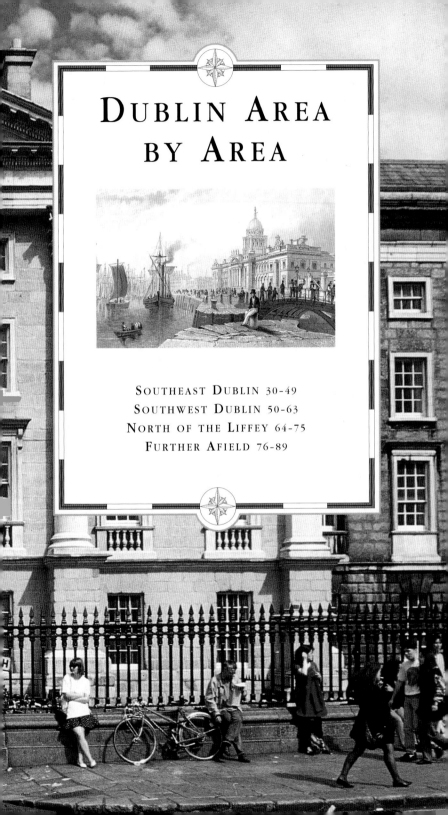

DUBLIN AREA BY AREA

SOUTHEAST DUBLIN

Window in the Government Buildings

THIS PART OF Dublin was virtually undeveloped until the founding of Trinity College in 1592. Even then, it was almost a hundred years before the land to the south was enclosed to create St Stephen's Green.

The mid-18th century saw the beginning of a construction boom in the area. During this time, public buildings such as the Old Library at Trinity College and Leinster House were built. Many of the buildings in Merrion Square still have their original features. Today, visitors are attracted to Southeast Dublin by the shops on Grafton Street and by the museums in the area, among them the excellent National Gallery and the National Museum with its displays of Irish Bronze Age gold treasures. The "Dead Zoo", as the fascinating Natural History Museum is known, has preserved its wonderful Victorian interior.

SIGHTS AT A GLANCE

Museums, Libraries and Galleries
Heraldic Museum ⑤
National Gallery pp46–9 ⑱
National Library ⑰
National Museum pp42–3 ⑭
Natural History Museum ⑮
Royal Hibernian Academy ⑳

Historic Buildings
Bank of Ireland ①
Government Buildings ⑬
Iveagh House ⑪
Leinster House ⑯
Mansion House ⑦
Newman House ⑩
Number 29 ㉑
Royal College of Surgeons ⑧
Trinity College pp36–7 ②

Historic Streets
Ely Place ⑫
Grafton Street ④
Merrion Square ⑲

Churches
St Ann's Church ⑥
St Teresa's Church ③

Parks and Gardens
St Stephen's Green ⑨

GETTING THERE
Buses 5, 7A, 8, 10, 13, 14A, 15A, 45 and 46 go along Nassau Street which is in walking distance of most of the sights in this area. If you are coming from further afield, the nearest DART station is Pearse Street.

KEY
■ Street-by-Street map *See pp32–3*
🚉 Railway station
🚉 DART station
🅿 Parking
ℹ Tourist Information

0 metres 250
0 yards 250

◁ **The lush gardens of Merrion Square**

Street-by-Street: Southeast Dublin

THE AREA AROUND COLLEGE GREEN, dominated by the façades of the Bank of Ireland and Trinity College, is very much the heart of Dublin. The alleys and malls cutting across busy pedestrianized Grafton Street boast many of Dublin's better shops, hotels and restaurants. Just off Kildare Street are the Irish Parliament, the National Library and the National Museum. To escape the city bustle many head for sanctuary in St Stephen's Green, which is overlooked by fine Georgian buildings.

← Dublin Castle

COLLEGE GREEN

GRAFTON ST

Bank of Ireland
This grand Georgian building was originally built as the Irish Parliament **1**

Statue of Molly Malone (1988)

Grafton Street
Bewley's Oriental Café is the social hub of this pedestrianized street, alive with talented buskers and pavement artists **4**

GRAFTON STREET   DUKE ST

St Ann's Church
The striking façade of the 18th-century church was added in 1868. The interior features lovely stained-glass windows **6**

ANNE ST. STH

STREET

Mansion House
This has been the official residence of Dublin's Lord Mayor since 1715 **7**

Fusiliers' Arch (1907)

DAWSON

ST STEPHEN'S GREEN NORTH

★ St Stephen's Green
The relaxing city park is surrounded by many grand buildings. In summer, lunchtime concerts attract tourists and workers alike **9**

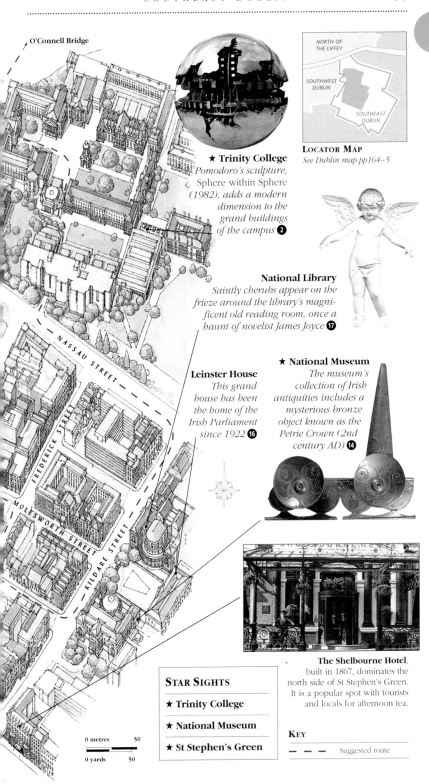

O'Connell Bridge

NORTH OF
THE LIFFEY

SOUTHWEST
DUBLIN

SOUTHEAST
DUBLIN

LOCATOR MAP
See Dublin map pp164–5

★ **Trinity College**
*Pomodoro's sculpture,
Sphere within Sphere
(1982), adds a modern
dimension to the
grand buildings
of the campus* ❷

National Library
*Saintly cherubs appear on the
frieze around the library's magnificent old reading room, once a
haunt of novelist James Joyce* ⓱

Leinster House
*This grand
house has been
the home of the
Irish Parliament
since 1922* ⓰

★ **National Museum**
*The museum's
collection of Irish
antiquities includes a
mysterious bronze
object known as the
Petrie Crown (2nd
century AD)* ⓮

NASSAU STREET

FREDERICK STREET

MOLESWORTH STREET

KILDARE STREET

The Shelbourne Hotel,
built in 1867, dominates the
north side of St Stephen's Green.
It is a popular spot with tourists
and locals for afternoon tea.

0 metres   50

0 yards   50

STAR SIGHTS

★ **Trinity College**

★ **National Museum**

★ **St Stephen's Green**

KEY

— — —   Suggested route

Original Chamber of the Irish House of Lords at the Bank of Ireland

Bank of Ireland ❶

2 College Green. **Map** D3. 🕻 661
5933 ext 2265. ⏰ 10am–4pm Mon–
Wed & Fri, 10am–5pm Thu. ⬤ public
hols. **House of Lords** 🎫 10:30am,
11:30am & 1:45pm Tue or by appt.

THE PRESTIGIOUS offices of
Ireland's national bank
began life as the first purpose-
built parliament house in
Europe. The original central
section was started by Irish
architect Edward Lovett
Pearce and completed in 1739
after his death. Sadly, Pearce's
masterpiece, the great octagonal chamber of the House
of Commons, was destroyed
by fire in 1792. The House of
Lords, however, remains
intact. Attendants lead tours
that point out the coffered
ceiling and oak panelling.
There are also huge tapestries
of the *Battle of the Boyne* and
the *Siege of Londonderry*,
and a splendid 1,233-
piece crystal chan-
delier that dates
from 1788.
  James Gandon
added the east
portico in 1785.
Further additions
were made
around 1797.
After the dissolu-
tion of the Irish
Parliament in
1800, the Bank of
Ireland bought
the building.
The present
structure was
completed in
1808 with the
transformation

of the former lobby of the
House of Commons into a
cash office and the addition
of a curving screen wall and
the Foster Place annexe.
  At the front of the bank on
College Green is a statue by
John Foley of Henry Grattan
(see p14), the most formidable
leader of the old parliament.

Trinity College ❷

See pp36–7.

St Teresa's Church ❸

Clarendon St or Johnson Court.
Map D4. 🕻 671 8466. ⏰ 6:45am–
6:30pm Mon–Fri, 6:45am–7:30pm Sat,
8:15am–7pm Sun.

THE FOUNDATION stone of
St Teresa's was laid in
1793, making it the first
post-Penal Law church to
be legally planned and
built in the city after
the passing of
the Catholic
Relief Act the
same year *(see
p14)*. The land
was bought by
a brewer named
John Sweetman
and was given to
the Discalced
Carmelite Fathers.
The church
did not in fact
open until
several years
later, in 1810.
The eastern
transept was

**Statue of the Virgin and child
in St Teresa's Church**

added in 1863 and the
western transept in
1876, at which stage it
reached the form it
remains in today.
  Located in the middle
of Dublin, St Teresa's is
a relatively busy place
of worship. Its T-shaped
interior means that, if
you enter through the
main door on Claren-
don Street and walk
through the church, you
will arrive in the tight
alleyway of Johnson
Court, a few yards from
the heart of bustling
Grafton Street. There
are seven stained-glass
windows in the church by
Phyllis Burke, which were
made in the 1990s, and a fine
sculpture of Christ by John
Hogan beneath the altar.

**Street musicians outside Brown
Thomas on Grafton Street**

Grafton Street ❹

Map D4.

THE SPINE OF DUBLIN'S most
popular and stylish shop-
ping district runs south from
Trinity College to the glass-
covered St Stephen's Green
Shopping Centre. At the north
end, at the junction with
Nassau Street, is a bronze
statue by Jean Rynhart of
Molly Malone (1988), the
celebrated "cockles and
mussels" street trader from
the traditional Irish folk song.
  This busy pedestrianized
strip, characterized by numerous energetic buskers and
talented street theatre artists,
boasts many shops, including
many British chain stores.
Its most exclusive, however,
is Brown Thomas, one of
Dublin's most elegant de-
partment stores *(see p136)*,
selling designer clothes and
exclusive perfumery.

Monkeys playing billiards outside the Heraldic Museum

Grafton Street's most famous landmark is Bewley's Oriental Café at No. 78 *(see p132).* Although not the oldest branch of this 150-year-old Dublin institution, this is Bewley's most popular location and a favourite meeting spot for Dubliners and visitors alike throughout the day. It stands on the site of Samuel Whyte's school, whose illustrious roll included Robert Emmet *(see p14),* leader of the 1803 Rebellion, and the Duke of Wellington.

Despite the removal of the old wooden pews, this large café retains its pleasant Victorian ambience, especially in the James Joyce Room upstairs. The balcony on the first floor, which looks down on the shop area at the entrance to the café, is a good spot for people-watching.

On many of the sidestreets off Grafton Street there are numerous pubs providing an alternative to Bewley's for the exhausted shopper, among them the famous Davy Byrne's *(see p132),* for years frequented by Dublin's literati.

Heraldic Museum and Genealogical Office ❺

2 Kildare St. **Map** E4. 603 0200.
10am–12:20pm, 2–4pm Mon–Fri.

THE GENEALOGICAL OFFICE helps anyone with an Irish background assemble facts about their ancestors, responding to great interest from North America. Inexpensive consultations are available but they recommend that the more you have found out about your ancestry beforehand (they offer a handy questionnaire) the better.

The Heraldic Museum offers a small but interesting collection of seals, stamps, regimental colours, coins, porcelain, paintings, family crests and county shields.

The building that houses the museum is a red-brick structure in the Venetian style, which is unusual for Dublin. On the exterior, it features some fanciful decorative aspects such as three monkeys playing billiards and bears playing violins just to the right of the entrance.

Window depicting Faith, Hope and Charity in St Ann's Church

St Ann's Church ❻

Dawson St. **Map** D4. 676 7727.
10am–4pm Mon–Fri (also for Sun service, phone to check).

FOUNDED IN 1707, St Ann's striking Romanesque façade was added by the architects Deane and Woodward in 1868. The best view of the façade is from Grafton Street, looking down Anne Street South. Inside the church are many colourful stained-glass windows that date back to the mid-19th century. St Ann's has a long tradition of charity work: in 1723 Lord Newton left a bequest specifically to buy bread for the poor. The original shelf used for the bread still stands adjacent to the altar.

There are numerous famous past parishioners of St Ann's including the Irish patriot Wolfe Tone *(see p14),* who was married here in 1785, Douglas Hyde, the first president of Ireland, and Bram Stoker (1847–1912), the author of *Dracula (see p20).*

The milling crowds filling the pedestrianized Grafton Street

Trinity College ❷

Trinity College coat of arms

TRINITY COLLEGE was founded in 1592 by Queen Elizabeth I on the site of an Augustinian monastery. Originally a Protestant college, it was not until the 1970s that Catholics started entering the university. Among the many famous students to attend the college were playwrights Oliver Goldsmith and Samuel Beckett, and political writer Edmund Burke. Trinity's lawns and cobbled quads provide a pleasant haven in the heart of the city. The major attractions are the Old Library and the *Book of Kells*, housed in the Treasury.

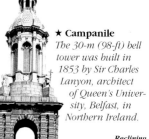

★ Campanile
The 30-m (98-ft) bell tower was built in 1853 by Sir Charles Lanyon, architect of Queen's University, Belfast, in Northern Ireland.

Reclining Connected Forms (1969) by Henry Moore

Dining Hall (1761)

Chapel *(1798)*
This is the only chapel in the Republic to be shared by all denominations. The painted window above the altar dates from 1867.

Parliament Square

Statue of Edmund Burke (1868) by John Foley

Main entrance

Statue of Oliver Goldsmith (1864) by John Foley

SAMUEL BECKETT (1906–89)

Nobel prizewinner Samuel Beckett was born at Foxrock, south of Dublin. In 1923 he entered Trinity, where he was placed first in his modern literature class. He was also a keen member of the college cricket team. Forsaking Ireland, Beckett moved to France in the early 1930s. Many of his works such as *Waiting for Godot* (1951) were written first in French, and then later translated, by Beckett, into English.

Provost's House (c. 1760)

Examination Hall
Completed in 1791 to a design by Sir William Chambers, the hall features a gilded oak chandelier and ornate ceilings by Michael Stapleton.

Library Square
The red-brick building (known as the Rubrics) on the east side of Library Square was built around 1700 and is the oldest surviving part of the college.

VISITORS' CHECKLIST

College Green. **Map** D3. ☎ 677 2941. 🚆 *DART to Tara Street.* 🚌 *14, 15, 46 & many other routes.* **Old Library and Treasury** ○ *9:30am– 5:30pm Mon–Sat (last adm: 5pm), noon–5pm Sun & some public hols (last adm: 4:30pm).* ● *10 days at Christmas.* 📷 🚫 ♿ 🎫 *by arrangement.* **Chapel** ○ *by appt.* **Douglas Hyde Gallery** ○ *for exhibitions only.*

Shop and entrance to Old Library

The Museum Building, completed in 1857, is noted for its Venetian exterior, and its magnificent multicoloured hall and double-domed roof.

New Square

Sphere within Sphere
(1982) was given to the college by its sculptor Arnaldo Pomodoro.

Berkeley Library Building by Paul Koralek (1967)

Fellows' Square

Entrance from Nassau Street

★ Treasury
This detail is from the Book of Durrow, *one of the other magnificent illuminated manuscripts housed in the Treasury along with the celebrated* Book of Kells *(see p38).*

The Douglas Hyde Gallery
was built in the 1970s to house temporary art exhibitions.

★ Old Library *(1732)*
The spectacular Long Room measures 64 m (210 ft) from end to end. It houses 200,000 antiquarian texts, marble busts of scholars and the oldest surviving harp in Ireland.

STAR FEATURES

★ **Old Library**

★ **Treasury**

★ **Campanile**

The Book of Kells

THE MOST RICHLY decorated of Ireland's illuminated manuscripts, the *Book of Kells*, may have been the work of monks from Iona, who fled to Kells, near Newgrange *(see pp112–3)*, in AD 806 after a Viking raid. The book, which was moved to Trinity College *(see pp36–7)* in the 17th century, contains the four gospels in Latin. The scribes who copied the texts embellished their calligraphy with intricate spirals as well as human figures and animals. Some of the dyes used were imported from as far as the Middle East.

Pair of moths

Stylized angel

The Greek letter "X"

The letter "I"

Interlacing motifs

Cat watching rats

The symbols of the four evangelists are used as decoration throughout the book. The figure of the man symbolizes St Matthew.

The letter that looks like a "P" is a Greek "R".

A full-page portrait of St Matthew, shown standing barefoot in front of a throne, precedes the opening words of his gospel.

Rats eating bread could be a reference to sinners taking Holy Communion. The symbolism of the animals and people decorating the manuscript is often hard to interpret.

MONOGRAM PAGE
This, the most elaborate page of the book, contains the first three words of St Matthew's account of the birth of Christ. The first word "XRI" is an abbreviation of "Christi".

The text is in a beautifully rounded Celtic script with brightly ornamented initial letters. Animal and human forms are often used to decorate the end of a line.

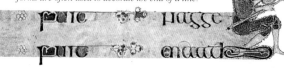

Mansion House ❼

Dawson St. **Map** E4. ● *to the public.*

SET BACK from Dawson Street with a neat cobbled fore-court, the Mansion House is an attractive Queen Anne-style building. It was built in 1710 for the aristocrat Joshua Dawson, after whom the street is named. The Dublin Corporation bought it from him five years later as the official residence of the city's Lord Mayor. A grey stucco façade was added in Victorian times.

The Dáil Éireann *(see p44)*, which adopted the Declaration of Independence, first met here on 21 January 1919. The building is now used mostly for civic functions and receptions.

Royal College of Surgeons ❽

Dawson St. **Map** E4. ● *to the public.* ⬛ *2pm Sun (Oct–May: groups only).*

ALTHOUGH THE WEST side of St Stephen's Green is its scruffiest, it is home to the most striking building of the square, namely the squat granite-faced Royal College of Surgeons. The college opened in 1810 and 15 years later its façade was extended from three to seven bays when a central pediment was added. On top of this are three statues which from left to right are Hygieia, goddess of health, Asclepius, god of

Royal College of Surgeons, which overlooks St Stephen's Green

medicine and son of Apollo, and Athena, the goddess of wisdom and patron of the arts. Today, the main entrance is through the modern exten-sion on York Street. The aca-demy has almost 1,000 students from all over the world.

The building itself played an important part in Irish his-tory. During the 1916 Easter Rising *(see p15)*, a section of the Irish Citizen Army under Michael Mallin and Countess Constance Markievicz were in control of the college. They were the last detachment of rebels to surrender and, although Mallin was execut-ed, Markievicz escaped sen-tence because of her gender and public status. She was later to become the first woman to be elected as an MP at Westminster in London. The front columns of the building still feature the old bullet holes, an ever-present reminder of its colourful past.

St Stephen's Green ❾

Map D5. ◯ *daylight hours.*

ORIGINALLY ONE of three ancient commons in the old city, St Stephen's Green was enclosed in 1664. The 9-ha (22-acre) green was laid out in its present form in 1880, using a grant given by Lord Ardilaun, a member of the Guinness family. Landscaped with flowerbeds, trees, a fountain and a lake, the green is dotted with memorials to eminent Dubliners, including Ardilaun himself. There is a bust of James Joyce *(see p21)*, and a memorial by Henry Moore (1967) dedicated to WB Yeats *(see p21)*. At the Merrion Row corner stands a massive monument (1967) by Edward Delaney to 18th-century nationalist leader Wolfe Tone – it is known locally as "Tonehenge". The 1887 bandstand still has free daytime concerts in summer.

The busiest side of the Green is the north, known during the 19th century as the Beaux' Walk and still home to several gentlemen's clubs. The most prominent building is the venerable Shelbourne Hotel *(see p167)*. Dating back to 1867, its entrance is adorn-ed by statues of Nubian prin-cesses and attendant slaves. It is well worth popping in for a look at the chandeliered foyer and for afternoon tea in the Lord Mayor's Lounge.

Dubliners relaxing by the lake in St Stephen's Green

Stucco work in the Apollo room of No. 85 in Newman House

Newman House ⑩

85 & 86 St Stephen's Green. **Map** D5.
🔟 706 7422. 🔘 Jun–Aug: Tue–Fri
12–5pm, Sat 2–5pm, Sun 11am–
2pm. 🔲

NUMBERS 85 AND 86 on the south side of St Stephen's Green are collectively known as Newman House, named for John Henry Newman, later Cardinal Newman and the first rector of the Catholic University of Ireland.

Founded as an alternative to the Protestant Trinity College, it became part of University College Dublin in the 1920s and is still owned by that institution.

During the 1990s it has seen one of the most painstaking and diligent restorations ever undertaken in the city. It is the much smaller No. 85, designed by Richard Castle in 1738, that contains the most beautiful rooms with plasterwork by the Franchini brothers. Of particular interest are the Apollo Room, with a figure of the god above the mantle, and the upstairs Saloon. In the late 1800s the Jesuits covered the naked plaster bodies on the ceiling of the Saloon with rudimentary plaster casts to conceal what they thought to be shameful nudity. One of the figures is still covered today. A classroom, decorated as it would have been in the days when James Joyce was a student

here, is open to the public, as is the study used by the poet Gerard Manley Hopkins, who was a professor here in the late 19th century. Other famous past pupils include the writer Flann O'Brien and former president Eamon de Valera.

Iveagh House and Iveagh Gardens ⑪

80 & 81 St Stephen's Green. **Map** D5.
🔘 to the public. **Gardens** ⬜ daily.

IVEAGH HOUSE, on the south of St Stephen's Green, was originally two free-standing town houses. No. 80 was designed in 1730s by Richard Castle – his first commission in the city. The houses were combined in the 1860s when Sir Benjamin Guinness bought the properties. None of the original façade remains as Guinness linked the properties under a Portland stone façade and had the family arms engraved on the pediment. The Guinness family also carried out much interior reconstruction,

Enjoying the secluded peace of Iveagh Gardens

including a large new ballroom, with a domed ceiling and liberal amounts of marble and onyx, added to the rear of the house. Iveagh House was given to the state by Rupert Guinness, the second Earl of Iveagh, in 1939. It is now used by the Department of Foreign Affairs, both as the office of the minister and as a venue for state receptions.

The rear of Iveagh House faces out onto the peaceful Iveagh Gardens, an almost secret Dublin park, which offers a quiet alternative to the busy St Stephen's Green. It owes its tranquility partly to the fact that its two entrances are discreet: one is behind the National Concert Hall on Earlsfort Terrace, the other is off Clonmel Street.

Ely Place ⑫

Map E5.

A CUL-DE-SAC with several well-preserved Georgian houses, Ely Place is at the end of Merrion Street Upper. Most of the houses along the street were built in the 1770s and Ely Place soon became one of the most desirable addresses in the city at this time. Behind its red brick façade, 8 Ely Place, known as Ely House, has elegant plasterwork by the stuccodore Michael Stapleton and an ornate staircase covered with engravings of characters from the tales of the Labours of Hercules below the banister rail.

Modern buildings seal the end of the street. The Royal Hibernian Academy Gallagher Gallery (see p45) was built in 1973 and may look somewhat out of place on this otherwise rather grand stretch, but it offers one of the best gallery spaces in the city, exhibiting mostly 20th-century Irish art.

Detail of stucco from Ely House, featuring the mythical dog Cerberus

The elegant, Neo-Classical façade of the Government Buildings

Government Buildings ⑬

Upper Merrion Street. **Map** E4.
(662 4888. ☐ Sat 10:30am–
12:30pm and 1:30–4:30pm. (Tickets
available from the National Gallery.)
✓ obligatory.

IN BETWEEN the Natural
History Museum and the
National Gallery on Upper
Merrion Street, facing the
Georgian town houses, stand
the imposing Government
Buildings, built in a Neo-
Georgian style.

The complex was opened
in 1911 as the Royal College
of Science (RCS) and it has
the distinction of being the
last major project planned by
the British in Dublin. In 1922
the Irish government took
over the north wing as offices
and the RCS became part of
University College Dublin.
Academic pursuits continued
here until 1989, when the
government moved into the
rest of the buildings and
ordered a massive restoration
of the façade. The city grime
on the Portland stone was
blasted away to restore it
to its original near-white
appearance.

The elegant domed buildings
are set apart from the street
by a cobbled courtyard and a
large colonnade with columns
that are strongly reminiscent of
Gandon's Custom House (see
p68). The tour takes in the
office of the Taoiseach (pronounced Tee-Shuck) and the
cabinet office. The interior is
decorated with examples of
works by contemporary Irish
artists, most notably a huge
stained-glass window, situated above the grand staircase,
called *My Four Green Fields*
by Dublin artist Evie Hone,
which depicts the island's four
provinces. This was
designed for the
1939 World's Fair in
New York. It was
displayed in the
Irish Pavilion there
and afterwards
returned to Dublin.
For a number of
years it lay packed
away, until the
1960s, when it was
put on display for a
while in the Dublin
Bus offices in
O'Connell Street. It
was finally moved
to its present home
in the Government
Buildings in 1991.

National Museum ⑭

See pp42–3.

Natural History Museum ⑮

Merrion St. **Map** E4. **(** 677 7444.
☐ 10am–5pm Tue–Sat, 2–5pm Sun.
● public hols. ♿ ground floor only.
✓ May–Sep.

KNOWN AFFECTIONATELY as the
"Dead Zoo" by Dublin
residents, this museum is
crammed with antique glass
cabinets containing stuffed animals from around the world.
The museum was opened to
the public in 1857 with an
inaugural lecture by Dr David
Livingstone on African fauna.
It remains virtually unchanged
from Victorian times.

On the ground floor, the
Irish room holds exhibits on
local wildlife. Inside the front
door are three skeletons of
the extinct giant deer known
as the "Irish elk". Also on this
floor are shelves with jars of
octopuses, leeches and worms,
preserved in embalming fluid.

The upper gallery is home
to the Blaschka Collection of
interesting glass models of
marine life, and a display
of buffalo and deer trophies.
Hanging from the ceiling are
the skeletons of a fin whale
and a humpback whale.

The advances made in taxi-
dermy over the years are em-
phasized by a stuffed rhino-
ceros and an Indian elephant,
both so heavily lacquered that
they seem to be covered in tar.

**Lawn and front entrance of the Natural History
Museum on Merrion Street Upper**

National Museum ⓮

THE NATIONAL MUSEUM OF IRELAND was built in the 1880s to the design of Sir Thomas Deane. Its splendid domed rotunda features marble pillars and a zodiac mosaic floor. The Treasury houses priceless items such as the Broighter gold boat, while an exhibition on Ireland's Bronze Age gold contains some beautiful jewellery. Many collections have now moved to the recently opened annexe of the museum at the impressive Collins Barracks (see pp84–5).

Egyptian Mummy

This mummy of the lady Tentdinebu is thought to date back to c.945–716 BC. Covered in brilliant colours, it is part of the stunning Egyptian collection.

★ Ór – Ireland's Gold

This is one of the most extensive collections of Bronze Age gold in Western Europe. This gold lunula (c.1800 BC), found in Athlone, is one of many pieces of ancient jewellery in this exhibition.

KEY TO FLOORPLAN

- ☐ The Road to Independence
- ☐ Ór – Ireland's Gold
- ☐ The Treasury
- ☐ Prehistoric Ireland
- ☐ Viking Exhibition
- ☐ Ancient Egypt
- ☐ Temporary exhibition space
- ☐ Non-exhibition space

Flag from 1916 Rising

The Road to Independence *exhibition covers historical events between 1900 and 1921. This flag flew over Dublin's GPO during the Easter Rising (see p15).*

Main entrance

GALLERY GUIDE

The ground floor holds The Treasury, Ór – Ireland's Gold *exhibition,* The Road to Independence *and the* Prehistoric Ireland *display. The first floor houses Viking artifacts and displays of silver, glass and ceramics. There may be other new displays, while some rooms may be closed to the public – this is due to the continuing reorganization of the museum.*

The domed rotunda, based on the design of the Altes Museum in Berlin, makes an impressive entrance hall.

The Treasury houses masterpieces of Irish crafts including the Ardagh Chalice.

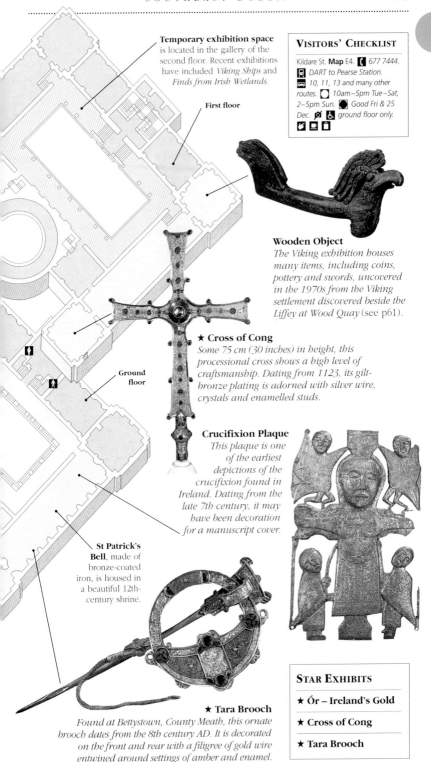

Temporary exhibition space
is located in the gallery of the
second floor. Recent exhibitions
have included *Viking Ships* and
Finds from Irish Wetlands.

First floor

Wooden Object
*The Viking exhibition houses
many items, including coins,
pottery and swords, uncovered
in the 1970s from the Viking
settlement discovered beside the
Liffey at Wood Quay (see p61).*

★ Cross of Cong
*Some 75 cm (30 inches) in height, this
processional cross shows a high level of
craftsmanship. Dating from 1123, its gilt-
bronze plating is adorned with silver wire,
crystals and enamelled studs.*

**Ground
floor**

Crucifixion Plaque
*This plaque is one
of the earliest
depictions of the
crucifixion found in
Ireland. Dating from the
late 7th century, it may
have been decoration
for a manuscript cover.*

**St Patrick's
Bell**, made of
bronze-coated
iron, is housed in
a beautiful 12th-
century shrine.

★ Tara Brooch
*Found at Bettystown, County Meath, this ornate
brooch dates from the 8th century AD. It is decorated
on the front and rear with a filigree of gold wire
entwined around settings of amber and enamel.*

STAR EXHIBITS

★ **Ór – Ireland's Gold**

★ **Cross of Cong**

★ **Tara Brooch**

Domed reading room on the first floor of the National Library

Leinster House ⑯

Kildare St. **Map** E4. **[** 681 3000.
⬤ to the public. ⬤ by arrangement,
ask at Kildare St entrance or phone
for details.

THIS STATELY MANSION houses
the *Dáil* and the *Seanad* –
the two chambers of the Irish
Parliament. It was originally
built for the Duke of Leinster
in 1745. Designed by Richard
Castle, the Kildare Street façade
resembles that of a large town
house. The rear, looking on to
Merrion Square, has the air of
a country estate. The Royal
Dublin Society bought the
building in 1815. The government obtained a part of it in
1922 and bought the entire
building two years later.
   Visitors can arrange to tour
the main rooms, including the
Seanad chamber.

National Library ⑰

Kildare St. **Map** E4. **[** 661 8811.
⬤ 10am–9pm Mon, 2–9pm Tue
& Wed, 10am–5pm Thu & Fri,
10am–1pm Sat. ⬤ public hols.

DESIGNED BY Sir Thomas
Deane, the National
Library was opened in 1890.
It was built to house the col-
lection of the Royal Dublin
Society *(see p83)*. In the
entrance hall are exhibitions
from the library's archive, in-
cluding manuscripts by George
Bernard Shaw, and politician

Daniel O'Connell *(see p14)*.
Prized exhibits include photographs of Victorian Ireland and
the 13th-century manuscript of
Giraldus Cambrensis's
Topographia Hiberniae.
   The first-floor Reading Room
has green-shaded lamps and
well-worn desks. To go in, ask
an attendant for a visitor's pass.

National Gallery ⑱

See pp46–9.

Merrion Square ⑲

Map F4.

MERRION SQUARE is one of
Dublin's largest and
grandest Georgian squares.
Covering about 5 ha (12 acres),
the square was laid out
by John Ensor
around 1762.
   On the
west of the
square are

**Statue of Oscar Wilde by Danny
Osbourne in Merrion Square**

the impressive façades of the
Natural History Museum, the
National Gallery and the front
garden of Leinster House.
However, this august trium-
virate does not compare with
the attractive Georgian town
houses on the other three
sides of the square. Many
have brightly painted doors
with original features such as
wrought-iron balconies, ornate
doorknockers and fanlights.
The oldest and finest houses
are on the north side.
   Many of the houses – now
predominantly used as office
space – have plaques detail-
ing the rich and famous who
once lived in them. These
include Catholic emancipation

leader Daniel O'Connell *(see p14)*, who lived at No. 58 and poet WB Yeats *(see p21)*, who lived at No. 82. Oscar Wilde *(see p21)* spent his childhood at No. 1.

The attractive central park features colourful flower and shrub beds. In the 1840s it served a grim function as an emergency soup kitchen, feeding the hungry during the Great Famine *(see p15)*. On the northwest side of the park stands the restored Rutland Fountain. It was originally erected in 1791 for the sole use of Dublin's poor.

Just off the square, at No. 24 Merrion Street Upper, is the birthplace of the Duke of Wellington, who, when he was teased about his Irish background, famously said, "Being born in a stable does not make one a horse."

Royal Hibernian Academy **❷⓿**

15 Ely Place. **Map** E5. ☎ *661 2558.* ⬜ *11am–5pm Mon–Wed, Fri & Sat, 11am–9pm Thu, 2–5pm Sun.* ⬤ *public hols.*

THE ACADEMY is one of the largest exhibition spaces in the city. It puts on touring exhibitions and mounts shows of painting, sculpture and other work by Ireland's best young art and design students. This modern brick-

The recreated Georgian kitchen of Number 29, Fitzwilliam Street Lower

and-plate-glass building does, however, look out of place at the end of Ely Place, an attractive Georgian cul-de-sac.

Number 29 **❷❶**

29 Fitzwilliam Street Lower. **Map** E5. ☎ *702 6165.* ⬜ *10am–5pm Tue–Sat, 2–5pm Sun.* ⬤ *Two weeks prior to Christmas.* 📷

NUMBER 29 IS A corner townhouse, built in 1794 for a Mrs Elizabeth Beattie whose late husband was a wine and paper merchant. While the period furniture comes from the collection of the National Museum, the main purpose of this exhibit is to give visitors a behind-the-scenes look at how middle-class Georgians went

about their daily business. Tours start with a short slide show and then work their way through the building from the cellar upwards. Along the way are mahogany tables, chandeliers, Turkish carpets and landscape paintings (by Thomas Roberts amongst others) but of most interest are some of the quirkier items. Guides point out rudimentary hostess trolleys, water filters and even a Georgian pushchair, as well as an early exercise machine, used to tone up the muscles for horse riding. A tea caddy takes pride of place in one of the reception rooms: at today's prices a kilo of tea would have cost IR£1,000 and hence the lady of the house kept the key to the caddy on her person at all times.

The elegant gardens in Merrion Square, a quiet backwater in the centre of Dublin

National Gallery ®

The Houseless Wanderer by **John Foley**

THIS PURPOSE-BUILT gallery was opened to the public in 1864. It houses many excellent exhibits, largely due to generous bequests, such as the Milltown collection of works of art from Russborough House *(see p100)*. Playwright George Bernard Shaw was also a benefactor, leaving a third of his estate to the gallery. More than 500 works are on display in the gallery and, although there is much emphasis on Irish art, every major school of European painting is well represented.

Stairs to temporary exhibitions

Pierrot
This Cubist-style work, by Spanish-born artist Juan Gris, is one of many variations he painted on the theme of Pierrot and Harlequin. This particular one dates from 1921.

First floor

Early Renaissance

★ **For the Road**
A whole room is dedicated to the works of Jack Yeats (1871–1957). This mysterious late painting reflects the artist's obsession with the Sligo countryside.

The Yeats Museum houses portraits by John B Yeats and works by son Jack B Yeats and his sisters.

The Shaw Room is an elegant hall, lined with full-length portraits, dating from the 17th century onwards, and lit by magnificent Waterford Crystal chandeliers.

GALLERY GUIDE

The collection is housed on two floors. On the ground floor are the Irish and British rooms: Room 32 has portraits of Irish sitters by artists from all schools. The first floor features works hung in broadly chronological order according to nation. The Italian, French, Dutch and Flemish collections account for most of the space.

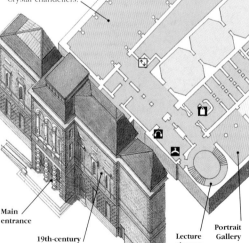

Main entrance

19th-century façade

Lecture theatre

Portrait Gallery

STAR PAINTINGS

★ **The Taking of Christ by Caravaggio**

★ **Castle of Bentheim by Ruisdael**

★ **For the Road by Jack Yeats**

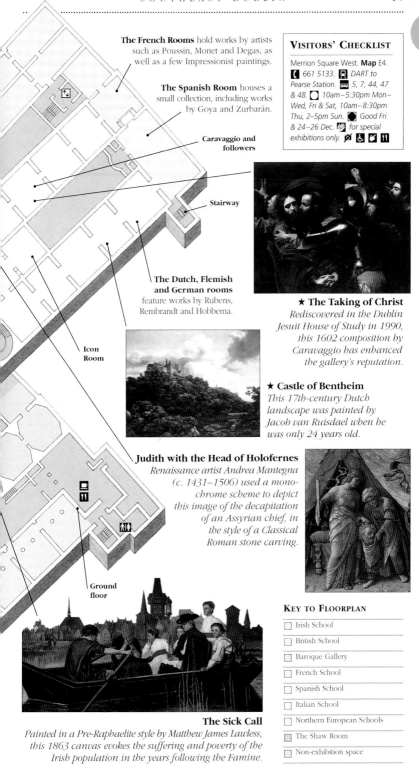

The French Rooms hold works by artists such as Poussin, Monet and Degas, as well as a few Impressionist paintings.

The Spanish Room houses a small collection, including works by Goya and Zurbarán.

Caravaggio and followers

Stairway

Icon Room

The Dutch, Flemish and German rooms feature works by Rubens, Rembrandt and Hobbema.

★ **The Taking of Christ**
Rediscovered in the Dublin Jesuit House of Study in 1990, this 1602 composition by Caravaggio has enhanced the gallery's reputation.

★ **Castle of Bentheim**
This 17th-century Dutch landscape was painted by Jacob van Ruisdael when he was only 24 years old.

Judith with the Head of Holofernes
Renaissance artist Andrea Mantegna (c. 1431–1506) used a mono-chrome scheme to depict this image of the decapitation of an Assyrian chief, in the style of a Classical Roman stone carving.

Ground floor

The Sick Call
Painted in a Pre-Raphaelite style by Matthew James Lawless, this 1863 canvas evokes the suffering and poverty of the Irish population in the years following the Famine.

KEY TO FLOORPLAN

- Irish School
- British School
- Baroque Gallery
- French School
- Spanish School
- Italian School
- Northern European Schools
- The Shaw Room
- Non-exhibition space

Exploring the National Gallery

THE EXHIBITIONS IN the gallery are laid out in a clear, easy-to-follow way and there are some excellent pieces of art on display. Modern Irish art, including the *Four Seasons* installation by Felim Egan, occupies the airy Atrium, a recent addition to the gallery's space. In addition to the major schools, there are rooms devoted to religious icons, and a modern print gallery which houses temporary exhibitions.

IRISH SCHOOL

THIS IS THE largest collection on display and the richest part of the gallery. Stretching back to the late 17th century, works range from landscapes such as *A View of Powerscourt Waterfall* by George Barret to paintings by Nathaniel Hone the Elder, including *The Conjuror*. Portraiture includes work by James Barry and Hugh Douglas Hamilton.

The Romantic movement made a strong impression on artists in the early 19th century; Francis Danby's *The Opening of the Sixth Seal*, an apocalyptic interpretation from the Book of Revelations, is the best example of this genre. Other examples are the Irish landscapes of James Arthur O'Connor.

In the late 19th century many Irish artists lived in Breton colonies, absorbing Impressionist influences. Roderic O'Conor's *Farm at Lezaven, Finistère* and William Leech's *Convent Garden, Brittany*, with its refreshing tones of green and white, are

Convent Garden, Brittany, by William Leech (1881–1968)

two of the best examples from this period.

The foundation in 1920 of the Society of Dublin Painters promoted work by the likes of Paul Henry and Jack B Yeats, also on display in the gallery. Other exponents of modern Irish works of art can be found on display at The Hugh Lane Gallery in Parnell Square *(see p71)*.

In 1999 a new Yeats gallery opened, displaying not just the work of Jack B Yeats but also other members of this talented Irish family.

BRITISH SCHOOL

WORKS DATING from the 18th century dominate in those rooms that are devoted to British artists. In particular William Hogarth, Thomas Gainsborough and Joshua Reynolds are well represented, accounting for over 15 items on display. Reynolds was one of the great portrait painters of his time and other portraits, by artists including Philip Reinagle, Francis Wheatley and Henry Raeburn, perfectly capture the family, military and aristocratic life of that period.

BAROQUE GALLERY

THIS LARGE ROOM accommodates 17th-century paintings, many by lesser-known artists. It also holds enormous canvases by more famous names such as Lanfranco, Jordaens and Castiglione, which are too big to fit into the spaces occupied by their respective schools. *The Annunciation* and *Peter Finding the Tribute Money* by Rubens are among the gallery's most eye-catching paintings.

FRENCH SCHOOL

THE PAINTINGS IN the rooms devoted to the French school are separated into the 17th and 18th centuries (in the Milltown Rooms) and the Barbizon, Impressionist, post-Impressionist and Cubist collections (in the Dargan Wing).

Among the earlier works is *The Annunciation*, a fine 15th-century panel by Jacques Yverni and the *Lamentation over the Dead Christ* by the 17th-century Nicolas Poussin.

The early 19th century saw the French colonization of North Africa. Many works were inspired by it, including *Guards at the Door of a Tomb* by Jean-Léon Gérôme. Another fine 19th-century work is *A Group of Cavalry in the Snow* by Ernest Meissonier.

The Impressionist paintings are always amongst the most popular in the gallery. These

A View of Powerscourt Waterfall by George Barret the Elder (c.1728–84)

A Group of Cavalry in the Snow by Ernest Meissonier (1815–91)

include Monet's *A River Scene, Autumn* from 1874. Works by Degas, Pissarro and Sisley are also displayed in this set of rooms. Jacques Emile Blanche's famous 1934 portrait of James Joyce is in Room 10.

Guards at the Door of a Tomb by Jean-Léon Gérôme (1824–1904)

SPANISH SCHOOL

Works from the Spanish school occupy comparatively little space, but they are rich and varied. One of the early pieces of note is El Greco's *St Francis Receiving the Stigmata*, a particularly dramatic work, dating from around 1595. Other notable acquisitions from this period are by Zurbarán, Velázquez and Murillo. There are four works by Francisco de Goya (1746–1828) on display including a portrait of the actress Doña Antonia Zárata. Pablo Picasso's *Still Life With A Mandolin* and *Pierrot* by Juan Gris represent 20th-century Spanish art.

ITALIAN SCHOOL

As a result of a successful purchasing strategy at the time of the gallery's inauguration, and various bequeathments, there is a strong collection of Italian art in the gallery.

Works of the Italian School spread over six rooms. Andrea Mantegna's *Judith with the Head of Holofernes* is done in *grisaille*, a technique that creates a stone-like effect. Famous pieces by Uccello, Titian, Moroni and Fontana hang in this section, but it is Caravaggio's *The Taking of Christ* (1602) which is the most important item. It was discovered by chance in a Dublin Jesuit house where it had hung in obscurity for many years. It was first hung in the National Gallery in 1993.

Constantinople School icon

NORTHERN EUROPEAN SCHOOLS

The early Netherlandish School is comprised largely of paintings with a religious theme. One exception is Brueghel the Younger's lively *Peasant Wedding* (1620). In the Dutch collection there are many 17th-century works, including some by Rembrandt. Other highlights include *A Wooded Landscape* by Hobbema and *Lady Writing a Letter With Her Maid* by Vermeer. Rubens and van Dyck are two more famous names here, but there are also fine works by lesser known artists, such as van Uden's *Peasants Merrymaking*. Portraits by such names as Faber and Pencz from the 15th and 16th centuries dominate the German collection, though Emil Nolde's colourful *Two Women in the Garden* dates from 1915.

OTHER COLLECTIONS

The impressive Shaw Room is home to some exceptionally fine historical portraits. One of the most interesting pieces is Reynolds' portrait of Charles Coote, the first Earl of Bellamont, dressed up in flamboyant pink ceremonial robes. Another famous picture here is *The Marriage of Strongbow and Aoife*, by Maclise.

Peasant Wedding by Pieter Brueghel the Younger (1564–1637)

SOUTHWEST DUBLIN

THE AREA around Dublin Castle was first settled in prehistoric times, and it was from here that the city grew. Dublin gets its name from the dark pool *(Dubh Linn)* which formed at the confluence of the Liffey and the Poddle, a river which originally ran through the site of Dublin Castle. It is now channelled underground. Archaeological excavations behind Wood Quay, on the banks of the river Liffey, reveal that the Vikings had a settlement here as early as AD 841.

Following Strongbow's invasion of 1170, a medieval city began to emerge; the Anglo-Normans built strong defensive walls around the castle.

Colourful logo of the children's centre, The Ark, in Temple Bar

A small reconstructed section of these old city walls can be seen at St Audoen's Church. More conspicuous reminders of the Anglo-Normans appear in the medieval Christ Church Cathedral and St Patrick's Cathedral. When the city expanded during the Georgian era, the narrow cobbled streets of Temple Bar became a quarter inhabited by skilled craftsmen and merchants. Today this area is considered to be the trendiest part of town, and is home to a variety of alternative shops and cafés. The Powerscourt Townhouse is an elegant 18th-century mansion that has been converted into one of the city's best shopping centres.

SIGHTS AT A GLANCE

Museums and Libraries
Chester Beatty Library and
  Gallery of Oriental Art ❷
Dublin Civic Museum ❻
Dublinia ⓭
Marsh's Library ❽

Historic Buildings
City Hall ❸
Dublin Castle pp54–5 ❶
Powerscourt Townhouse ❺
Tailors' Hall ⓫

Historic Areas
Temple Bar pp56–7 ❹

Churches
Christ Church Cathedral
  pp62–3 ⓮
St Audoen's Church ⓬
St Patrick's Cathedral ❾
St Werburgh's Church ❿
Whitefriar Street Carmelite
  Church ❼

KEY

▨	Street-by-Street map *See pp52–3*
🅿	Parking

**GETTING
AROUND**
Buses 11, 16A, 16B and 19A go to streets adjacent to Temple Bar. Numbers 49A, 49B, 54A, 65A, 65B and 123 go past St Patrick's and Christ Church cathedrals.

◁ **Colourful street in bustling Temple Bar**

Street-by-Street: Southwest Dublin

D ESPITE ITS WEALTH of ancient buildings,
such as Dublin Castle and Christ Church
Cathedral, this part of Dublin lacks the sleek
appeal of the neighbouring streets around
Grafton Street. In recent years, however,
redevelopment has rejuvenated the area,
especially around Temple Bar, where the
attractive cobbled streets are lined with shops,
futuristic arts centres, galleries, bars and cafés.

Sunlight Chambers
were built in 1900 for
the Lever Brothers
company. The
delightful
terracotta deco-
ration on the
façade advertises
their main business
of soap manufacturing.

Wood Quay is where the
Vikings established their first
permanent settlement in Ireland
around 841.

**Dublin Viking
Adventure**

★ **Christ Church Cathedral**
*Huge family monuments,
including that of the
19th Earl of Kildare,
can be found in
Ireland's oldest cath-
edral, which also has a
fascinating crypt* ⑭

St Werburgh's Church
*An ornate interior hides behind
the somewhat drab exterior of
this 18th-century church* ⑩

Dublinia
*Medieval Dublin is
the subject of this
interactive museum,
located in the
former Synod Hall
of the Church of
Ireland. It is linked
to Christ Church by
a bridge* ⑬

City Hall
*Originally built as the
Royal Exchange in
1779, the city's muni-
cipal headquarters is
fronted by a huge
Corinthian portico* ❸

★ **Dublin Castle**
*The Drawing Room, with its
Waterford crystal chandelier, is
part of a suite of luxurious rooms
built in the 18th century for the
Viceroys of Ireland* ❶

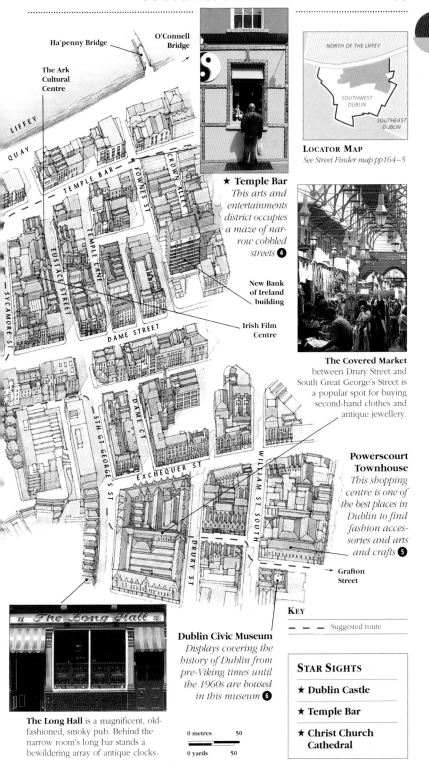

Ha'penny Bridge

O'Connell Bridge

The Ark Cultural Centre

LIFFEY

QUAY

TEMPLE BAR

FOWNES ST

CROW ALLEY

SYCAMORE ST

EUSTACE STREET

TEMPLE LANE

DAME STREET

STH GT GEORGE'S ST

DAME CT

EXCHEQUER ST

DRURY ST

WILLIAM ST SOUTH

★ **Temple Bar**
This arts and entertainments district occupies a maze of narrow cobbled streets ❹

New Bank of Ireland building

Irish Film Centre

The Covered Market
between Drury Street and South Great George's Street is a popular spot for buying second-hand clothes and antique jewellery.

Powerscourt Townhouse
This shopping centre is one of the best places in Dublin to find fashion accessories and arts and crafts ❺

Grafton Street

KEY

– – – Suggested route

STAR SIGHTS

★ **Dublin Castle**

★ **Temple Bar**

★ **Christ Church Cathedral**

Dublin Civic Museum
Displays covering the history of Dublin from pre-Viking times until the 1960s are housed in this museum ❻

The Long Hall is a magnificent, old-fashioned, smoky pub. Behind the narrow room's long bar stands a bewildering array of antique clocks.

0 metres   50

0 yards   50

LOCATOR MAP
See Street Finder map pp164–5

NORTH OF THE LIFFEY

SOUTHWEST DUBLIN

SOUTHEAST DUBLIN

Dublin Castle ❶

F OR SEVEN CENTURIES Dublin Castle was a symbol of English rule, ever since the Anglo-Normans built a fortress here in the 13th century. Nothing remains of the original structure except the much-modified Record Tower. Following a fire in 1684, the Surveyor-General, Sir William Robinson, laid down the plans for the Upper and Lower Castle Yards in their present form. On the first floor of the south side of the Upper Yard are the luxury State Apartments, including St Patrick's Hall. These rooms, with Killybegs carpets and chandeliers of Waterford glass, served as home to the British-appointed Viceroys of Ireland.

St Patrick by Edward Smyth

Figure of Justice
Facing the Upper Yard above the main entrance from Cork Hill, this statue aroused much cynicism among Dubliners, who felt she was turning her back on the city.

★ **Throne Room**
Built in 1740, this room contains a throne said to have been presented by William of Orange after his victory at the Battle of the Boyne (see p13).

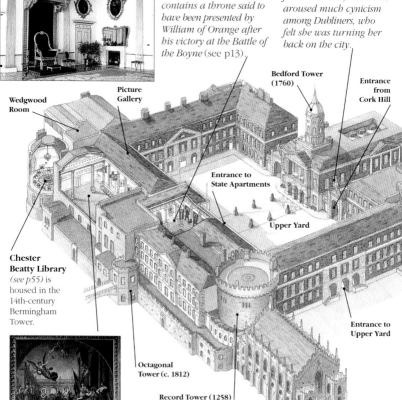

Wedgwood Room

Picture Gallery

Bedford Tower (1760)

Entrance from Cork Hill

Entrance to State Apartments

Upper Yard

Chester Beatty Library
(see p55) is housed in the 14th-century Bermingham Tower.

Entrance to Upper Yard

Octagonal Tower (c. 1812)

Record Tower (1258)

★ **St Patrick's Hall**
This hall, with its banners of the now defunct Knights of St Patrick, has ceiling paintings by Vincenzo Valdré (1778), symbolizing the relationship between Britain and Ireland.

The Church of the Most Holy Trinity was completed in 1814 by Francis Johnston. The 100 heads on the exterior of this Neo-Gothic church were carved by Edward Smyth.

ROBERT EMMET

Robert Emmet (1778–1803),
leader of the abortive 1803
rebellion, is remembered
as a heroic champion of
Irish liberty. His plan was
to capture Dublin Castle
as a signal for the country
to rise up against the Act
of Union (see p14). Emmet
was caught and publicly
hanged, but the defiant,
patriotic speech he made
from the dock helped to
inspire future generations
of Irish freedom fighters.

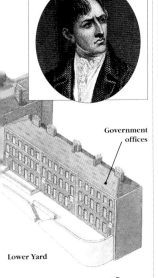

Government
offices

Lower Yard

Dame Street

STAR FEATURES

★ **St Patrick's Hall**

★ **Throne Room**

**Manuscript (1874) from the Holy Koran written by calligrapher Ahmad
Shaikh in Kashmir, Chester Beatty Library**

Chester Beatty Library and Gallery of Oriental Art **❷**

Bermingham Tower, Dublin Castle.
Map C4. **[** 677 7129. **□** ring for
details.

THIS COLLECTION of Oriental
manuscripts and art was
bequeathed to Ireland by the
American mining magnate and
art collector Sir Alfred Chester
Beatty, who died in 1968.
This generous act no doubt
led to his selection as Ireland's
first honorary citizen in 1957.

During his lifetime Beatty
accumulated almost 300 copies
of the Koran, representing the
works of master calligraphers
from Iran, Turkey and the
Arab world. Other exhibits
include 6,000-year-old
Babylonian stone tablets,
Greek papyri from the 2nd
century AD and biblical
material in Coptic, the original
language of Egypt.

In the Far Eastern collection
is a display of Chinese jade
books – each leaf is made from
thinly cut jade. Other displays
include Chinese snuff bottles
and imperial robes. Burmese
and Siamese art is represented
in the collection of 18th-
century Parabaiks, books of
folk tales illustrated with
colourful paintings. The
Japanese collection includes
paintings and books from the
16th to the 18th centuries.

Not to be overlooked is the
collection of western European
manuscripts. One of the most

beautiful is the Coëtivy Book of
Hours, an illuminated French
prayer book, dating from the
15th century. There is also a
collection of printed books,
many with fine engravings.

City Hall **❸**

Lord Edward St. **Map** C3. **●** to the
public.

DESIGNED BY Thomas Cooley,
this imposing building
was built between 1769 and
1779 as the Royal Exchange.
It was taken over by Dublin
Corporation in 1852 as a meeting place for the city council,
a role it keeps to this day.

Beyond the façade is the
entrance rotunda with its
attractive illuminated dome.
The city's coat-of-arms and
motto Obedientia Civium
Urbis Felicitas (Happy the city
where citizens obey) is depicted in mosaic form on the floor
of the rotunda. A pair of magnificent oval staircases leads
up to the Council Chamber.

Façade of City Hall

Temple Bar **4**

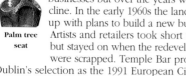

Palm tree seat

THE COBBLED streets between Dame Street and the Liffey are named after Sir William Temple who acquired the land in the early 1600s. The term "bar" meant a riverside path. In the 1800s it was home to small businesses but over the years went into decline. In the early 1960s the land was bought up with plans to build a new bus station. Artists and retailers took short term leases but stayed on when the redevelopment plans were scrapped. Temple Bar prospered and Dublin's selection as the 1991 European City of Culture has added impetus to its transformation. Today it is an exciting place, with bars, restaurants, shops and galleries.

Modern, floor-lit entrance hall of the Irish Film Centre

Exploring Temple Bar
For a first-time visitor, the most dramatic way to enter Temple Bar is through the **Merchants' Arch** opposite Ha'penny Bridge (see p75). Underneath the arch is a short, dark alley lined with bazaar-like retail outlets. The alley then opens out into the modern airy space of **Temple Bar Square**, a popular lunchtime hangout. In the southwest corner is the **Temple Bar Gallery and Studios**, a renovated factory that combines exhibition and studio spaces. Along the east side of the square is the colourful **Crown Alley** with its brightly-painted stores and cafés.

Curved Street is the heart of Temple Bar with its modern cultural institutions. The **Temple Bar Music Centre**, a resource centre and music venue, is here. The **DESIGNyard** has exhibitions of, and sells, modern Irish jewellery and furniture from

Ireland's top designers. A good source of information about the area is the **Temple Bar Information Centre** where you can pick up maps and leaflets about galleries and restaurants.

In the evening, there is a huge choice of restaurants, bars and pubs to choose from and entertainment ranges from avant-garde performance art at the **Project Arts Centre**, to musicals, plays and rock concerts at the **Olympia Theatre**. The Kitchen, a club owned by Bono, and the Edge of U2, situated under the band's Clarence Hotel offer the latest dance sounds.

Bird from DESIGNyard

Temple Bar Information Centre
18 Eustace Street. ⚫ 671 5717.
⚪ daily. www.temple-bar.ie

Irish Film Centre
6 Eustace Street. ⚫ 679 5744.
⚪ daily.
Opened in November 1992, this was the first major cultural project completed in Temple Bar. A neon art sign indicates the main entrance which runs through a floor-lit corridor before opening into an airy atrium where visitors can browse in the bookstore or have a snack. Irish film-making has come to the fore in recent years with such international hits as *The Commitments* (1991). The centre's two screens focus on cult, arthouse and independent films as well as showing archive screenings and documentaries. The IFC's programme also includes seminars and workshops, seasons on various themes, nations or directors, and it hosts the Junior Dublin Film Festival each year.

Arthouse Multimedia Centre for the Arts
Curved Street. ⚫ 605 6800.
Exhibition areas ⚪ daily.
Standing on Curved Street opposite the Temple Bar Music Centre, Arthouse is a centre for the arts, bringing art and technology together through multimedia. On the ground floor and in the basement, exhibition space is host to touring displays. Arthouse also offers training courses, workshops and seminars in multimedia. There is an Internet café, Cyberia, on the top floor of the building.

Shoppers in the streets of Temple Bar

Meeting House Square

Named after a Quaker place of worship which once stood here, this outdoor performance space is a wonderful asset to the city. In the summer there are lunchtime and evening classical concerts, with the orchestra playing on a stage which folds away into a wall when it is not being used. There are also outdoor screenings of films (these are free, but it is necessary to get a ticket from the Temple Bar Information Centre in advance), family events, and an organic food market is held every Saturday.

Cheese stall at the weekly organic market in Meeting House Square

Gallery of Photography

Meeting House Square. **🎟** *671 4654.* **⏰** *Mon–Sat.*
The only gallery in the country devoted solely to photography, this bright, contemporary space runs exhibitions, workshops and special events. Its bookshop stocks a good array of photos and postcards from the exhibitions.

National Photographic Archive

Meeting House Square. **🎟** *603 0200.* **⏰** *Mon–Fri.*
Housed in the Photography Centre which opened in 1998, the NPA spreads over three floors of exhibition space.

The exhibitions, covering a vast range of subjects, change four times a year. The photographs come from the National Library's archives of around a quarter of a million pictures.

Dublin's Viking Adventure

Essex Street West. **🎟** *679 6040.* **⏰** *Mar–Oct: Tue–Sat.* **♿**
This multimedia reconstruction of life in Dublin during the 9th century is, appropriately, adjacent to Wood Quay, where the Vikings first settled. The entertaining tours start off with visitors boarding a boat which runs on rollers through a "storm" before docking at a Viking village complete with re-created houses and actors

dressed in period costume. The special effects are authentic right down to the smells. Guides then lead visitors through corridors explaining the Wood Quay dig and into a room of Viking artifacts. There is also a film show for visitors to watch, projected onto the side of a replica longship. In the evenings, a feast of Irish food and entertainment is laid on around the longship – tickets must be purchased in advance.

Situated directly opposite the Viking Adventure are excavation sites of Viking dwellings. It is hoped that part of this area will be open to public view in the future.

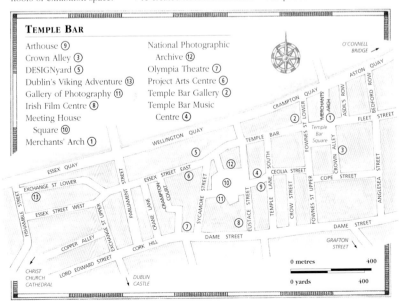

TEMPLE BAR

Arthouse ⑨
Crown Alley ③
DESIGNyard ⑤
Dublin's Viking Adventure ⑬
Gallery of Photography ⑪
Irish Film Centre ⑧
Meeting House Square ⑩
Merchants' Arch ①

National Photographic Archive ⑫
Olympia Theatre ⑦
Project Arts Centre ⑥
Temple Bar Gallery ②
Temple Bar Music Centre ④

0 metres 400

0 yards 400

The light and airy interior of Powerscourt Townhouse shopping centre

Powerscourt Townhouse **5**

South William St. **Map** D4. 679 4144. 9am–6pm Mon–Sat (9am–7pm Thu), noon–6pm Sun. *See also Shopping in Dublin pp134–9.*

COMPLETED IN 1774 by Robert Mack, this grand mansion was originally built as the city home of Viscount Powerscourt, who also had a country estate at Enniskerry just south of Dublin. Granite from the Powerscourt estate was used in its construction. Today the building houses one of Dublin's best shopping centres. Inside it still features the original grand mahogany staircase, and finely detailed plasterwork by stuccodore Michael Stapleton.

The building became a drapery warehouse in the 1830s, and major restoration in the 1960s turned it into a centre of specialist galleries, antique shops, jewellery stalls, cafés and other shop units. The central courtyard, topped by a glass dome, is popular with many Dubliners as a place to have a snack and a coffee.

The Townhouse can also be reached by an entrance on the narrow Johnson Court alley, just off bustling Grafton Street.

Dublin Civic Museum **6**

58 South William St. **Map** D4. 679 4260. 10am–6pm Tue–Sat, 11am–2pm Sun. 10 days at Christmas & public hols.

THIS SMALL MUSEUM, housed in the former Georgian City Assembly House, depicts Dublin's history from Viking times through to the 20th century by means of photographs, paintings, old newspaper cuttings and an

Shoes of an Irish Giant in Dublin Civic Museum

assortment of very unusual objects, including the old shoes of an Irish giant. One of the star exhibits is the head from the 40-m (134-ft) high Nelson Pillar. This massive monument was erected in 1808, and predated Nelson's Column in London's Trafalgar Square by several decades. It loomed high over O'Connell Street until it was destroyed in an explosion by anti-British protestors on 8 March 1966.

Whitefriar Street Carmelite Church **7**

56 Aungier St. **Map** C4. 475 8821. 8am–6:30pm Mon & Wed–Fri, 8am–9pm Tue, 8am–7pm Sat, 8am–7:30pm Sun.

DESIGNED BY George Papworth, this Catholic church was built in 1827. It stands on the site of a 16th-century Carmelite priory of which nothing remains.

In contrast to the two Church of Ireland cathedrals, St Patrick's and Christ Church, which are usually full of tourists, this church is frequented by local worshippers. Every day they come to light candles to various saints, including St Valentine – the patron saint of lovers. His remains, previously buried in the cemetery of St Hippolytus in Rome, were offered to the church as a gift from Pope Gregory XVI in 1836. Today they rest beneath the commemorative statue to the saint, which stands in the northeast corner of the church beside the high altar.

Nearby is a Flemish oak statue of the Virgin and Child, dating from the late 15th or early 16th century. It may have belonged to St Mary's Abbey *(see p74)* and is believed to be the only wooden statue of its kind to escape destruction when Ireland's monasteries were sacked during the time of the Reformation *(see p12).*

Statue of Virgin and child in Whitefriar Street Carmelite Church

The entrance to Marsh's Library, adjacent to St Patrick's Cathedral

Marsh's Library ❽

St Patrick's Close. **Map** B4.
📞 454 3511. ⏰ 10am–12:45pm & 2–5pm Mon & Wed–Fri, 10:30am–12:45pm Sat. ● 10 days at Christmas & public hols. 📷

BUILT IN 1701 for Archbishop Narcissus Marsh, this is the oldest public library in Ireland. It was designed by Sir William Robinson, architect of the Royal Hospital Kilmainham *(see p82)*.

To the rear of the library are wired alcoves where readers were locked in with rare books. The collection of books from the 16th–18th centuries includes a volume of Clarendon's *History of the Rebellion*, with margin notes by Jonathan Swift.

St Patrick's Cathedral ❾

St Patrick's Close. **Map** B4. 📞 475 4817. ⏰ Apr–Oct: 9am–6pm Mon–Fri, 9am–5pm Sat, 10–11am & 12:15–3pm Sun; Nov–Mar: 9am–6pm Mon–Fri, 9am–4pm Sat, 10am–11am & 12:15–3pm Sun. 📷

IRELAND'S LARGEST CHURCH was founded beside a sacred well where St Patrick is said to have baptized converts around AD 450. The original building was just a wooden chapel and remained so until 1192 when Archbishop John Comyn rebuilt it in stone.

In the mid-17th century, Huguenot refugees from France arrived in Dublin, and were given the Lady Chapel by the Dean and Chapter as

JONATHAN SWIFT (1667–1745)

Jonathan Swift was born in Dublin and educated at Trinity College *(see pp36–7)*. He left for England in 1689, but returned in 1694 when his political career failed. He began a life in the church, becoming Dean of St Patrick's in 1713. In addition, he was a prolific political commentator – his best-known work, *Gulliver's Travels*, contains a bitter satire on Anglo-Irish relations. Swift's personal life, particularly his friendship with two younger women, Ester Johnson, better known as Stella, and Hester Vanhomrigh, attracted criticism. In later life, he suffered from Menière's disease – an illness of the ear which led many to believe he was insane.

their place of worship. The chapel was separated from the rest of the cathedral and used by the Huguenots until the late 18th century. Today St Patrick's is the Protestant Church of Ireland's national cathedral.

Much of the present building dates back to work completed between 1254 and 1270. The cathedral suffered over the centuries from desecration, fire and neglect but, thanks to Sir Benjamin Guinness, it underwent extensive restoration during the 1860s. The building is 91 m (300 ft) long; at the western end is a 43-m (141-ft) tower, restored by Archbishop Minot in 1370 and now known as Minot's Tower. The spire was added in the 18th century.

The interior is dotted with memorial busts, brasses and monuments. A leaflet available at the front desk helps identify and locate them. Famous citizens remembered in the church include the harpist Turlough O'Carolan (1670–1738), Douglas Hyde (1860–1949), the first President of Ireland and of course Jonathan Swift and his beloved Stella.

At the west end of the nave is an old door with a hole in it – a relic from a feud between the Lords Kildare and Ormonde in 1492. The latter took refuge in the Chapter House, but a truce was soon made and a hole was cut in the door by Lord Kildare so that the two could shake hands in friendship.

St Patrick's Cathedral with Minot's Tower and spire

Nave of St Werburgh's Church, showing gallery and organ case

St Werburgh's Church ⑩

Entrance through 7–8 Castle St.
Map C4. **☎** 478 3710. ☐ 10am–4pm Mon–Fri, ring bell if doors locked.

BUILT ON LATE 12th-century foundations, St Werburgh's was designed by Thomas Burgh in 1715, after an act of parliament which appointed commissioners to build a new church. Around eighty-five people made donations. By 1719 the church was complete but had an unfinished tower. Then in 1728 James Southwell bequeathed money for a clock and bells for the church on condition that the tower was completed within three years of his death. It was finally finished in 1732. After a fire in 1754 it was rebuilt with the financial help of George II. It served as the parish church of Dublin Castle, hosting many state ceremonies, including the swearing-in of viceroys. However, this role was later taken over by the Church of the Most Holy Trinity within the castle walls.

Beyond the shabby pallor of its exterior walls lies some fine decorative work. There are massive memorials to members of the Guinness family, and a finely carved Gothic pulpit by Richard Stewart. Also worth seeing are the 1767 organ case and the beautiful stuccowork in the chancel.

Beneath the church lie 27 vaults including that of Lord Edward Fitzgerald, who died during the 1798 Rebellion (see p14), and also Sir James Ware. The body of Fitzgerald's captor, Major Henry Sirr, is in the graveyard. John Field, the creator of the nocturne, was baptized here in 1782.

Tailors' Hall ⑪

Back Lane. **Map** B4. ● to the public.

DUBLIN'S ONLY surviving guildhall preserves a delightful corner of old Dublin in an otherwise busy redevelopment zone. Built in 1706, it stands behind a limestone arch in a quiet cobbled yard. The building is the oldest guildhall in Ireland and was used by various trade groups including hosiers, saddlers and barber-surgeons as well as tailors. It was regarded as the most fashionable venue in Dublin for social occasions such as balls and concerts for many years until the New Music Hall in Fishamble Street opened and the social scene transferred to there. It also hosted many political meetings – the Protestant leader of the United Irishmen, Wolfe Tone, famously made a speech at the convention of the Catholic Committee on 2nd December 1792 before the 1798 rebellion (see p14).

The building closed in the early 1960s as a result of neglect, but a successful appeal by Desmond Guinness saw the hall completely refurbished. Since 1985 is has been the home of An Taisce (the Irish National Trust).

Façade of Tailors' Hall, today the home of the Irish National Trust

St Audoen's Church ⑫

High St. **Map** B3. ● for restoration.

DESIGNATED A national monument and currently under restoration, St Audoen's is Dublin's earliest surviving medieval church. The 12th-century tower is believed to be the oldest in Ireland, and its three bells date from 1423. The 15th-century nave also remains intact.

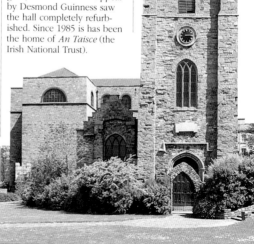

The 12th-century tower of St Audoen's Church, the oldest in Ireland

The church stands in an attractive churchyard with well-maintained lawns and shrubs. To the rear, steps lead down to St Audoen's Arch, the last remaining gateway of the old city. Flanking the gate are restored sections of the 13th-century city walls.

Next door stands St Audoen's Roman Catholic Church, which was begun in 1841 and completed in 1847. It was built by Patrick Byrne, of Talbot Street, who studied at the Dublin Society School. The parish priest, Patrick Mooney, completed the plasterwork and also installed the organ. In 1884 the dome of the church collapsed and was replaced with a plaster circle. The portico was added to the building in 1899. The Great Bell, dedicated on All Saints Day in 1848 and known as The Liberator after Daniel O'Connell, rang to announce his release from prison and also tolled on the day of his funeral. The two large Pacific clam shells by the front door of the church hold holy water. In the basement there is an audio-visual presentation on pre-Viking Ireland.

Former Synod Hall, now home to the Dublinia Exhibition

Dublinia ⑬

St Michael's Hill. **Map** B3. **[** 679 4611. **○** Apr–Sep: 10am–5pm daily; Oct–Mar: 11am–4pm Mon–Sat, 10am–4:30pm Sun. **●** 24–26 Dec. **◪** includes entry to Christ Church Cathedral via bridge. **♿**

MANAGED BY the non-profit-making Medieval Trust, the Dublinia exhibition covers the formative period of Dublin's history from the arrival of the Anglo-Normans in 1170 to the closure of the monasteries in the 1540s. The exhibition is housed in the Neo-Gothic Synod Hall, which, up until 1983, was home to the ruling body of the Church of Ireland. The building and the bridge linking it to Christ Church Cathedral date from the 1870s. Before Dublinia was

established in 1993, the Synod Hall was briefly converted into a nightclub.

The exhibition is entered via the basement where an audiotape-guided tour takes visitors through exhibits of life-size reconstructions, complete with realistic sounds and smells. These depict major events in Dublin's history, such as the Black Death and the rebellion of Silken Thomas *(see p12)*. The ground floor houses a large scale model of Dublin as it was around 1500, and reconstructions including the inside of a late medieval merchant's kitchen. There is also a display of artifacts from the Wood Quay excavation. This was the site of the first Viking settlement in Ireland. Excavations in the 1970s revealed remains of Norse and Norman villages, and artifacts includ-

Medieval key in the Dublinia exhibition

ing pottery, swords, coins and leatherwork. Many of these finds are on display at the National Museum *(see pp42–3)* as well as here in Dublinia. However, the city chose not to develop the Wood Quay site, but instead built two large civic offices there. If you go to Wood Quay today all you will find is a plaque and an unusual picnic site by the Liffey in the shape of a Viking longboat.

Also in the exhibition are information panels on the themes of trade, merchants and religion. On the first floor is the wood-panelled Great Hall, where there is a multi-screen presentation, set up to illustrate Dublin's medieval history.

Mid 13th-century jug in Dublinia

The Malton Room contains a set of prints by James Malton, the English artist who spent ten years in Dublin and did work for James Gandon in the 18th century. The 60-m (200-ft) high St Michael's Tower above Dublinia offers one of the best vantage points across the city.

Reconstruction of a Viking street in Dublinia

Christic Church Cathedral ⓮

CHRIST CHURCH CATHEDRAL was commissioned in 1172 by Strongbow, Anglo-Norman conqueror of Dublin (see p12), and Archbishop Laurence O'Toole. It replaced an earlier wooden church built by the Vikings in 1038. At the time of the Reformation (see p12), the cathedral passed to the Protestant Church of Ireland. By the 19th century it was in a bad state of repair, but was completely remodelled by architect George Street in the 1870s. In the crypt are monuments removed from the cathedral during its restoration.

★ **Medieval Lectern**
This beautiful brass lectern was hand-wrought during the Middle Ages. It stands on the left-hand side of the nave, in front of the pulpit. The matching lectern on the right-hand side is a copy, dating from the 19th century.

The Lord Mayor's pew is usually kept in the north aisle, but is moved to the front of the nave when used by Dublin's civic dignitaries. It features a carving of the city arms and a stand for the civic mace.

Great Nave
The 25-m (68-ft) high nave has some fine early Gothic arches. On the north side, the original 13th-century wall leans out by as much as 50 cm (18 in) due to subsidence.

Entrance

★ **Strongbow Monument**
The large effigy in chain armour is probably not Strongbow. However, his remains are buried in the cathedral and the curious half-figure may be part of his original tomb.

The bridge to the Synod Hall was added when the cathedral was being rebuilt in the 1870s.

STAR FEATURES

★ **Strongbow Monument**

★ **Crypt**

★ **Medieval Lectern**

Chapel of St Laud
The casket on the wall contains the heart of St Laurence O'Toole. The chapel features original medieval floor tiles.

VISITORS' CHECKLIST

Christ Church Place. **Map** B3.
677 8099. 50, 66, 77 & many other routes. 10am–5pm daily (6pm in summer).
26 Dec. **Donation.**
12.45pm Mon–Fri, 11am and 3.30pm Sun. Choral Evensong: 6pm Wed & Thu, 5pm Sat.

The Lady Chapel is used for Eucharist celebrations and is the chapel of the St John Ambulance Brigade.

★ **Crypt**
The cavernous crypt contains several oddities, including this mummified cat and rat, found in an organ pipe in the 1860s.

Stairs to crypt

Crypt

The foundations of the original Chapter House date back to the early 13th century.

Romanesque Doorway
Leading to the south transept, this ornately carved doorway is one of the finest examples of 12th-century Irish stonework.

TIMELINE

1000	1200	1400	1600	1800
1038 Construction of original wooden Viking cathedral	**1240** Completion of stone cathedral	**1600** Shopkeepers rent crypt space	**1689** King James II of England worships in cathedral	**1983** Cathedral ceases using Synod Hall
		1541 King Henry VIII alters constitution of cathedral		
1172 St Laurence O'Toole and Strongbow commission the new stone cathedral	*Meeting takes place between Lambert Simnel and the Earl of Kildare*	**1742** Choir participates in first performance of Handel's *Messiah* **1487** Coronation of 10-year-old Lambert Simnel as "King of England"		**1871** Major rebuilding of the cathedral begins, including Synod Hall and bridge

NORTH OF THE LIFFEY

DUBLIN'S NORTHSIDE was the last part of the city to be developed during the 18th century. The city authorities envisioned an area of leafy avenues, but the reality of today's traffic has rather spoiled their original plans. Nonetheless, O'Connell Street is an impressive thoroughfare, lined with department stores, monuments and historic public buildings.

Sign outside the Winding Stair Bookshop

Some of these buildings, such as James Gandon's glorious Custom House and majestic Four Courts, together with the famous General Post Office *(see p69)*, add grace to the area.

The Rotunda Hospital, Europe's first purpose-built maternity hospital, is another fine building. Dublin's two most celebrated theatres, the Abbey and the Gate, act as cultural magnets, as does the Dublin Writers' Museum and also the James Joyce Cultural Centre, two museums that are dedicated to writers who spent most of their lives in the city.

SIGHTS AT A GLANCE

Historic Buildings
Custom House ❶
Four Courts ❶❷
King's Inns ❾
Tyrone House ❹

Historic Streets and Bridges
Ha'penny Bridge ❶❻
O'Connell Street ❸
Parnell Square ❼
Smithfield ❿

Theatres
Abbey Theatre ❷

Churches
St Mary's Church ❶❺
St Mary's Pro-Cathedral ❺
St Michan's Church ❶❸

Museums and Galleries
Old Jameson Distillery ❶❶
James Joyce Cultural Centre ❻
World of Wax ❽
St Mary's Abbey Exhibition ❶❹

GETTING AROUND
Buses 3, 10, 11A, 13, 16A, 16B, 19A, 22A, 22B and 123 go along O'Connell Street and round Parnell Square. To get to St Michan's Church, Smithfield and Old Jameson Distillery, take a number 67A, 68, 69, 79 or 90.

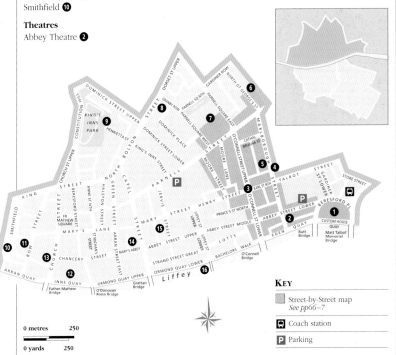

KEY

▨	Street-by-Street map *See pp66–7*
🚌	Coach station
🅿	Parking

◁ **The impressive columns of the General Post Office on O'Connell Street**

Street-by-Street: Around O'Connell Street

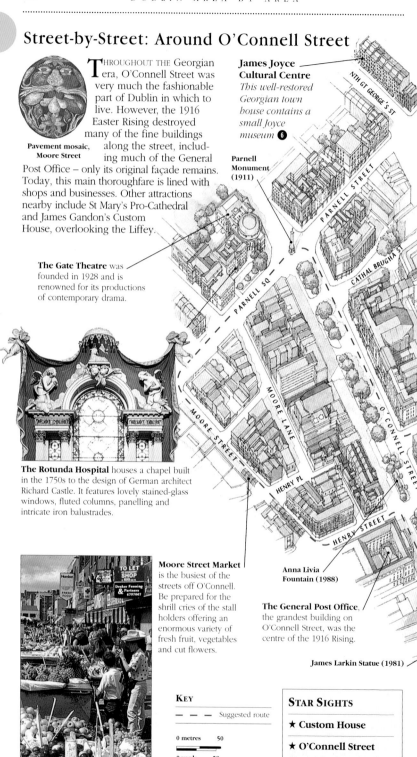

THROUGHOUT THE Georgian era, O'Connell Street was very much the fashionable part of Dublin in which to live. However, the 1916 Easter Rising destroyed many of the fine buildings along the street, including much of the General

Pavement mosaic, Moore Street

Post Office – only its original façade remains. Today, this main thoroughfare is lined with shops and businesses. Other attractions nearby include St Mary's Pro-Cathedral and James Gandon's Custom House, overlooking the Liffey.

James Joyce Cultural Centre
This well-restored Georgian town house contains a small Joyce museum **6**

Parnell Monument (1911)

The Gate Theatre was founded in 1928 and is renowned for its productions of contemporary drama.

The Rotunda Hospital houses a chapel built in the 1750s to the design of German architect Richard Castle. It features lovely stained-glass windows, fluted columns, panelling and intricate iron balustrades.

Moore Street Market is the busiest of the streets off O'Connell. Be prepared for the shrill cries of the stall holders offering an enormous variety of fresh fruit, vegetables and cut flowers.

Anna Livia Fountain (1988)

The General Post Office, the grandest building on O'Connell Street, was the centre of the 1916 Rising.

James Larkin Statue (1981)

KEY

– – – Suggested route

0 metres   50

0 yards   50

STAR SIGHTS

★ **Custom House**

★ **O'Connell Street**

St Mary's Pro-Cathedral
*Built around 1825, this is
Dublin's main place of
worship for Catholics. The
plaster relief above the
altar in the sanctuary
depicts* The Ascension **5**

The statue of James Joyce (1990), by
Marjorie Fitzgibbon, commemorates one
of Ireland's most famous novelists. Born in
Dublin in 1882, he catalogued the people
and streets of Dublin in *Dubliners* and in
his most celebrated work, *Ulysses.*

LOCATOR MAP
See Street Finder map pp164–5

NORTH OF
THE LIFFEY

SOUTHWEST
DUBLIN

SOUTHEAST
DUBLIN

Abbey Theatre
*Ireland's national
theatre is known
throughout the world
for its productions by
Irish playwrights,
such as Sean O'Casey
and JM Synge* **2**

★ O'Connell Street
*This monument to Daniel
O'Connell by John Foley took
19 years to complete from the
laying of its foundation
stone in 1864* **3**

CUSTOM HOUSE QUAY

Butt Bridge

LIFFEY

**O'Connell
Bridge**

**Trinity
College**

★ Custom House
*This striking head, by
Edward Smyth, symbolizes
the River Liffey. It is one of
14 carved keystones that
adorn the building* **1**

Illuminated façade of the Custom House reflected in the Liffey

Custom House ❶

Custom House Quay. **Map** E2.
❶ *to the public.*

THIS MAJESTIC BUILDING was designed as the Custom House by the English architect James Gandon. However, just nine years after its completion, the 1800 Act of Union *(see p14)* transferred the custom and excise business to London, rendering the building practically obsolete. In 1921, supporters of Sinn Fein celebrated their election victory by setting light to what they saw as a symbol of British imperialism. The fire blazed for five days causing extensive damage. Reconstruction took place in 1926, although further deterioration meant that the building was not completely restored until 1991, when it re-opened as government offices.

The main façade is made up of pavilions at each end with a Doric portico in its centre. The arms of Ireland crown the two pavilions, and a series of 14 allegorical heads by Dublin sculptor Edward Smyth form the keystones of arches and entrances. These heads depict Ireland's main rivers

and the Atlantic Ocean. A statue of Commerce tops the central copper dome.

The best view of the building is from the south of the Liffey beyond Matt Talbot Bridge, especially at night.

Logo of the Abbey Theatre

Abbey Theatre ❷

Lower Abbey St. **Map** E2. ☎ 878 7222. ☐ *for performances only.* **Box office** ☐ *10:30am–7pm Mon–Sat. See also Entertainment pp140–5.*

FOUNDED in 1898 with WB Yeats and Lady Gregory as co-directors, the Abbey staged its first play in 1904. The early

years of this much lauded national theatre witnessed works by WB Yeats, JM Synge and Sean O'Casey. Many were controversial: nationalist sensitivities were severely tested in 1926 in the premiere of O'Casey's *The Plough and the Stars*, when the flag of the Irish Free State appeared on stage in a scene which featured a pub frequented by prostitutes.

The Abbey Theatre remains best known for its excellent productions of early 20th-century Irish work, though in recent years it has done much to encourage new writing talent, particularly in the small Peacock Theatre downstairs. One of the most acclaimed performances in the main theatre was Brian Friel's *Dancing At Lughnasa* (1990). The walls in the theatre bar are lined with portraits of famous names that were once connected with the theatre.

O'Connell Street ❸

Map D1–D2.

O'CONNELL STREET is very different from the original plans of Irish aristocrat Luke Gardiner. When he bought the land in the 18th century, Gardiner envisioned a grand residential parade with an elegant mall running along its centre. Such plans were short-lived. The

O'Connell Bridge spanning the Liffey, viewed from the Butt Bridge

construction of Carlisle (now O'Connell) Bridge in 1790 transformed the street into the city's main north-south route. Also, several buildings were destroyed during the 1916 Easter Rising and the Irish Civil War. Since the 1960s many of the old buildings have been replaced by the plate glass and neon of fast food joints and amusement arcades.

A few venerable buildings remain, such as the General Post Office (1818), Gresham Hotel (1817), Clery's department store (1822) and the Royal Dublin Hotel, part of which occupies the street's only original town house.

A walk down the central mall is the most enjoyable way to see the street's mix of architectural styles. At the south end stands a huge monument to Daniel O'Connell *(see p14)*, unveiled in 1882. The street, which throughout the 19th century had been called Sackville Street, was renamed for O'Connell in 1922. Higher up, almost facing the General Post Office, is an expressive statue of James Larkin (1867–1943),

Clock outside Clery's department store

leader of the Dublin general strike in 1913. The next statue is of Father Theobald Mathew (1790– 1856), founder of the Pioneer Total Abstinence Movement. At the north end of the street is the obelisk-shaped monument to Charles Stewart Parnell (1846– 91), who was leader of the Home Rule Party and known as the "uncrowned King of Ireland" *(see p15)*. Also on O'Connell Street, at the junction of Cathedral Street, is the Anna Livia Millennium Fountain, which was unveiled during the city's millennium celebrations in 1988. It is supposed to represent the River Liffey but most Dubliners dismiss it simply as the "Floozie in the Jacuzzi".

Tyrone House **4**

Marlborough Street. **Map** D2.
4 *to the public.*

CONSIDERED TO BE the most important Dublin building by German-born Richard Castle (also known as Cassels) after Leinster House, this Palladian-style structure was completed around 1740 as a town house for Sir Marcus Beresford, later Earl of Tyrone. Its interior features elaborate plasterwork by the Swiss Francini brothers, as well as a grand mahogany staircase. The premises were bought by the government in the 1830s and today house a section of the Department of Education; the minister has one of the most ornate state offices in what used to be a reception room.

Austere Neo-Classical interior of St Mary's Pro-Cathedral

St Mary's Pro-Cathedral **5**

Marlborough St. **Map** D2. **📞** 874 5441. **⏰** 9:30am–5pm daily.

DEDICATED in 1825 before Catholic emancipation was fully effected *(see p14)*, St Mary's is Dublin's Catholic cathedral. Its backstreet site was the best the city's Anglo-Irish leaders would allow.

The façade is based on the Temple of Theseus in Athens. Its six Doric columns support a pediment with statues of St Laurence O'Toole, 12th-century Archbishop of Dublin and patron saint of the city, St Mary and St Patrick. The most striking feature of the interior is the intricately carved high altar.

St Mary's is home to the famous Palestrina Choir, started in 1902. In 1904 the great Irish tenor, John McCormack, began his career with the choir, which can be heard every Sunday at 11am.

THE GENERAL POST OFFICE (GPO)

Built in 1818 halfway along O'Connell Street, the GPO became a symbol of the 1916 Irish Rising. Members of the Irish Volunteers and Irish Citizen Army seized the building on Easter Monday, and Patrick Pearse *(see p15)* read out the Proclamation of the Irish Republic from its steps. Shelling from the British finally forced the rebels out after a week. At first, many Irish people viewed the Rising unfavourably. However, as WB Yeats wrote, matters "changed utterly" and a "terrible beauty was born" when, during the

***Irish Life* magazine cover showing the 1916 Easter Rising**

following weeks, 14 of the leaders were shot at Kilmainham Gaol *(see p79)*. Inside the GPO is a sculpture of the Irish mythical warrior Cuchulainn, dedicated to those who died.

James Joyce Cultural Centre ❻

35 North Great George's St. **Map** D1.
█ 878 8547. ⬤ 9:30am–5pm Mon–
Sat, noon–5pm Sat & Sun. ⬤ Good
Fri & 23–27 Dec. 🖼 🔲

ALTHOUGH BORN IN Dublin, Joyce spent most of his adult life in Europe. He used Dublin as the setting for his major works, including *Ulysses, A Portrait of the Artist as a Young Man* and *Dubliners.*

This centre is located in a 1784 town house which was built for the Earl of Kenmare. Michael Stapleton, one of the greatest stuccodores of his time, contributed to the plasterwork, of which the friezes are particularly noteworthy.

The main literary display is an absorbing set of biographies of around 50 characters from *Ulysses,* who were based on real Dublin people. Professor Dennis J Maginni, a peripheral character in *Ulysses,* ran a dancing school from this town house. Leopold and Molly Bloom, the central characters of *Ulysses,* lived a short walk away at No. 7 Eccles Street. The centre also organizes walking tours of Joyce's Dublin, so a visit is a must for all Joycean zealots.

At the top of the road, on Great Denmark Street, is the Jesuit-run Belvedere College attended by Joyce between 1893 and 1898. He recalls his unhappy schooldays there in *A Portrait of the Artist as a Young Man.* The college's interior contains some of Stapleton's best and most colourful plasterwork (1785).

**Portrait of James Joyce (1882–
1941) by Jacques Emile Blanche**

Parnell Square ❼

ONCE AS AFFLUENT as the now-restored squares to the south of the Liffey, Parnell Square is today sadly neglected. However, it still holds many points of interest, including the historic Gate Theatre and the peaceful Garden of Remembrance. There are hopes that this once-elegant part of the city will one day be renovated and restored to its original splendour.

Stained-glass window (c. 1863) in the Rotunda Hospital's chapel

Gate Theatre

1 Cavendish Row. **Map** D1.
█ 874 4368. ⬤ for performances
only. **Box office** █ 874 4045.
⬤ 10am–7pm Mon–Sat. See also
***Entertainment in Dublin** pp140– 5.*

Originally the grand supper room in the Rotunda, today the Gate Theatre is renowned for its staging of contemporary international drama in Dublin. It was founded in 1928 by Hilton Edwards and Mícheál Mac Liammóir. The latter is now best remembered for *The Importance of Being Oscar,* his long-running one-man show about the writer Oscar Wilde *(see p21).* An early success was Denis Johnston's *The Old Lady Says No,* so-called because of the margin notes made on one of his scripts by Lady Gregory, founding director of the Abbey Theatre *(see p68).* Although still noted for staging productions of new plays, the Gate's current output often includes classic Irish plays including Sean O'Casey's *Juno and the Paycock.*

Entrance to the Gate Theatre

Many famous names in the acting world got their first break at the Gate Theatre, including James Mason and a teenage Orson Welles.

Rotunda Hospital

Parnell Square West. **Map** D1.
█ 873 0700.

Standing in the middle of Parnell Square is Europe's first purpose-built maternity hospital. Founded in 1745 by Dr Bartholomew Mosse, the design of the hospital is similar to that of Leinster House *(see p44).* The German-born architect Richard Castle designed both buildings. At the east end of the hospital is the Rotunda, after which the hospital is named. It was built in 1764 by John Ensor as Assembly Rooms to host fundraising functions and concerts. Franz Liszt gave a concert here in 1843.

On the first floor is a chapel featuring striking stained-glass windows and Rococo plasterwork and ceiling (1755) by the stuccodore Bartholomew

Cramillion. On the other side of the road from the hospital is Conway's Pub. Opened in 1745, it has been popular with expectant fathers for years.

Garden of Remembrance

Parnell Square. **Map** C1.
◯ *dawn–dusk daily.*

At the northern end of Parnell Square is a small, peaceful park, dedicated to the men and women who have died in the pursuit of Irish freedom. The Garden of Remembrance marks the spot where several leaders of the Easter Rising were held overnight before being taken to Kilmainham Gaol (*see p79*), and is also where the Irish Volunteers movement was formed in 1913.

Designed by Daithí Hanly, the garden was opened by President Eamon de Valera (*see p16*) in 1966, to mark the 50th anniversary of the Easter Rising. In the centre is a cruciform pool with a mosaic depicting broken swords, shields and spears, symbolizing peace. At one end of the garden is a large bronze sculpture by Oisín Kelly (1971) of the legendary *Children of Lir*, the daughters of King Lir who were changed into swans by their jealous stepmother.

Gallery of Writers at Dublin Writers Museum

Dublin Writers Museum

18 Parnell Square North. **Map** C1.
📞 872 2077. ◯ *10am–5pm (Jun–Aug: 10am–6pm) Mon–Sat, 11am–5pm Sun & public hols.* ● *25 & 26 Dec.* ▦

Opened in 1991, the museum occupies an 18th-century town house. There are displays relating to Irish literature over the last thousand years, although there is little about writers in the latter part of the 20th century. The exhibits include paintings, manuscripts, letters, rare editions and mementos of Ireland's finest authors. There are many temporary exhibits and a lavishly decorated Gallery of Writers upstairs. The museum also hosts frequent poetry readings and lectures.

Children of Lir **in the Garden of Remembrance**

An excellent restaurant, the Chapter One (*see p129*), and a specialist bookstore, providing an out-of-print search service, add to the relaxed and friendly ambience of this interesting museum.

Hugh Lane Municipal Gallery of Modern Art

Charlemont House, Parnell Square North. **Map** C1. 📞 874 1903.
◯ *9:30am–6pm Tue–Thu, 9:30am–5pm Fri & Sat, 11am–5pm Sun.* ● *23–25 Dec & public hols.*

Noted art collector Sir Hugh Lane donated his valuable collection of Impressionist paintings, including *Le Concert aux Tuileries* by Manet and *Sur La Plage* by Degas, to Dublin Corporation in 1905. However, the failure to find a suitable location for them prompted Lane to consider transferring his gift to the National Gallery in London. The Corporation then proposed Charlemont House, the town house of Lord Charlemont, who built Marino Casino (*see p86*) and Lane relented. However, in 1915, before Lane's revised will could be witnessed, he died on board the torpedoed liner *Lusitania.* This led to a 50-year dispute which has been resolved by Dublin Corporation and the National Gallery swapping the collection every five years.

As well as the Lane bequest the gallery also has a sculpture hall with work by Rodin and others. There is also an extensive collection of modern Irish canvases including Michael Farrell's *Madonna Irlanda* (1977) and Patrick Graham's *Ireland III* (1982).

Sur la Plage (c. 1876) by Edgar Degas, Hugh Lane Municipal Gallery

The impressive façade of the King's Inns, on Constitution Hill

National Wax Museum ❽

Granby Row, Parnell Square. **Map** C1.
☎ 872 6340. ◯ Mon–Sat 10am–
5:30pm, Sun noon–5:30pm. ♿

JUST OFF THE northwest edge of Parnell Square, this museum firmly sets its sights on attracting children. Significant space is given over to fairytale and cartoon characters such as the Flintstones, Ninja Turtles and the Simpsons. Further amusement comes in the form of a hall of mirrors while the dimly-lit Chamber of Horrors is good fun. The largest area traces Ireland's history and culture with characters from the past almost to the present day. The wax dummies of all the figures, from Wolfe Tone to recent President Mary Robinson, make the subjects look incredibly young – including the Reverend Ian Paisley and Pope John Paul II (who appears complete with replica Popemobile). Irish cycling legend Sean Kelly is set racing up a steep climb.

Many of the displays, encased behind glass screens, offer an audio definition of their cultural or historical importance; a useful feature as some of the subjects are not particularly well known outside Ireland. The final section groups together several leading lights in the entertainment world including U2, Garth Brooks and Madonna.

King's Inns ❾

Henrietta St/Constitution Hill.
Map B1. ◖ to the public.

THIS CLASSICALLY proportioned public building was founded in 1795 as a place of both residence and study for barristers in Dublin. The King's Inns was the name taken by the Irish lawyers' society upon Henry VIII declaring himself King of Ireland. To build it, James Gandon, famous as the architect of the Custom House (see p68), chose to seal off the end of Henrietta Street, which was Dublin's first Georgian street and, at the time, one of the city's most fashionable addresses. Francis Johnston added the graceful cupola in 1816, and the building was finally completed in 1817. Inside there is a fine Dining Hall, and the Registry of Deeds (formerly the Prerogative Court). The west

Statue at the entrance to King's Inns

façade has two doorways flanked by elegant Classical caryatids (statues used in place of pillars) carved by sculptor Edward Smyth. The male figure, holding book and quill, is representative of the law.

Sadly, much of the area around Constitution Hill today is less attractive than it was in Georgian times. However, the King's Inns' gardens, which are open to the public, are still pleasant to stroll around.

Smithfield ❿

Map A2.

LAID OUT in the mid-17th century as a marketplace, this vast, cobbled expanse is a welcome respite from central Dublin's traffic-laden streets. Most of the time Smithfield is relatively tranquil, though on the first Sunday of each month it springs to life when it hosts the long-established horse and pony sale. Although you will not see

Children riding saddle-free through the cobbled streets of Smithfield market

any thoroughbreds here – none of the animals on sale is likely to run in the Irish Derby – the atmosphere alone makes this event well worth a visit if you are in the city on the first Sunday in the month. The occasion is a delightful cameo of Dublin life and the scene of young children riding horses bareback chaotically over the cobblestones and adults haggling over prices is an eye-opening experience – far removed from the chic environs of Temple Bar.

Horses tethered at Smithfield market

Old Jameson Distillery ⑪

Bow St. **Map** A2. 📞 *807 2355.* 🕐 *daily 9.30am–6pm (last tour at 5pm).* ⬤ *25 Dec and Good Fri.* 📷 ♿

PROOF OF significant investment in the emerging Smithfield area of Dublin's northside is evident in this large exhibition, set in a restored building that formed part of John Jameson's distillery. Whiskey was produced here from 1780 until 1971. While the place is run by Irish Distillers Limited, who are obviously keen to talk up their products (the four main names are Jameson, Paddy, Bushmills and John Power), it is an impressive, entertaining and educational experience. Visits start with a video, *Uisce Beatha* (the Water of Life; *uisce* meaning "water" and the origin of the word

Sampling different whiskeys at the Old Jameson Distillery

"whiskey"). Further whiskey-related facts are then explained to visitors in the 20-minute tour. This moves around displays set out as a working distillery with different rooms devoted to the various stages of whiskey production, from grain storage right through to bottling. The tour guides are particularly keen to point how the barley drying process differs from that used in the production of Scotch whisky: in Ireland the grain is dried through clean dry air while in Scotland it is smoked over peat. They claim that this results in a smoother Irish tipple compared to its more smoky Scottish counterpart. At the end of the tour, visitors can test this claim in the nicely-appointed bar.

IRISH WHISKEY

It is widely claimed that the Irish were the first to produce whiskey. This is quite possibly the case, since the monks spreading Christianity across Europe supposedly learnt the skills of distillation in the East where perfume was made. Some even believe that it was St Patrick who introduced the art. In the late 1800s and early 1900s Irish whiskey was superseded somewhat by the lighter blended Scotch. In addition, sales suffered in the United States as a result of the Prohibition. Today however, Irish whiskeys are enjoying a comeback and provide fierce competition for Scotch whiskies.

Jameson 1780, at 12 years old, has a classic smooth Jameson character. It is a hearty taste of Dublin's distilling heritage.

Old Bushmills *is a blended whiskey made from just one malt and a single grain. The end result is a pleasant blend of malty sweetness and aromatic dryness.*

Paddy is the classic whiskey of Cork, Ireland's second city. It is firm-bodied, with the crisp finish typical of native Cork whiskeys.

Power and Son's Gold Label Irish, sometimes known as "Three Swallows", is a well-balanced and malty whiskey. Originally from Dublin, today it is very much a national brand.

James Gandon's Four Courts overlooking the River Liffey

Four Courts ⑫

Inns Quay. **Map** B3. 〖 *872 5555.*
◯ *10am–1pm, 2–4:30pm Mon–Fri
(when courts in session).*

Cᴏᴍᴘʟᴇᴛᴇᴅ ɪɴ 1802 by James
Gandon, this majestic
building was virtually gutted
120 years later during the Irish
Civil War *(see p15)* when
government forces bombard-
ed anti-Treaty rebels into
submission. The adjacent
Public Records Office, with
documents dating back to the
12th century, was destroyed
by fire. In 1932, the main
buildings were restored using
Gandon's original design. A
copper-covered lantern dome
rises above the six-columned
Corinthian portico, which is
crowned with the figures of
Moses, Justice and Mercy.
This central section is flanked
by two wings containing the
four original courts: Common
Pleas, Chancery, Exchequer

and King's Bench. It is possible
to walk in to the central waiting hall under the grand dome.
An information panel to the
right of the entrance gives
details of the building's
history and functions.

St Michan's Church ⑬

Church St. **Map** B3. 〖 *872 4154.*
◯ *mid-Mar–Oct: 10am–12:45pm &
2–4:45pm Mon–Fri, 10am–12:45pm
Sat; Nov–mid-Mar: 12:30–3:30pm
Mon–Fri, 10am–12:45pm Sat.* 🖼 🖼

Lᴀʀɢᴇʟʏ ʀᴇʙᴜɪʟᴛ in 1686 on
the site of an 11th-century
Hiberno-Viking church, the
dull façade of St Michan's
hides a more exciting interior.
Deep in its vaults lie a number
of bodies that have barely
decomposed because of the
dry atmosphere created by the
church's magnesian limestone
walls. Their wooden caskets,

however, have cracked open,
revealing the preserved bodies,
complete with skin and hair.
Among those thought to have
been mummified in this way
are the brothers Henry and
John Sheares, leaders of the
1798 rebellion *(see p14)*, who
were executed that year.
  Other, less gory, attractions
include the magnificent wood
carving of fruits and violins and
other instruments above the
choir. There is also an organ
(1724) on which Handel is
said to have played.

St Mary's Abbey Exhibition ⑭

Meetinghouse Lane. **Map** C2.
〖 *872 1490.* ◯ *mid-Jun–mid-Sep:
10am–5pm Wed.* 🖼

Fᴏᴜɴᴅᴇᴅ ʙʏ Benedictine
monks in 1139, but then
transferred to the Cistercian
order just eight years later,
this was one of
the largest and
most important
monasteries in
medieval Ireland.
When it was
built, the sur-
rounding land
was peaceful
countryside; to-
day, what is left
of this historically
important abbey
is hidden away in

Detail of wood carving (c. 1724) at St Michan's Church

the sprawling backstreets that are found on the north side of the river Liffey.

As well as having control over extensive estates, including whole villages, mills and fisheries, the abbey acted as state treasury and meeting place for the Council of Ireland. It was during a council meeting in St Mary's that "Silken Thomas" Fitzgerald *(see p12)* renounced his allegiance to Henry VIII and marched out to raise the short-lived rebellion of 1534. The monastery was dissolved a few years later in 1539 and, during the 17th century, the site served as a quarry. Stone from St Mary's was pillaged and used in the construction of Essex Bridge (which was later replaced by Grattan Bridge in 1874), just to the south of the abbey.

Sadly, all that remains of the abbey today is the vaulted chamber of the old Chapter House. This houses a display on the history of the abbey and a model of how it would have looked 800 years ago.

The old vaulted Chapter house in St Mary's Abbey

St Mary's Church 🄯

Mary Street (at Wolfe Tone Street).
Map C2. ☎ *872 4088.*

IN AMONGST THE produce stalls and family-run stores in the warren of streets to the west of O'Connell Street stands what was once one of the most important society churches in 18th and 19th century Dublin. Dating back to 1697, its design is usually credited to Sir William Robinson, the Surveyor General who also built the beautiful Royal Hospital Kilmainham *(see p82)*, and it is reckoned to be the first church in the city with a gallery. Famous

Impressive organ in St Mary's Church

past parishioners here include Arthur Guinness, who got married here in 1793, and Wolfe Tone, the leader of the United Irishmen, who was born within a stone's throw of the church and baptised here in the 1760s. The cross street and the small park to the rear of the church are named in his honour today. The playwright Sean O'Casey was also baptized at St Mary's in 1880. Church services finally ceased in the mid-1980s and, in recent years, St Mary's has gone through many incarnations, including a bookshop, with cheap shelves standing where the pews once were. The church has recently been renovated and turned into a pub. However, the impressive stained-glass windows and the organ remain intact.

Detail of carving in St Mary's Church

Ha'penny Bridge 🄰

Map D3.

LINKING Temple Bar and Liffey Street on the north bank of the river, this attractive high-arched foot bridge is made of cast-iron and is used by thousands of people every day to cross Dublin's river. It was built by John Windsor, an ironworker from Shropshire, England. One of Dublin's most popular and most photographed sights, it was originally named the Wellington Bridge, after the Duke of Wellington. Its official name today is in fact the Liffey Bridge, but it is also known simply as the Metal Bridge. Originally opened in 1816, the bridge got its better-known nickname from the halfpenny toll that was first levied on it. The toll was scrapped in 1919 but the nickname stuck and is still used with some fondness by Dubliners and visitors alike.

A recent restoration job on the bridge, which included the installation of original period lanterns, has made it even more attractive. This is particularly true at night when it is lit up as people cross over it to go through Merchant's Arch and into the bustling nightlife of the Temple Bar area *(see pp56–7)* with all its pubs, clubs and restaurants.

The Ha'penny Bridge looking from Temple Bar to Liffey Street

FURTHER AFIELD

THERE ARE many interesting sights just outside Dublin. In the western suburbs is the Museum of Modern Art, housed in the splendid setting of the Royal Hospital Kilmainham. Phoenix Park, Europe's largest city park, offers the opportunity for a stroll in a leafy setting. Further north are the National Botanic Gardens, home to over 20,000 plant species from around the world. Nearby, Marino Casino is a fine example of Palladian architecture. The magnificent coastline is easily admired by taking the DART railway. The highlight of the riviera-like southern stretch is around Dalkey village, especially lovely Killiney Bay. One of the many Martello towers built as defences now houses a museum to James Joyce. To the northeast, slightly further from the centre, is Malahide Castle, once home of the Talbot family.

Michael Collins' gravestone

SIGHTS AT A GLANCE

Museums and Galleries
Collins Barracks **5**
Fry Model Railway Museum **14**
Guinness Hop Store **4**
James Joyce Tower **17**
Kilmainham Gaol **3**
Royal Hospital Kilmainham **6**
Shaw's Birthplace **7**
Waterways Visitors' Centre **9**

Parks and Gardens
Dublin Zoo **2**
Glasnevin Cemetery **12**
National Botanic Gardens **11**
Phoenix Park **1**

Historic Buildings
Malahide Castle **13**
Marino Casino **10**

Towns and Villages
Ballsbridge **8**
Dalkey **18**
Dun Laoghaire **16**
Howth **15**
Killiney **19**

CENTRAL DUBLIN

GREATER DUBLIN AND ENVIRONS

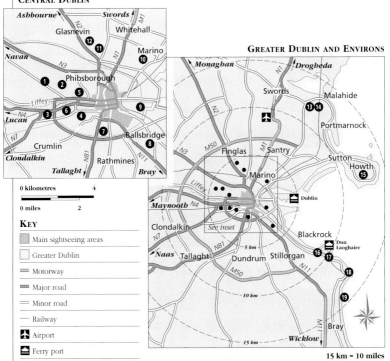

KEY

Main sightseeing areas
Greater Dublin
Motorway
Major road
Minor road
Railway
Airport
Ferry port

0 kilometres   4
0 miles   2

15 km = 10 miles

◁ **Boat moored in Dun Laoghaire harbour at dusk**

Phoenix Park ●

Park Gate, Conyngham Rd, Dublin 8.
🚌 *10, 25, 26, 37, 38, 39.* ○ *6:30am–
11pm daily.* **Phoenix Park Visitor
Centre** 🄲 *677 0095.* ○ *Mar–May
& Oct: 9:30am–5:30pm daily; Jun–
Sep: 9:30am–6:30pm daily; Nov to
mid-Mar: 9:30am–4:30pm Sat & Sun.*

A LITTLE to the west of the
city centre, ringed by a
wall 11 km (7 miles) long, is
Europe's largest enclosed city
park. Phoenix Park is over
700 ha (1700 acres) in size.
The name "Phoenix" is said to
be a corruption of the Gaelic
Fionn Uisce, meaning "clear
water". This refers to a spring
that rises near the **Phoenix
Column** which, to add
confusion, is crowned by a
statue of the mythical bird.
Phoenix Park originated in
1662, when the Duke of

**The Phoenix Column marking the
site of the *Fionn Uisce* spring**

Ormonde turned the land into
a deer park. Deer still roam in
the park today. In 1745 it was
landscaped and opened to the
public by Lord Chesterfield.
   Near Park Gate is the lakeside **People's Garden** – the
only part of the park which
has been cultivated. It was
created in 1864. A little further
on is **Dublin Zoo**.
   In addition to the
Phoenix Column, the
park has two other
conspicuous monu-
ments. The **Welling-
ton Testimonial**, a
63-m (204-ft) obelisk,

was begun in 1817 and completed in 1861. It allegedly
took so long to be built
because the Duke of Wellington fell out of public favour
during that time. Its bronze
bas-reliefs were made from
captured French cannons.
The 27-m (90-ft) steel **Papal
Cross** marks the spot where
the Pope celebrated Mass in
front of one million people
in 1979. Buildings within the
park include two 18th-century
houses. **Áras an Uachtaráin**,
the Irish President's official
residence, was built in 1751
and for a period of time was
home to various British viceroys until it became the residence of the president in
1937. The other is **Deerfield**,
the residence of the US Ambassador and once the home
of Lord Cavendish, the British
Chief Secretary for Ireland
who was murdered in 1882
by an Irish nationalist. The
only building open to the
public is **Ashtown Castle**,
a restored 17th-century tower
house which contains the
Phoenix Park Visitor Centre.

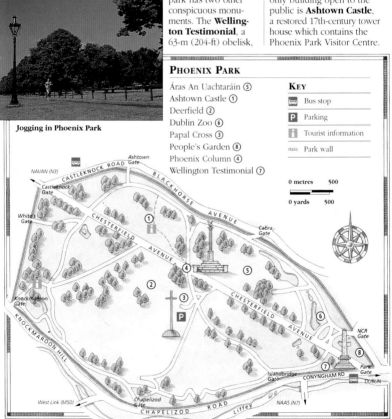

Jogging in Phoenix Park

PHOENIX PARK

Áras An Uachtaráin ⑤
Ashtown Castle ①
Deerfield ②
Dublin Zoo ⑥
Papal Cross ③
People's Garden ⑧
Phoenix Column ④
Wellington Testimonial ⑦

KEY

🚌 Bus stop

🅿 Parking

🄷 Tourist information

⊔⊔⊔⊔ Park wall

0 metres   500

0 yards   500

Orang-utang mother and baby at Dublin Zoo

Five times the size of Hyde Park in London and over double the size of New York's Central Park, Phoenix Park is large enough to accommodate playing fields for Gaelic football, hurling and polo, and running and cycling trails. It also has a motor racing track and facilities for horse riding.

Visitors at the giraffe compound in Dublin Zoo

Dublin Zoo ❷

Phoenix Park, Dublin 8. 🖀 677 1425. 🚌 10 from O'Connell St or 25 & 26 from Middle Abbey Street. ◻ Apr–Oct: Mon–Sat 9.30am–6pm, Sun 10.30am–6pm; Nov–Mar: Mon–Fri 9.30am–4pm, Sat 9.30am–5pm, Sun 10.30am–5pm. ♿

OPENED IN 1830 with one wild boar and an admission price of 6d (2.5 pence), Dublin Zoo was one of the world's first zoos and was the birthplace of the lion that roars at the beginning of MGM movies. The big cat compound in the southeast sector of Phoenix Park, set around two lakes, has been recently renovated. The lion breeding programme began here in 1857.

Nowhere is the zoo's venerable status better seen than in the old, ornate South America House, home to such enchanting creatures as golden lion tamarins, squirrel monkeys and two-toed sloths. Dublin Zoo has always prided itself on its breeding programme and today it concentrates on several endangered species including the snow leopard. Education is another important aspect of the zoo's work: a Discovery Centre where exhibits include the world's biggest egg, and a Meet The Keeper programme where you can see the animals being fed and chat to the keepers. Another attraction for children is the Zoo Train that runs all day in summer and at weekends in winter. Several hairy two-humped Bactrian camels, a pair of polar bears and a pool of hippos are among the most popular sights.

Kilmainham Gaol ❸

Inchicore Rd, Kilmainham, Dublin 8. 🖀 453 5984. 🚌 23, 51, 51A, 78, 79. ◻ May–Sep: 9:30am–6pm daily; Oct–Apr: 9:30am–5pm Mon–Fri, 10am–4:30pm Sun. ● 25 & 26 Dec. ♿ 🅿

ALONG TREE-LINED avenue runs from the Royal Hospital Kilmainham to the grim, grey bulk of Kilmainham Gaol.

The building dates from 1789, but was restored in the 1960s.

During its 130 years as a prison, it housed many of those involved in the fight for Irish independence, including Robert Emmet (see p14) and Charles Stewart Parnell (p15). The last prisoner held during the Civil War was Eamon de Valera (p16), the future President of Ireland, who was released on 16 July 1924, just prior to the Gaol's closure.

The tour of the Gaol starts in the chapel, where Joseph Plunkett married Grace Gifford just a few hours before he faced the firing squad for his part in the 1916 Rising (see p15). The tour ends in the prison yard where Plunkett's badly wounded colleague James Connolly, unable to stand up, was strapped into a chair before being shot. It also passes the dank cells of those involved in the 1798, 1803, 1848 and 1867 uprisings, as well as the punishment cells and hanging room. Fourteen of the 16 executions that took place in the few days after the Easter Rising were carried out here. There is a video presentation, and in the central hall are exhibits depicting various events which took place in the Gaol until it finally closed in 1924. There are also personal mementoes of some of the former inmates.

Standing in the courtyard is the Asgard, the ship that was used to deliver arms from Germany to the Nationalists in 1914. It famously broke through the British blockade in order to do so.

Doorway and gates of the historic Kilmainham Gaol

Sampling Guinness at the Hop Store

Guinness Hop Store ❹

Crane St, Dublin 8. **[** 453 6700 ext 5155. **▦** 78A, 68A, 123. **◯** Apr–Oct: 9:30am–5pm Mon–Sat, 10:30am–4:30pm Sun; Nov–Mar: 9:30am–4pm Mon–Sat, 12–4pm Sun. **●** Good Fri, 25 & 26 Dec. **▨ ▣ ♿**

T HE "WORLD OF GUINNESS" exhibition is housed in a 19th-century warehouse, which was used for storing bales of hops until the 1950s.

A self-guided tour takes the visitor through displays which chronicle 200 years of brewing at St James's Gate. The tour starts in a Victorian kieve (or mash tun), and goes on to examine all other stages of the brewing process. Displays show how production has changed over the years from when Arthur Guinness took over the backstreet brewery in 1759, to today's state-of-the-art techniques. There is also a cooperage display with life-size models showing the skills involved in making the wooden barrels used for storage. Since the 1950s metal containers have been used.

On the ground floor, in the Transport Gallery, is a narrow-gauge steam locomotive which once ferried materials around the factory site. Other displays include models of the company's fleet of barges that plied the Grand Canal, ocean tankers, and the once-familiar dray horses which transported the stout to the ports.

The tour ends with an audio-visual show on the company's development, followed by a visit to the sampling bar where you can enjoy a couple of glasses of draught Guinness.

The Brewing of Guinness

Label from a
Guinness bottle

G UINNESS IS A BLACK BEER, known as "stout", renowned for its distinctive malty flavour and smooth, creamy head. From its humble beginnings over 200 years ago, the Guinness brewery site at St James's Gate now covers 26 ha (65 acres) and has its own water and electricity supply. It is the largest brewery in Europe and exports beers to more than 120 countries. Other brands owned by Guinness include Harp Lager and Smithwick's Ale.

HOW GUINNESS IS MADE
The four main ingredients used to brew Guinness are barley, hops, yeast and water which, contrary to popular belief, comes from the Wicklow Mountains rather than the River Liffey.

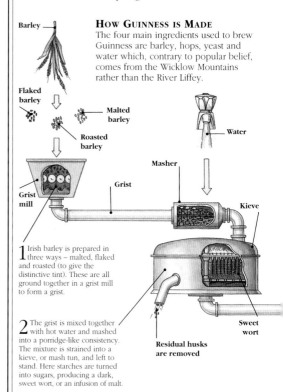

Barley

Flaked barley

Malted barley

Roasted barley

Grist mill

Grist

Masher

Water

Kieve

Sweet wort

Residual husks are removed

1 Irish barley is prepared in three ways – malted, flaked and roasted (to give the distinctive tint). These are all ground together in a grist mill to form a grist.

2 The grist is mixed together with hot water and mashed into a porridge-like consistency. The mixture is strained into a kieve, or mash tun, and left to stand. Here starches are turned into sugars, producing a dark, sweet wort, or an infusion of malt.

Guinness advertising has become almost as famous as the product itself. Since 1929, when the first advertisement announced that "Guinness is Good for You", poster and television advertising campaigns have employed many amusing images of both animals and people.

ARTHUR GUINNESS

In December 1759, 34-year-old Arthur Guinness signed a 9,000-year lease at an annual rent of £45 to take over St James's Gate Brewery, which had lain vacant for almost ten years.

Arthur Guinness

At the time the brewing industry in Dublin was at a low ebb – the standard of ale was much criticized and in rural Ireland beer was virtually unknown, as whiskey, gin and poteen were the more favoured drinks. Furthermore, Irish beer was under threat from imports. Guinness started brewing ale, but was also aware of a black ale called porter, produced in London. This new beer was so called because of its popularity with porters at Billingsgate and Covent Garden markets. Guinness decided to stop making ales and develop his own recipe for porter (the word "stout" was not used until the 1920s). So successful was the switch that he made his first export shipment in 1769.

Engraving (c. 1794) of a satisfied customer

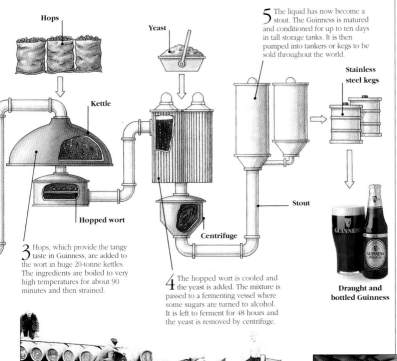

Hops

Yeast

Kettle

Hopped wort

5 The liquid has now become a stout. The Guinness is matured and conditioned for up to ten days in tall storage tanks. It is then pumped into tankers or kegs to be sold throughout the world.

Stainless steel kegs

Stout

3 Hops, which provide the tangy taste in Guinness, are added to the wort in huge 20-tonne kettles. The ingredients are boiled to very high temperatures for about 90 minutes and then strained.

Centrifuge

4 The hopped wort is cooled and the yeast is added. The mixture is passed to a fermenting vessel where some sugars are turned to alcohol. It is left to ferment for 48 hours and the yeast is removed by centrifuge.

Draught and bottled Guinness

The Guinness brewery has relied heavily on water transport since its first export was shipped to England in 1769. The barges which, up until 1961, made the short trip with their cargo down the Liffey to Dublin Port, were a familiar sight on the river. Once at port, the stout would be loaded onto huge tanker ships for worldwide distribution.

Steel kettles used in modern-day brewing

The elegant façade of the Royal Hospital Kilmainham

National Museum at Collins Barracks ❺

See pp84–5.

The Royal Hospital Kilmainham ❻

Kilmainham, Dublin 8. 【 671 8666.
🚌 24, 78, 90. **Irish Museum of Modern Art** ◯ 10am–5:30pm Tue–Sat, noon–5:30pm Sun & public hols. ◯ Good Fri & 24–26 Dec. 🗗

I RELAND'S FINEST SURVIVING 17th-century building was laid out in 1680, and styled on Les Invalides in Paris. It was built by Sir William Robinson, who also built Marsh's Library (*see p59*), as a home for 300 wounded soldiers, rather than as a hospital as its name suggests. It retained this role until 1927 and was the first such institution in the British Isles, erected even before the famous Chelsea Hospital in London. When it was completed, people were so impressed by its elegant Classical symmetry that it was suggested it would be better used as the main campus of Trinity College. In contrast to the functional design of the building, the Baroque chapel has fine wood carvings and intricate heraldic stained glass. The plaster ceiling is a replica of the original, which fell down in 1902.

In 1991, the hospital's former residential quarters were converted to house the

Irish Museum of Modern Art. Corridors were painted white and floors were uniformly covered in grey to create a stunning home for the museum. Since its opening the museum has established a collection through purchases, donations and long-term loans. The exhibits, which include a cross section of Irish and international art, are shown on a rotating basis and there are regular temporary exhibitions.

Shaw's Birthplace ❼

33 Synge St, Dublin 8. 【 475 0854.
🚌 16, 19, 22. ◯ May–Oct: 10am–1pm, 2–5pm Mon–Sat, 11:30am–1pm, 2–6pm Sun & public hols. 🗗

P LAYWRIGHT and Nobel prize-winner George Bernard Shaw was born in this Victorian house on 26 July 1856. In 1876 he followed his mother to London. She had left four years earlier with her daughters, fed up with her

The recreated Victorian kitchen in Shaw's Birthplace

husband's drinking habits. It was in London that Shaw met his wife-to-be Charlotte Payne-Townsend. He remained in England until his death.

Inside the house, visitors can see the young Shaw's bedroom and the kitchen where the author remembered he drank "much tea out of brown delft left to 'draw' on the hob until it was pure tannin". Also on view are the nursery, the maid's room and the drawing room, all furnished in period style.

Although there is little in the museum on Shaw's productive years, the house does give an interesting insight into the lives of a typical middle-class Victorian family.

GEORGE BERNARD SHAW

Born in Dublin in 1856, Shaw moved to England at the age of 20 where he began his literary career somewhat unsuccessfully as a critic and novelist. It was not until his first play was produced in 1892 that his career finally took off. One of the most prolific writers of his time, Shaw's many works include *Heartbreak House*, *Man and Superman*, and, perhaps most famously, *Pygmalion*, which was later adapted into the successful musical *My Fair Lady*. He often attacked conventional thinking and was a supporter of many causes, including vegetarianism and feminism. He lived an abstemious life and died in 1950 at the age of 94.

Ballsbridge ❽

Co Dublin. 🚌 *5,7, 7A, 8, 18, 45.*

LAID OUT mostly between 1830 and 1860, the suburb of Ballsbridge is a very exclusive part of Dublin, attracting many wealthy residents. Many of the streets are named after military heroes. Running off Pembroke Road the elegant tree-lined streets such as Raglan Road and Wellington Road are lined with prestigious red-brick houses. The area is also home to several foreign embassies – look for the striking cylindrical US Embassy building at the junction of Northumberland and Eglin roads – as well as a number of upmarket hotels and guesthouses.

Close to Baggot Street Bridge is a statue of the poet Patrick Kavanagh, depicted reclining on a bench. This attractive stretch of the Grand Canal at Lower Baggot Street was one of the poet's favourite parts of Dublin.

The southeast sector of Ballsbridge, just across the River Dodder, is dominated by the Royal Dublin Society Showgrounds (often simply abbreviated to RDS). Founded in 1731 to promote science, the arts and agriculture, the Royal Dublin Society was an instrumental mover behind the creation of most of Ireland's national museums

Late 18th-century engraving of a passenger ferry passing Harcourt Lock on the Grand Canal, taken from a painting by James Barralet

DUBLIN'S CANALS

The affluent Georgian era witnessed the building of the Grand and Royal canals linking Dublin with the River Shannon and the west coast. These two canals became the main arteries of trade and public transport in Ireland from the 1760s until the coming of the railways, which took much of the passenger business, almost a century later. However, the canals continued to carry freight until after World War II, finally closing to commercial traffic in 1960. Today the canals are well maintained and used mainly for pleasure-boating, cruising and fishing.

and galleries. The two major events at the sprawling yet graceful showgrounds are the Spring Show in May and the Horse Show in August *(see p25)*. Throughout the rest of the year the showground plays host to various conventions, exhibitions and concerts.

The Lansdowne Road stadium, the home of the Irish national rugby team, is another Ballsbridge landmark. Rugby supporters in the team's orange, green and white colours can often be seen in the area.

Stretch of the Grand Canal near the Waterways Visitors' Centre

Waterways Visitors' Centre ❾

Grand Canal Quay, Dublin 2.
📞 677 7510. 🚌 *3.* 🕐 *Jun–Sep: 9:30am–6:30pm daily; Oct–May: 12:30–5pm Wed–Sun.* ⬛ *25 Dec.* ♿ 📷 *on request.*

FIFTEEN MINUTES' walk from Trinity College along Pearse Street, the Waterways Visitors' Centre overlooks the Grand Canal Basin. Audio-visual displays and models illustrate the history of Ireland's inland waterways. One of the most interesting focuses on their construction: in the 18th century, canals were often called "navigations" and the men who built them were "navigators", a term shortened to "navvies". There are also exhibits on the wildlife found in the canals and surrounding marshlands.

The Royal Dublin Showground at Ballsbridge

The National Museum at Collins Barracks ❺

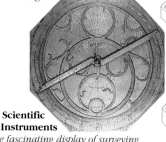

Silver coffee pot

COMMISSIONED BY William III in 1700, this was the largest barracks in his domain, with living accommodation for over 5,000 soldiers. Originally known as Dublin Barracks it was renamed Collins Barracks after Michael Collins *(see p16)* following Irish independence. This refurbished annexe of the National Museum *(see pp42–3)* displays the fine exhibits, from furniture to silver, by making full use of up-to-date technology including a multimedia catalogue and clever lighting. Currently occupying only two blocks, the museum is planned to extend eventually to fill all four wings.

Scientific Instruments
The fascinating display of surveying and navigation instruments includes this astrolabe (c.1580–90), which was made in Prague by Erasmus Habermel.

★ Irish Silver
This silver-gilt bowl by Thomas Bolton dates from 1703. Also known as a monteith, it was used for cooling wine glasses.

Ground floor

West Block

Entrance

STAR EXHIBITS

- ★ **William Smith O'Brien Gold Cup**
- ★ **Irish Silver**
- ★ **The Fonthill Vase**

Skinners Alley Chair
Dating back to c.1730, this gilt chair is part of the furniture collection and was made for the Protestant aldermen of Skinners Alley who were removed from the Dublin Assembly by James II.

★ **The Fonthill Vase**
This beautiful 14th-century Chinese vase takes its name from Fonthill Abbey, near Salisbury in England, one of its many homes before it came to this museum.

VISITORS' CHECKLIST

Benburb Street, Dublin 7.
677 7444. 25, 25A, 66, 67, 90. 10am–5pm Tue–Sat, 2–5pm Sun. 25 Dec, Good Fri.

★ **William Smith O'Brien Gold Cup**
After an uprising in 1848, O'Brien was sent to Australia and imprisoned. On his release he was presented with this 22-carat gold cup by his supporters in Australia.

Third floor

Second floor

First floor

South Block

Main entrance

GALLERY GUIDE
Furniture, silver and scientific instrument collections are in the South Block. In the West Block the Out of Storage exhibits include musical instruments and glass. The Curators' Choice section displays 25 unusual objects, individually chosen by the curators of the museum for their cultural significance.

KEY TO FLOORPLAN

☐ Irish Silver
☐ Period Furniture
☐ Scientific Instruments
☐ Fonthill Vase
☐ Irish Country Furniture
☐ Out of Storage
☐ The Museum at Work
☐ Exhibition Development
☐ Origin of National Collections
☐ Curators' Choice
☐ Temporary exhibition space
☐ Non-exhibition space

Crucifixion Stone
Part of the Curators' Choice, this was found in County Meath. It dates from the time of Catholic persecution, c.1740.

Marino Casino ⓾

Fairview Park, off Malahide Rd,
Dublin 3. 📞 833 1618. 🚌 20A, 20B,
27, 42, 42B, 43. ⏰ May–Oct: 10am–
6:30pm daily; Nov, Feb–Apr: noon–
4pm Wed & Sun. 📷 🎫 obligatory.

THIS DELIGHTFUL little villa,
built by Sir William
Chambers in the 1760s for
Lord Charlemont, now sits
next to a busy road. Originally built as a summer house
for the Marino Estate, the villa
survives today although the
main house was pulled down
in 1921. The Casino is
acknowledged to be
one of the finest
examples of
Palladian archi-
tecture in
Ireland. Some
fascinating innovative
features were used in its
construction, including
chimneys disguised as urns
and hollow columns that
accommodate drains. Outside,
four fine carved stone lions,
thought to be by English
sculptor Joseph Wilton, stand
guard at each of the corners.

The building's squat, compact
exterior conceals eight rooms
built on three floors around a
central staircase. The ground
floor comprises a spacious hall

and a saloon, with beautiful
silk hangings, parquet floor-
ing and a coffered ceiling. On
the first floor is the State Room,
decorated in green and white.

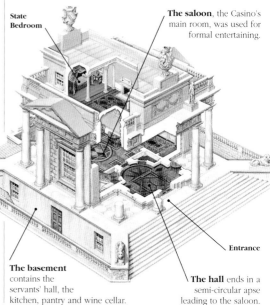

State
Bedroom

The saloon, the Casino's
main room, was used for
formal entertaining.

Entrance

The basement
contains the
servants' hall, the
kitchen, pantry and wine cellar.

The hall ends in a
semi-circular apse
leading to the saloon.

Spectacular giant water lilies in the Lily
House, National Botanic Gardens

National Botanic Gardens ⓫

Botanic Ave, Glasnevin, Dublin 9.
📞 837 4388. 🚌 13, 19, 19A, 134.
⏰ Mar–Oct: 9am–6pm Mon–Sat,
11am–6pm Sun; Nov–Feb: 10am–
4:30pm Mon–Sat, 11am–4:30pm
Sun. ⏺ 25 Dec.

OPENED IN 1795, these
gardens are home to
Ireland's foremost centre of
botany and horticulture. They

still possess an old-
world feel, thanks to
the beautiful cast-iron
Palm House and
other curvilinear
glasshouses. These
were built between
1843 and 1869 by
Richard Turner, who
was also responsible
for the Palm House at
Kew Gardens, Lon-
don, and the glass-
houses in Belfast's
Botanic Gardens.
The 20-ha (49-acre)
park contains over
20,000 different plant species.
A particularly attractive feature is the colourful display
of Victorian carpet bedding.
Other highlights include a
renowned rose garden and
rich collections of cacti and
orchids. Pampas grass and the
giant lily were first grown in
Europe here.
   One path, known as Yew
Walk, has trees that date back
to the early 18th century and
there is also a giant redwood
that towers to 30 m (100 ft).

Glasnevin Cemetery ⓬

Finglas Rd, Glasnevin. 📞 830 1133.
⏰ daily. 🚌 40 from Parnell St.

ORIGINALLY KNOWN as
Prospect Cemetery, this
is Ireland's largest graveyard,
with approximately 1.2

Impressive gravestones in
Glasnevin Cemetery

million people buried here.
It was established by Daniel
O'Connell in 1832 and was
viewed as a great achievement
on his part, since Catholics
were previously unable to
conduct graveside ceremonies
because of the Penal Laws.

O'Connell's endeavours
have been rewarded with the
most conspicuous monument
– a 51 m (167 ft) tall round-
tower in the early Irish Christian style stands over his crypt.

While the maze of head-
stones exhibits a tremendous
variety of designs, none, apart
from O'Connell's, has been
allowed by the cemetery's
committee to be too resplen-
dent. However the graves
conjure up a very Irish feel
with high crosses and insignia
such as shamrocks, harps
and Irish wolfhounds.

The most interesting sector
is the oldest part by Prospect
Square, on the far right-hand
side. Look for the two watchtowers built into the medieval-
looking walls. These were
erected as lookouts for the
bodysnatchers hired by 19th
century surgeons. Before the
Anatomy Act permitted corpses
to be donated to science, this
was the only way medical
students could learn. Staff at
the cemetery office will gladly
give directions to graves of
famous people such as
Charles Stewart
Parnell, Eamon
De Valera, Michael
Collins and Brendan
Behan. A small
Republican plot holds
the remains of Countess
Constance Markievicz
and Maud Gonne
MacBride, while the grave
of poet Gerard Manley
Hopkins is situated in
the Jesuit Plot.

Glasnevin also
reveals some interesting
landscaping; the paths
that run between the
plots follow the same routes
as the original woodland
trails. Copses of mature sycamore and oak have been
maintained while some of
the more interesting imports
among the thousand trees
to be found here include a
Californian Giant Sequoia
and a Cedar of Lebanon.

The oak-beamed Great Hall at Malahide Castle

Malahide Castle ⑬

Malahide, Co Dublin. 🚉 🚌 42.
📞 846 2184. ⏰ Apr–Oct: 10am–5pm
Mon–Sat, 11am–6pm Sun & public
hols; Nov–Mar: 10am–5pm Mon–Fri,
2–5pm Sat, Sun & public hols. ♿

NEAR THE SEASIDE dormitory
town of Malahide stands
a huge castle set in 100 ha
(250 acres) of grounds. The
castle's core dates from the
14th century but later
additions, such as its
rounded towers, have
given it a classic fairy-
tale appearance. Origin-
ally a fortress, the building served as a stately
home for the Talbot family
until 1973. They were
staunch supporters of
James II: the story goes
that, on the day of the
Battle of the Boyne
in 1690 *(see p13)*, 14
members of the family
breakfasted here; none
came back for supper.
Guided tours take in the
impressive oak-beamed Great
Hall and the Oak Room with
its carved panelling as well
as the castle's collection of
18th-century Irish furniture.
Part of the Portrait Collection,
on loan from the National
Gallery *(see pp46–9)*, can be
seen at the castle. It includes

**Candelabra
at Malahide
Castle**

portraits of the Talbot family,
as well as other figures such
as Wolfe Tone *(see p14)*.

Fry Model Railway ⑭

Malahide Castle grounds, Malahide,
Co Dublin. 🚌 42 from Beresford
Place, near Busaras. 🚉 from Connolly
Station. 📞 846 3779. ⏰ Jun–Sep:
10am–6pm Mon–Fri, 10am–5pm Sat,
2–6pm Sun & public hols (Apr & May:
Mon–Thu, Sat, Sun & public hols);
Oct–Mar: 2–5pm Sat, Sun & public
hols. ♿ combined ticket with
Malahide Castle available.

SET IN THE grounds of Malahide Castle, this collection
of handmade models of Irish
trains and trams was started
by Cyril Fry, a railway engineer and draughtsman, in the
1920s. It is one of the largest
such displays in the world.
Running on a 32 mm-wide
(0-gauge) track, each detailed
piece is made to scale and
journeys through a landscape
featuring the major Dublin
landmarks, including the River
Liffey with model barges. As
well as historic trains, there
are also models of the DART
line, buses and ferries. A
smaller room exhibits static
displays of memorabilia and
larger scale models.

Howth ⑮

Co Dublin. 🚊 *DART.* **Howth Castle grounds** ○ *8am–sunset daily.*

Yachts anchored in Dun Laoghaire harbour

THE COMMERCIAL fishing town of Howth marks the northern limit of Dublin Bay. Before Dun Laoghaire, or Kingstown as it was known then, took over, Howth was the main harbour for Dublin. Howth Head, a huge rocky mass, has lovely views of the bay. A footpath runs around the tip of Howth Head, which is known locally as the "Nose". Nearby is Baily Lighthouse (1814). Sadly, much of this area – some of Ireland's prime real estate – has suffered from building development.

To the west of the town is Howth Castle, which dates back to Norman times. Its grounds are particularly beautiful in May and June when the rhododendrons and azaleas are in full bloom.

A short boat ride out from the harbour is the rocky islet, Ireland's Eye, which is a bird sanctuary where puffins nest. Boat trips from Howth run there throughout the summer.

Dun Laoghaire ⑯

Co Dublin. 🚊 *DART.* **National Maritime Museum of Ireland** 🄲 *280 0969.* ○ *May–Sep: 1–5pm Tue–Sun (Oct: 1–5pm Sun).* 📷

IRELAND'S MAJOR passenger ferry port and yachting centre, with its brightly painted villas, parks and palm trees, makes a surprising introduction to Ireland, usually known for its grey dampness. On a warm, sunny day it exudes a decidedly continental feel.

It was once known as Kingstown, after a visit from King George IV of England in 1821. The name lasted for around 100 years, up until the Free State was established in 1921. The harbour at Dun Laoghaire was designed by John Rennie and built between 1817 and 1859. A rail connection with the centre of Dublin was established in 1834. As a result of the railway being built, however, the original *dún* or fort after which Dun Laoghaire is named, was destroyed.

Many visitors to Ireland head straight out of Dun Laoghaire (pronounced Dunleary) upon alighting from the ferry and head for Dublin or the countryside. However, the town offers some magnificent walks around the harbour and to the lighthouse along the east pier. The outlying villages of Sandycove and Dalkey can be reached via "The Metals"; a footpath that runs along the disused railway.

Located in the Mariners' Church, built in 1837, is the **National Maritime Museum**. Exhibits tell the story of Robert Halpin, who captained the *Great Eastern*, the steam vessel built in 1858 by the English engineer Brunel, that successfully laid the first transatlantic telegraph cable in 1866. Also on show in the museum are an enormous clockwork-driven lighthouse lens formerly used at Howth, and a longboat used by French officers during Wolfe Tone's unsuccessful invasion at Bantry in 1796.

Martello Tower at Howth Head just north of Dublin

James Joyce Tower ⑰

Sandycove, Co Dublin. 280 9265.
DART to Sandycove. Apr–Oct:
10am–1pm & 2–5pm Mon–Sat,
2–6pm Sun & public hols.

STANDING ON a rocky pro-
montory above the village
of Sandycove is this Martello
tower. It is one of 15 defensive towers which were
erected between Dublin and
Bray in 1804 to withstand a
threatened invasion by
Napoleon. They were
named after a tower on
Cape Mortella in Corsica.
One hundred years later
James Joyce *(see p21)* stayed
in this tower for a week as
the guest of Oliver St John
Gogarty, poet and model for
the *Ulysses* character Buck
Mulligan. Gogarty rented
the tower for a mere
£8 per year. Today,
inside the squat 12-m
(40-ft) tower's granite
walls is a small mu-
seum with some of
Joyce's correspon-
dence, personal
belongings, such as
his guitar, cigar case
and walking stick, **Guitar at James**
and his death mask. **Joyce Tower**
There are also photo- **Guitar**
graphs and several
first editions of his works,
including a deluxe edition
(1935) of *Ulysses* illustrated by
Henri Matisse. The roof, originally a gun platform but
later used as a sunbathing
deck by Gogarty, affords mar-
vellous views across Dublin
Bay. Directly below the tower
is the Forty Foot Pool, which
was traditionally an all-male
nude bathing spot, but is
now open to both sexes.

Dalkey ⑱

Co Dublin. DART.

DALKEY WAS ONCE known as
the "Town of Seven
Castles", but only two of these
fortified mansions, dating
from the 15th and 16th
centuries, now remain.
They are both on the main
street of this attractive village
whose tight, winding lanes
and charming villas give it a
Mediterranean feel.
A little way offshore is tiny
Dalkey Island, a rocky bird
sanctuary with a Martello
tower and a medieval
Benedictine church,
both now in a poor
state of repair. In sum-
mer the island can be
reached by a boat
ride from the town's
Coliemore Harbour.
The island was, at
one time, held by
Danish pirates. In the
18th century, a Dublin
club used to gather
on the island to crown
a mock "King of Dalkey" and
his officers of state. Originally
done simply for fun, the cere-
mony was stopped in 1797 by
Lord Clare when it became a
political issue. It began again
in the late 1970s.

**Shopfronts lining the main street
of Dalkey village**

Killiney ⑲

Co Dublin. DART to Dalkey or
Killiney.

SOUTH OF DALKEY, the coastal
road climbs uphill before
tumbling down into the
winding leafy lanes around
Killiney village. The route
offers one of the most scenic
vistas on this stretch of the east
coast, with views that are often compared to those across
the Bay of Naples in Italy.
Howth Head is clearly visible
to the north, with Bray Head
(see p108) and the foothills
of the Wicklow Mountains
(see p105) to the south. There
is another exhilarating view
from the top of windswept
Killiney Hill Park, off Victoria
Road. It is well worth tackling
the steep trail up from the
village to see it. Down below
is the popular pebbly beach,
Killiney Strand.

View southwards from Killiney Hill over Killiney Bay towards the Wicklow Mountains

BEYOND DUBLIN

BEYOND DUBLIN

A SHORT WAY *out of central Dublin, the beautiful Irish countryside offers a wealth of pretty villages, dramatic mountains and elegant stately homes to visit. South of Dublin, the coastline down to Dun Laoghaire and beyond, with its dramatic backdrop of the Wicklow Mountains, is stunning. To the north can be found traces of some of the earliest residents in the area – the Celts.*

North of Dublin, the fertile Boyne Valley in County Meath was settled during the Stone Age. The remains of ancient sites from this early civilization fill the area and include New-grange, the finest Neolithic tomb in Ireland. In Celtic times, the focus shifted south to the Hill of Tara, the seat of the High Kings of Ireland and the Celts' spiritual and political capital. Tara's heyday was in the 3rd century AD, but it retained its importance until the Norman invasion in the 1100s.

Norman castles, such as the immense fortress at Trim in County Meath, attest to the shifting frontiers around the region of English influence known as the Pale *(see p100)*. By the end of the 16th century, this area

Coracle from the Millmount Museum in Drogheda

incorporated nearly all the counties in the Midlands. The Boyne Valley returned to prominence in 1690, when the Battle of the Boyne ended in a landmark Protestant victory over the Catholics *(see p13)*.

The area to the south of Dublin had the strongest English influence in all of Ireland. From the 18th century onwards, wealthy Anglo-Irish families were drawn to what they saw as a stable zone, and felt confident enough to build fine mansions like the Palladian masterpieces of Russborough, Newbridge and Castletown.

For a refreshing breath of fresh air, stroll along the cliffs at Bray Head, or follow one of the invigorating walking routes in the Wicklow Mountains.

Traditional kitchen in Newbridge House

◁ **View towards the sea beyond Ardgillan Castle**

Exploring Beyond Dublin

THE COUNTRYSIDE AROUND Dublin is stunning and offers everything from stately homes to ancient burial sites and dramatic mountains to seaside villages. The Wicklow Mountains have excellent walking territory and are also home to some of the best sights, such as the elegant gardens of Powerscourt House and the monastic complex at Glendalough. The coastal stretch to the south of Dublin towards Bray is particularly scenic.

The lush gardens at Ardgillan Demesne, situated on the coast north of Dublin

SIGHTS AT A GLANCE

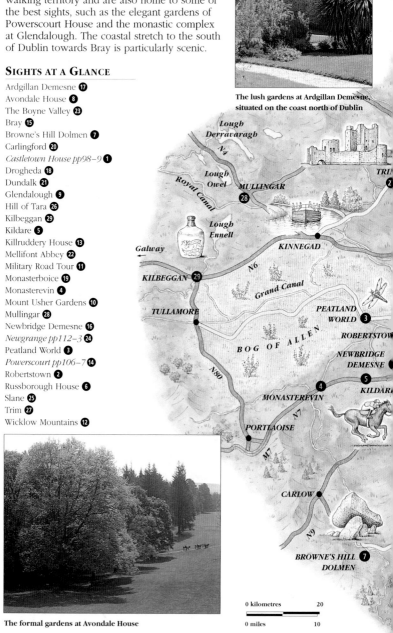

The formal gardens at Avondale House

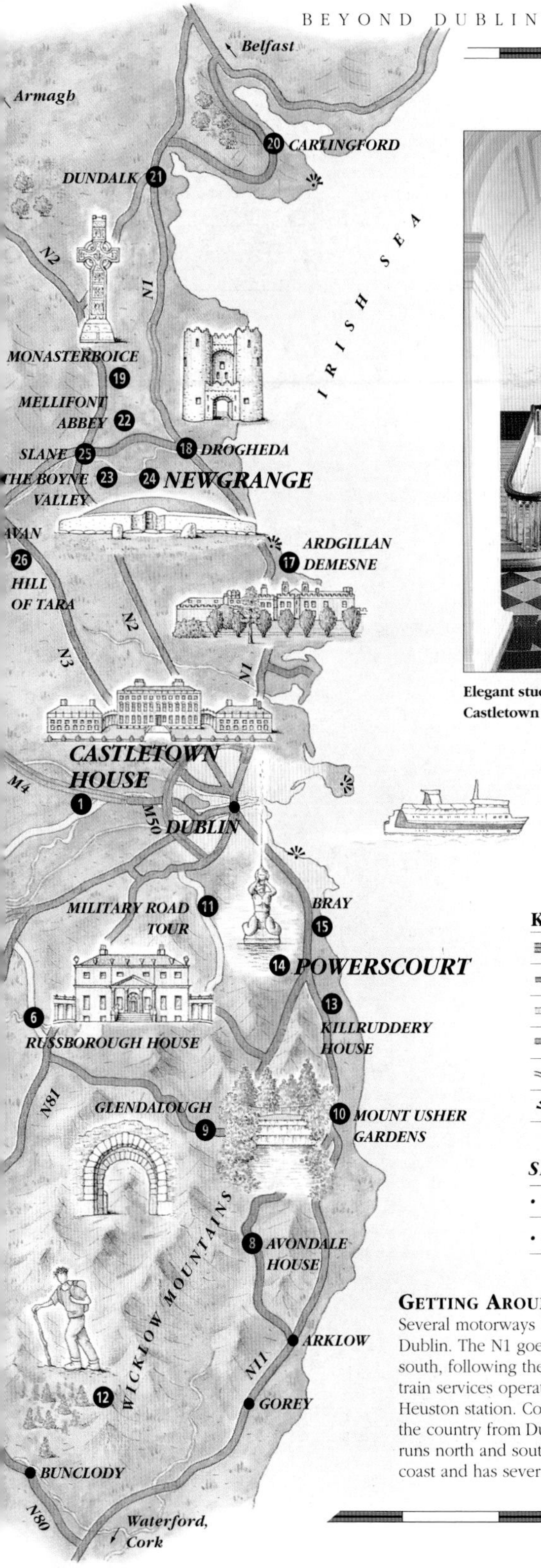

Belfast

Armagh

CARLINGFORD 20

DUNDALK 21

N2

N1

I R I S H   S E A

MONASTERBOICE

MELLIFONT 19
ABBEY 22

SLANE 25

THE BOYNE 23 24 NEWGRANGE
VALLEY

18 DROGHEDA

AVAN

26

HILL
OF TARA

N2

N3

N1

CASTLETOWN
HOUSE
1

M4

M50

DUBLIN

ARDGILLAN 17
DEMESNE

Elegant stuccoed hall and staircase in
Castletown House

MILITARY ROAD 11
TOUR

BRAY
15

14 POWERSCOURT

13

KILLRUDDERY
HOUSE

6

RUSSBOROUGH HOUSE

N81

GLENDALOUGH
9

10 MOUNT USHER
GARDENS

8 AVONDALE
HOUSE

W I C K L O W   M O U N T A I N S

ARKLOW

N11

12

GOREY

BUNCLODY

N80

Waterford,
Cork

KEY

▬▬▬ Motorway

▬▬ Major road

▭▭▭ Minor road

▭▭▭ Scenic route

≈ River

✲ Viewpoint

SEE ALSO

• *Where to Stay* pp118–123

• *Where to Eat* pp124–131

GETTING AROUND

Several motorways and main roads fan out from
Dublin. The N1 goes north to Dundalk, the N11
south, following the scenic coastline. Regular fast
train services operate across the country from
Heuston station. Coach services also run all across
the country from Dublin. The DART railway line
runs north and south from the city along the
coast and has several stops in central Dublin.

Castletown House ❶

See pp98–9.

Robertstown ❷

Co Kildare. 🚗 *240.* 🚎

TEN LOCKS WEST along the Grand Canal from Dublin, Robertstown is a characteristic 19th-century canalside village, with warehouses and cottages flanking the waterfront. Freight barges plied the route until about 1960, but pleasure boats have since replaced them. Visitors can take barge cruises from the quay and the Grand Canal Company's Hotel, built in 1801 for canal passengers, is now used for banquets.

Near Sallins, about 8 km (5 miles) east of Robertstown, the canal is carried over the River Liffey along the **Leinster Aqueduct**, an impressive structure built in 1783.

Peatland World ❸

Lullymore, Co Kildare. 📞 *045 860133.* 🚌 🚌 *to Newbridge.* ⏰ *9am– 4:30pm Mon–Fri (Apr–Oct: 2–6pm Sat, Sun also).* ⬤ *10 days at Christmas.* 📷 ♿ *limited.*

ANYONE INTERESTED in the natural history of Irish bogs should visit Peatland World, an exhibition housed in an old farm at Lullymore, 9 km (6 miles) northeast of Rathangan. It lies at the heart of the Bog of Allen, a vast expanse of raised bog that extends across the counties of Offaly, Laois and Kildare. The exhibition is devoted to

Japanese Gardens at Tully near Kildare

explaining the history and ecology of the bog, and features displays of flora and fauna as well as archaeological finds from the surrounding area. Guided walks across the peatlands are also organized to introduce visitors to the bog's delicate ecosystem and the careful conservation work that is being done.

Stacking peat for use as fuel

Monasterevin ❹

Co Kildare. 🚗 *2,200.* 🚎

THIS GEORGIAN market town lies west of Kildare, where the Grand Canal crosses the River Barrow. Waterborne trade brought prosperity to Monasterevin in the 18th century, but the locks now see little traffic. However, you can still admire the aqueduct, which is a superb example of canal engineering.

Moore Abbey, next to the church, was built in the 18th century on the site of a Cistercian monastery which was founded by St Evin, but the grand Gothic mansion owes a great deal to Victorian remodelling. Originally the ancestral seat of the earls of Drogheda, in the 1920s Moore Abbey became the home of the internationally celebrated Irish tenor, John McCormack. It has now been turned into a hospital.

Kildare ❺

Co Kildare. 🚗 *4,200.* 🚌 🚎 ℹ️ *Market House (May–Sep: 045 522696).* 🛒 *Thu.*

THE CHARMING and tidy town of Kildare is dominated by **St Brigid's Cathedral**, which commemorates the saint who founded a religious community on this site in AD 490. Unusually, monks and nuns lived

The Grand Canal Company's Hotel in Robertstown

here under the same roof, but this was not the only unorthodox practice associated with the community. Curious pagan rituals, including the burning of a perpetual fire, continued until the 16th century. The fire pit is visible in the grounds today. So too is a round tower, which was probably built in the 12th century and has a Romanesque doorway. The cathedral was rebuilt in the Victorian era, but the restorers largely adhered to the original 13th-century design.

⚐ St Brigid's Cathedral
Market Square. 📞 045 521229.
◯ May–Oct: daily. 🅿 donation. ♿

ENVIRONS: Kildare lies at the heart of racing country: the Curragh racecourse is nearby, stables are scattered all around and bloodstock sales take place at Kill, northeast of town.
The **National Stud** is a state-run bloodstock farm at Tully, just south of Kildare. It was founded in 1900 by an eccentric Anglo-Irish colonel called William Walker. He sold his foals on the basis of their astrological charts, and put skylights in the stables to allow the horses to be "touched" by sunlight or moonbeams. Walker received the title Lord Wavertree in reward for bequeathing the farm to the British Crown in 1915.
Visitors can explore the 400-ha (1,000-acre) grounds and watch the horses being exercised. Mares are normally kept in a separate paddock from the stallions, though a "teaser" stallion is introduced to discover when the mares come into season.

HORSE RACING IN IRELAND
Ireland has a strong racing culture and, thanks to its non-elitist image, the sport is enjoyed by all. Much of the thoroughbred industry centres around the Curragh, a grassy plain in County Kildare stretching unfenced for more than 2,000 ha (5,000 acres). This area is home to many of the country's studs and training yards, and every morning horses are put through their paces on the gallops. Most of the major flat races, including the Irish Derby, take place at the Curragh racecourse just east of Kildare. Other popular fixtures are held at nearby Punchestown – most famously the steeplechase festival in April – and at Leopardstown, which also hosts major National Hunt races *(see p27)*.

Finishing straight at the Curragh racecourse

Breeding stallions wait in the covering shed: each one is expected to cover 50 mares per season. There is a special foaling unit where the mare and foal can remain undisturbed for a few days after the birth.
The farm has its own forge and saddlery, and also a Horse Museum. Housed in an old stable block, this illustrates the importance of horses in Irish life. Exhibits include the frail skeleton of Arkle, the champion steeplechaser who raced to fame in the 1960s.
Sharing the same estate as the National Stud are the **Japanese Gardens**, created by Lord Wavertree at the height of the Edwardian penchant for Orientalism. The gardens were laid out in 1906–10 by a Japanese landscape

gardener called Tassa Eida, with the help of his son Minoru and 40 assistants. The impressive array of trees and shrubs includes maples, mulberries, bonsai, magnolias, cherry trees and sacred bamboos.
The gardens take the form of an allegorical journey from the cradle to the grave, beginning with the Gate of Oblivion (a cave) and leading to the Gateway of Eternity, a contemplative Zen rock garden. The route incorporates a variety of rockeries, symbolic stone lanterns and miniature bridges.

♣ National Stud and Japanese Gardens
Tully. 📞 045 521617.
◯ Feb–Nov: 9:30am–6pm daily. 🅿 ♿
🔲 Stud only. ▣ ▢

St Brigid's Cathedral and roofless round tower in Kildare town

Castletown House ❶

UILT IN 1722–32 for William Conolly, the Speaker of the Irish Parliament, Castletown was the work of Florentine architect Alessandro Galilei and gave Ireland its first taste of Palladianism. The magnificent interiors date from the second half of the 18th century. They were commissioned by Lady Louisa Lennox, wife of William Conolly's great-nephew, Tom, who took up residence here in 1758. Castletown stayed in the family until 1965, when it was taken over by the Irish Georgian Society. The state now owns the house and it is open to the public.

Conolly crest on an armchair

★ **Long Gallery**
Pompeiian-style friezes adorn the cobalt-blue walls of this magnificent room. The niches frame statues of figures from Classical mythology.

Green Drawing Room

Red Drawing Room
The room takes its name from the red damask on the walls, which is probably French and dates from the 1820s. This exquisite mahogany bureau was made for Lady Louisa in the 1760s.

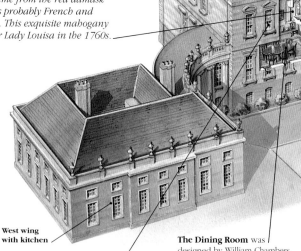

West wing with kitchen

Boudoir Wall Paintings
The boudoir's decorative panels, moved here from the Long Gallery, were inspired by the Raphael Loggia in the Vatican.

The Dining Room was designed by William Chambers, architect of the Marino Casino *(see p86)*. The mantelpiece and door cases show his strong Neo-Classical inspiration.

★ **Print Room**
In this, the last surviving print room in Ireland, Lady Louisa indulged her taste for Italian engravings. In the 18th century it was fashionable for ladies to paste prints directly on to the wall and frame them with elaborate festoons.

VISITORS' CHECKLIST

Celbridge, Co Kildare.
628 8252. 67, 67A from Dublin. Reopening late spring 1999. Apr–Sep: 10am–6pm Mon–Fri, 11am–6pm Sat, 2–6pm Sun & public hols; Oct: 10am–5pm Mon–Fri, 2–5pm Sun; Nov–Mar: 2–5pm Sun.
obligatory.

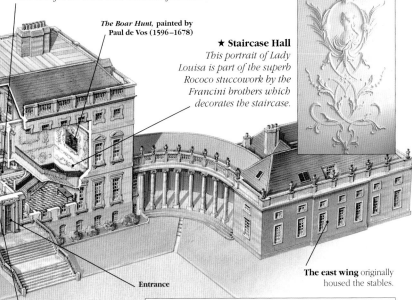

The Boar Hunt, painted by
Paul de Vos (1596–1678)

★ **Staircase Hall**
This portrait of Lady Louisa is part of the superb Rococo stuccowork by the Francini brothers which decorates the staircase.

The east wing originally housed the stables.

Entrance

The Entrance Hall is an austere Neo-Classical room. Its most decorative feature is the delicate carving on the pilasters of the upper gallery.

STAR FEATURES

★ **Long Gallery**

★ **Print Room**

★ **Staircase Hall**

CONOLLY'S FOLLY

This folly, which lies just beyond the grounds of Castletown House, provides the focus of the view from the Long Gallery. Speaker Conolly's widow, Katherine, commissioned it in 1740 as a memorial to her late husband, and to provide employment after a harsh winter. The unusual structure of superimposed arches crowned by an obelisk was designed by Richard Castle, architect of Russborough House *(see p100)*.

Saloon in Russborough House with original fireplace and stuccowork

Russborough House ❻

Blessington, Co Wicklow. ☎ *045 865239.* 🚌 *65 from Dublin.* ⏺ *May–Sep: daily; Easter–Apr & Oct: Sun & public hols.* 📷 ✓ ♿

THIS PALLADIAN MANSION, built in the 1740s for Joseph Leeson, Earl of Milltown, is one of Ireland's finest houses. Its architect, an anglicized German called Richard Castle, also designed Powerscourt House *(see pp106–7)* and is credited with introducing the Palladian style that grew to be so popular to Ireland.

Unlike many grand estates in the Pale, Russborough has survived magnificently, both inside and out. The house claims the longest frontage in Ireland, with a façade adorned by heraldic lions and curved colonnades. The interior is even more impressive. Many rooms feature superb stucco decoration, which was done largely by the Italian Francini brothers, who also worked on Castletown House *(see pp98–9)*. The best

Vernet seascape in the drawing room

examples are found in the music room, saloon and library, which are embellished with exuberant foliage and cherubs. Around the main staircase, a riot of Rococo plasterwork depicts a hunt, with hounds clasping garlands of flowers. The stucco mouldings in the drawing room were designed especially to enclose marine scenes by the French artist, Joseph Vernet (1714–89). The paintings were sold in 1926, but were tracked down more than 40 years afterwards and returned to the house.

Russborough House has many other treasures to be seen, including finely worked fireplaces made of Italian marble, imposing mahogany doorways and priceless collections of silver, porcelain and Gobelins tapestries.

Such riches aside, one of the principal reasons to visit Russborough is to see the **Beit Art Collection**, famous for its Flemish, Dutch and Spanish Old Master paintings. These include superb works by Goya, Velázquez, Hals, Rubens and Vermeer. Sir Alfred Beit, who bought the house in 1952, inherited the pictures from his uncle – also named Alfred Beit and co-founder,

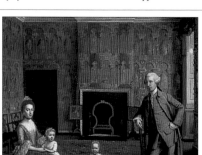

An 18th-century family enjoying the privileged lifestyle that was typical within the Pale

THE HISTORY OF THE PALE

The term "Pale" refers to an area around Dublin which marked the limits of English influence from Norman to Tudor times. The frontier fluctuated but, at its largest, the Pale stretched from Dundalk in County Louth to Waterford town. Gaelic chieftains outside the area could keep their lands provided they agreed to raise their heirs within the Pale.

The Palesmen supported their rulers' interests and considered themselves the upholders of English values. This widened the gap between the Gaelic majority and the Anglo-Irish, foretelling England's doomed involvement in the country. Long after its fortifications were dismantled, the idea of the Pale lived on as a state of mind. The expression "beyond the pale" survives as a definition of those outside the bounds of civilized society.

along with Cecil John Rhodes, of the de Beer diamond mining empire in Kimberley, South Africa. In 1974, several masterpieces were taken by the IRA, but fortunately they were later retrieved. In 1986, more pictures disappeared in a second robbery, and a number of these are still missing. Only a selection of paintings is on view at any one time, while others are on permanent loan to the National Gallery in the centre of Dublin (see pp46–9). Other

Avondale House, with its colourful gardens in the foreground

paintings from the National Gallery are also exhibited in the house from time to time.

Russborough enjoys a fine position near the village of **Blessington**, which has a good view of the Wicklow Mountains. The house lies in the midst of wooded parkland rather than elaborate gardens. As Alfred Beit said of Irish Palladianism, "Fine architecture standing in a green sward was considered enough".

ENVIRONS: The **Poulaphouca Reservoir**, which was formed by the damming of the River Liffey, extends south from Blessington. The placid lake is popular with watersports enthusiasts, especially during the summer months, while others come simply to enjoy the lovely views of the nearby Wicklow Mountains.

Browne's Hill Dolmen **❼**

Co Carlow. 🚏 🚌 to Carlow. 🅿 daily.

IN A FIELD 3 km (2 miles) east of Carlow, along the R726, stands a huge dolmen boasting the biggest capstone in Ireland. It stands in the area of Browne's Hill, where there is a stone house dating from 1763. Weighing a reputed 100 tonnes, this massive stone is embedded in the earth at one end and supported at the other by three much smaller stones. Dating back to 2000 BC, the Dolmen is thought to mark the tomb of a local chieftain. A path from the road skirts the field before reaching it.

Browne's Hill Dolmen, famous for its enormous capstone

Avondale House **❽**

Co Wicklow. 📞 0404 46111.
🚏 🚌 to Rathdrum. **House** 🅿 daily.
🎫 Good Fri & 23–28 Dec. 🚫
Grounds 🅿 daily.

LYING JUST south of Rathdrum, Avondale House was the birthplace of the 19th-century politician and patriot, Charles Stewart Parnell (see p15). It was built in 1779 by Samuel Hayes, a barrister. It passed into the hands of the Parnell family in 1795 and Charles Stewart Parnell was born here on 27 June 1846. The Georgian mansion now houses a museum dedicated to Parnell and the fight for Home Rule. The

Parnell's chair in Avondale House

state now owns Avondale and runs a forestry school here, but the public is free to explore the grounds, which stretch to 200 ha (500 acres) around the house. Known as **Avondale Forest Park**, the former estate includes an impressive arboretum which was first planted in the 18th century and has many additions made to it since 1900.

There are some lovely walks through the woods, including the magnificent Great Ride, which is one of the best, with pleasant views along the River Avonmore. There is also much wildlife in the area, including hares, rabbits and otters.

Glendalough ❾

Co Wicklow. 🚌 *St Kevin's Bus from Dublin.* **Ruins** ⭕ *daily.* 📷 *in summer.* **Visitors' Centre** 📞 *0404 45325.* ⭕ *daily.* ⬤ *23–31 Dec.* 🎞️ ♿

THE STEEP, WOODED slopes of Glendalough, the "valley of the two lakes", harbour one of Ireland's most atmospheric monastic sites. Established by St Kevin in the 6th century, the settlement was sacked time and again by the Vikings but nevertheless flourished for over 600 years. Decline set in only after English forces partially razed the site in 1398, though it functioned as a monastic centre until the Dissolution of the Monasteries in 1539 *(see p12).* Pilgrims kept on coming to Glendalough even after that, particularly on St Kevin's feast day, 3 June, which was often a riotous event.

The age of the buildings is uncertain, but most date from the 8th to 12th centuries. Many were restored during the 1870s.

Remains of the Gatehouse, the original entrance to Glendalough

View along the Upper Lake at Glendalough

The main group of ruins lies east of the Lower Lake, but the earliest buildings associated with St Kevin are by the Upper Lake. Here, where the scenery is much wilder, it is possible to enjoy more the tranquillity of Glendalough and to escape the crowds which inevitably descend on the site. Try to arrive as early as possible in the day, particularly during the peak tourist season. Enter the monastery through the double stone arch of the **Gatehouse**, the only surviving example in Ireland of a gateway into a monastic enclosure.

A short walk leads to a graveyard with a **Round tower** in one corner. Reaching 33 m (110 ft) in height, this is one of the finest of its kind in the country. Its cap was rebuilt in the 1870s using stones found inside the tower. The roofless **Cathedral** nearby dates mainly from the 12th century and is

St Kevin's Kitchen

the valley's largest ruin. At the centre of the churchyard stands the tiny **Priest's House**, whose name derives from the fact that it was a burial place for local clergy. The worn carving of a robed figure above the door is thought possibly to be St Kevin, flanked by two disciples. East of here, **St Kevin's Cross** dates from the 12th century and is one of the best preserved of Glendalough's various High Crosses. Made of granite, the cross may once have marked the boundary of the monastic cemetery. Below, nestled in the lush valley, a minuscule oratory with a steeply pitched stone roof is a charming sight. Erected in the 11th century or even earlier, it is popularly known as **St Kevin's Kitchen**; this is perhaps because its belfry, which is thought to be a later addition, resembles a chimney. One of the earliest churches at Glendalough, **St Mary's**,

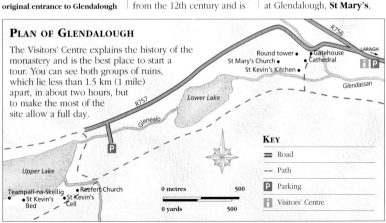

PLAN OF GLENDALOUGH

The Visitors' Centre explains the history of the monastery and is the best place to start a tour. You can see both groups of ruins, which lie less than 1.5 km (1 mile) apart, in about two hours, but to make the most of the site allow a full day.

Round tower • • Gatehouse
St Mary's Church • • Cathedral
St Kevin's Kitchen •

R756
LARAGH
🛈 P

Glendassan

Lower Lake

R757

Glenealo

Upper Lake

Teampall-na-Skellig • Reefert Church
• St Kevin's • St Kevin's
Bed Cell

0 metres   500
0 yards   500

KEY

▰▰	Road
--	Path
P	Parking
🛈	Visitors' Centre

St Kevin at Glendalough

St Kevin was born in 498, a descendant of the royal house of Leinster. He rejected his life of privilege, however, choosing to live instead as a hermit in a cave at Glendalough. He later founded a monastery here, and went on to create a notable centre of learning devoted to the care of the sick and the copying and illumination of manuscripts. St Kevin attracted many disciples to Glendalough during his lifetime, but the monastery became more celebrated as a place of pilgrimage after his death in around 618.

Colourful legends about the saint make up for the dearth of facts about him. That he lived to the age of 120 is just one of the stories told about him. Another tale claims that one day, when St Kevin was at prayer, a blackbird laid an egg in one of his outstretched hands. The saint remained in the same position until it was hatched.

Round tower at Glendalough

lies across a field to the west. Some traces of Romanesque moulding are visible outside the east window. The path along the south bank of the river leads visitors to the Upper Lake. This is the site of more monastic ruins and is also the chief starting point for walks through the valley and to a number of abandoned lead and zinc mines.

Situated in a grove not far from the Poulanass waterfall are the ruins of the **Reefert Church**, a simple Romanesque building. Its unusual name is a corruption of *Righ Fearta*, meaning "burial place of the kings"; the church may mark the site of an ancient cemetery.

Near here, on a rocky spur overlooking the Upper Lake, stands **St Kevin's Cell**, the ruins of a beehive-shaped structure which is thought to have once been the home of the hermit.

There are two sites on the south side of the lake which cannot be reached on foot but are visible from the shore on the other side. **Teampall-na-Skellig**, or the "church on the rock", was supposedly built on the site of the first church that was founded by St Kevin at Glendalough. To the east of it, carved into the cliff, is **St Kevin's Bed**. This small cave, in fact little more than a rocky ledge, is thought possibly to

have been used as a tomb in the Bronze Age, but it is more famous as St Kevin's favourite retreat. It was from this point that the saint allegedly rejected the advances of a naked woman by picking her up and throwing her into the lake.

Mount Usher Gardens ⑩

Ashford, Co Wicklow. ☎ 0404 40205. ☐ to Ashford. ☐ Mar–Nov: daily. ☑ ☑ limited.

Set on the banks of the River Vartry just east of Ashford are the Mount Usher Gardens. They were designed in 1868 by a Dubliner, Edward Walpole, who imbued them with his strong sense of romanticism.

The 8 hectares (19 acres) of beautiful gardens are laid out in a wild, informal style and contain around 4,000 different species of plants including rare shrubs and trees, from Chinese conifers and bamboos to Mexican pines and pampas grass. The Maple Walk is particularly glorious in the autumn when the changing colours of the trees are spectacular. In spring the rhododendron collection is brilliant with reds and pinks.

The river provides the main focus of the Mount Usher Gardens and, amid the exotic and lush vegetation, the visitor can usually catch a glimpse of herons standing on the many weirs and little bridges that cross the river.

Mount Usher Gardens, on the banks of the River Vartry

A Tour of the Military Road ⓫

Rare red squirrel

T HE BRITISH BUILT the Military Road through the heart of the Wicklow Mountains during a campaign to flush out Irish rebels after an uprising in 1798 *(see p14)*. Now known as the R115, this winding road takes you through the emptiest and most rugged landscapes of County Wicklow. Beautiful countryside, in which deer and other wildlife flourish, is characteristic of the whole of this tour.

Powerscourt Waterfall ⑨
The River Dargle cascades 130 m (425 ft) over a granite escarpment to form Ireland's highest waterfall.

Glencree ①
The former British barracks in Glencree are among several found along the Military Road.

Great Sugar Loaf ⑧
The granite cone of Great Sugar Loaf Mountain can be climbed in under an hour from the car park on its southern side.

Sally Gap ②
This remote pass is surrounded by a vast expanse of blanket bog dotted with pools and streams.

Lough Tay ⑦
Stark, rocky slopes plunge down to the dark waters of Lough Tay. Though it lies within a Guinness-owned estate, the lake is accessible to walkers.

Glenmacnass ③
After Sally Gap, the road drops into a deep glen where a waterfall spills dramatically over rocks.

Roundwood ⑥
The highest village in Ireland at 238 m (780 ft) above sea level, Roundwood enjoys a fine setting. Its main street is lined with pubs, cafés and craft shops.

Glendalough ④
This ancient lakeside monastery *(see pp102–3)*, enclosed by wooded slopes, is the prime historical sight in the Wicklow Mountains.

TIPS FOR DRIVERS

Length: 96 km (60 miles).
Stopping-off points: There are several pubs and cafés in Enniskerry (including Poppies, an old-fashioned tearoom), and also in Roundwood, but this area is better suited for picnics. There are numerous marked picnic spots south of Enniskerry.

0 kilometres   5

0 miles   3

KEY

 Tour route

 Other roads

⚜ Viewpoint

Vale of Clara ⑤
This picturesque wooded valley follows the River Avonmore. It contains the tiny village of Clara, which consists of two houses, a church and a school.

Map labels: DUBLIN, Enniskerry, Powerscourt, R115, Glencree, R760, Dargle, R755, Great Sugar Loaf, R759, R755, Lough Dan, Vartry Reservoir, R115, Glenmacnass, Annamoe, R756, Laragh, Avonmore, R755, Clara, RATHDRUM

Wicklow Mountains ⑫

Co Wicklow. 🚊 to Rathdrum & Wicklow. 🚌 to Enniskerry, Wicklow, Glendalough, Rathdrum & Avoca. ℹ️ Rialto House, Fitzwilliam Square, Wicklow (0404 69117).

THE INACCESSIBILITY of the rugged Wicklow Mountains meant that they once provided a safe hideout for opponents of English rule. Rebels who took part in the 1798 uprising sought refuge here. The building of the **Military Road**, started in 1800, made the area slightly more accessible, but the mountains are still thinly populated. There is little traffic to disturb enjoyment of the exhilarating scenery of rock-strewn glens, lush forest and bogland where heather gives a purple sheen to the land. Turf-cutting is still a thriving cottage industry, and you can often see peat stacked up by the road. Numerous walking trails weave through these landscapes. Among them is the **Wicklow Way**, which extends 132 km (82 miles) from Marlay Park in Dublin to Clonegal in County Carlow. It is marked but not always easy to follow, so do not set out without a good map. Although no peak exceeds 915 m (3,000 ft), the Wicklow Mountains can be dangerous in bad weather.

Hiking apart, there is plenty to see and do in this region. A good starting point for exploring the northern area is the picture-postcard estate

View across the Long Ponds to Killruddery House

village of **Enniskerry**, close to Powerscourt (see pp106–7). To the south, you can reach Glendalough (see pp102–3) and the **Vale of Avoca**. The beauty of this gentle valley was captured in the poetry of Thomas Moore (1779–1852): "There is not in the wide world a valley so sweet as that vale in whose bosom the bright waters meet" – a reference to the confluence of the Avonbeg and Avonmore rivers, the so-called **Meeting of the Waters** beyond Avondale House (see p101). Nestled among wooded hills at the heart of the valley is the hamlet of Avoca, where the **Avoca Handweavers** produce colourful tweeds in the oldest hand-weaving mill in Ireland, in operation since 1723.

Further north, towards the coast near Ashford, the River Vartry rushes through the deep chasm of the **Devil's Glen**. On entering the valley, the river falls 30 m (100 ft) into a

pool known as the Devil's Punchbowl. There are good walks around here, with fine views of the coast.

🏠 **Avoca Handweavers**
Avoca. 📞 0402 35105. ☐ daily. 🔴 25 & 26 Dec. 🍴 🏠

Killruddery House ⑬

Bray, Co Wicklow. 📞 286 3405. ☐ May–Jun & Sep: daily (pm only). ♿ limited.

KILLRUDDERY HOUSE lies just to the south of Bray, in the shadow of Little Sugar Loaf Mountain. Built in 1651, it has been the family seat of the Earls of Meath ever since, although it was remodelled in the 19th century.

The house contains some good carving and stuccowork, but it is a rather faded stately home. The real charm stems from its formal gardens, laid out in the 1680s by a French gardener named Bonet, who also worked at Versailles.

The gardens, planted with great precision, feature romantic parterres and an array of different hedges, trees and shrubs. The sylvan theatre, a small enclosure surrounded by a bay hedge, is the only known example in Ireland.

The garden centres on the Long Ponds, a pair of canals which extend 165 m (550 ft) and were once used to stock fish. Beyond, an enclosed pool leads to a Victorian arrangement of paths flanked by statues and hedges of yew, beech, lime and hornbeam.

Colourful moorland around Sally Gap in the Wicklow Mountains

Powerscourt 🕐

Laocöon statue on upper terrace

THE GARDENS AT POWERSCOURT are probably the finest in Ireland, both for their design and their dramatic setting at the foot of Great Sugar Loaf Mountain. The house and grounds were commissioned in the 1730s by Richard Wingfield, the first Viscount Powerscourt. The gardens fell into decline but, in 1840, the original scheme was revived. New ornamental gardens were completed in 1858–75 by the seventh Viscount, who added gates, urns and statues collected during his travels on the Continent. Gutted by an accidental fire in 1974, the ground floor and the ballroom on the first floor have been renovated.

Bamberg Gate
Made in Vienna in the 1770s, this gilded wrought-iron gate was brought to Powerscourt by the seventh Viscount from Bamberg Cathedral in Bavaria.

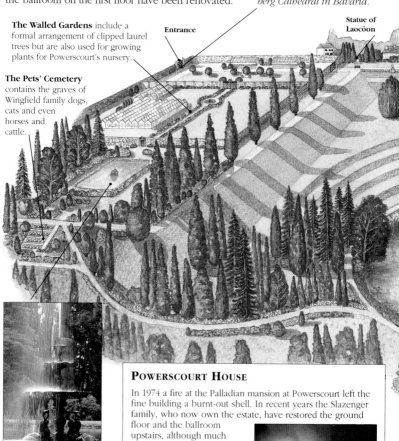

The Walled Gardens include a formal arrangement of clipped laurel trees but are also used for growing plants for Powerscourt's nursery.

Entrance

Statue of Laocöon

The Pets' Cemetery contains the graves of Wingfield family dogs, cats and even horses and cattle.

Dolphin Pond
This pool, designed as a fish pond in the 18th century, is enclosed by exotic conifers in a lovely secluded garden.

POWERSCOURT HOUSE

In 1974 a fire at the Palladian mansion at Powerscourt left the fine building a burnt-out shell. In recent years the Slazenger family, who now own the estate, have restored the ground floor and the ballroom upstairs, although much work remains to be done to the rest of the house. Originally built in 1731 on the site of a Norman castle, the house was designed by Richard Castle, also the architect of Russborough House (see p100).

Powerscourt ablaze in 1974

★ **The Perron**
This superb Italianate stairway, added in 1874, leads down to the Triton Lake, which is guarded by two statues of the winged horse Pegasus and the emblem of the Wingfield family.

VISITORS' CHECKLIST

Enniskerry, Co Wicklow.
286 7676. 85 from Bray, 44 from Dublin to Enniskerry.
9:30am–5:30pm daily (open until dusk in summer).

Pebble Mosaic
Many tonnes of pebbles were gathered from nearby Bray beach to build the Perron and to make this mosaic on the terrace.

The Italian Garden
is laid out on terraces which were first cut into the steep hillside in the 1730s.

The Pepper Pot Tower was built in 1911.

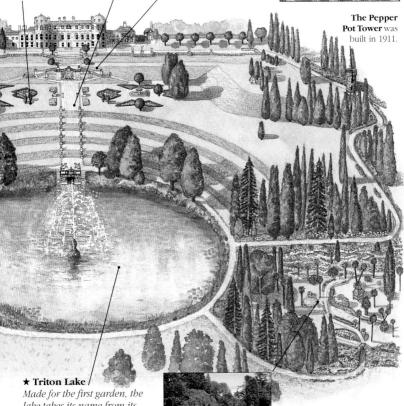

★ **Triton Lake**
Made for the first garden, the lake takes its name from its central fountain, which is modelled on a 17th-century work by Bernini in Rome.

★ **Japanese Gardens**
These enchanting Edwardian gardens, created out of bogland, contain Chinese conifers and bamboo trees.

STAR FEATURES

★ **The Perron**

★ **Japanese Gardens**

★ **Triton Lake**

Bray ⑮

Co Wicklow. 🏘 *33,000.* 🚉 *DART.*
🚌 🛈 *Old Court House, Main St*
(286 7128).

ONCE A REFINED Victorian resort, Bray is nowadays a brash holiday town, with amusement arcades and fish-and-chip shops lining the seafront. Its beach attracts huge crowds in summer, including many young families. Anyone in search of peace and quiet can escape to nearby Bray Head, where there is scope for bracing cliffside walks. Bray also makes a good base from which to explore the Wicklow Mountains *(see p105)*, the delightful coastal villages of Killiney and Dalkey *(see p89)* and Powerscourt House and Gardens *(see pp106–7)*.

Tourist road train on the seafront esplanade at Bray

Newbridge Demesne ⑯

Donabate, Co Dublin. 📞 *843 6534.*
🚉 *to Donabate.* 🚌 *33B from Eden Quay.* **House and Courtyard**
🕙 *Apr–Sep: Tue–Sun & public hols;*
Oct–Mar: Sat, Sun & public hols (pm only). ⬛ *25 & 26 Dec.* 🎟 *combined ticket with Malahide Castle available.*
🎥 *house only (obligatory).* ♿ *courtyard only.* **Park** 🕙 *daily.*

NEWBRIDGE IS ON the edge of the seaside village of Donabate, 19 km (12 miles) north of Dublin and a short drive from the airport. The house itself is a delight for enthusiasts of Georgian architecture and decor. The house was designed by George Semple in 1737 for

Connemara Pony stabled at Newbridge House

Archbishop Charles Cobbe, and it remained the family home until 1986, when it was bought by the local council. The Cobbe family retains the use of the upstairs quarters.

The highlight of the house tour is the Red Drawing Room, one of the best preserved Georgian rooms in the country. Its rich red decor is complemented by fine plasterwork by Richard Williams and by some impressive portrait and landscape paintings. Its contents have remained unaltered since at least the 1820s.

Also on view are the sizeable, airy dining room, a large kitchen with a huge stock of utensils, and the Museum of Curiosities – a small room filled to the rafters with artifacts collected from 1790 onwards by Cobbe family members on foreign travels. Housed in cabinets, some of which date back to the late 1700s, are unusual and bizarre items such as delicately carved ostrich eggs, snakeskins, stuffed animals and the mummified ear of an Egyptian bull.

The cobbled courtyard has been restored and now has displays of aspects of late 18th-century life, including dairy production, carpentry and forging, all of which are popular with children. It also houses rare goat and pony breeds, including the native Connemara pony, as well as a pleasant tea room and, incongruously, the Lord Chancellor's intricately detailed ceremonial carriage which is on loan from the National Museum *(see pp42–3)*. This is thought to be one of the best examples of carriage-work in existence.

Footpaths wind through the woodland, and the elegant, rolling grounds of Newbridge, which are landscaped in the style of an English estate.

Ardgillan Demesne ⑰

Balbriggan, Co Dublin. 📞 *849 2212.*
🚌 *33 via Rush and Skerries.* **Castle and Gardens** 🕙 *Jul–Aug: daily;*
Sep–Jun: Tue–Sun & public hols.
⬛ *23 Dec–2 Jan.* 🎥 🎟 *obligatory.*
♿ *except kitchen.* **Park** 🕙 *daily.*

IN BETWEEN THE very likeable resort towns of Skerries and Balbriggan, the Ardgillan Demesne is set on a high stretch of coastline and offers a particularly pleasant vantage

The elegant façade of Newbridge House

Stately drawing room in Ardgillan Castle

point for stunning views over Drogheda Bay. Its sweeping and expansive grounds, which cover 78 ha (194 acres), incorporate various ornamental gardens, including a rose garden and a walled kitchen garden, as well as rolling pasture and dense woodland (the name Ardgillan means "high wooded area").

In the grounds stands Ardgillan Castle, which was built in 1738 by the Reverend Robert Taylor. The rooms on the ground floor are all furnished in Georgian and Victorian styles and the basement kitchen also retains its original decor. Upstairs there is an exhibition space which houses a permanent collection of old maps.

Gramophone in the Millmount Museum

Drogheda ⓲

Co Louth. 🚶 25,000. 🚉 🚌
🅗 West St (mid-Jun–mid-Sep: 041 37070). 🚌 Sat.

IN THE 14TH CENTURY, this historic Norman port situated near the mouth of the River Boyne was one of Ireland's most important towns. It was first captured by the Danes in AD 911 and later heavily fortified by the Normans. However, the place seems never to have fully recovered from a vicious attack by the English general Oliver Cromwell in 1649, during which 3,000 citizens were killed after refusing to surrender. Although it looks rather dilapidated today, the town has retained its original street plan and has a rich medieval heritage. Little remains of Drogheda's Norman defences but **St Lawrence Gate**, a fine 13th-century barbican, has survived. The **Butter Gate** is the only other surviving gate. Near St Lawrence Gate there are two churches called **St Peter's**. The one belonging to the Church of Ireland, built in 1753, is the more striking and has some splendid gravestones. The Catholic church, on West Street and dating from 1791, is worth visiting just to see the embalmed head of Oliver Plunkett, an archbishop who was martyred in 1681. It is displayed in an elaborate glass case beside its certificate of authenticity, dated 1682.

South of the river you can climb Millmount, a Norman motte that is topped by a Martello tower. As well as providing a good view, this is the site of the **Millmount Museum**, which contains an interesting display of artifacts relating to the town and its history, as well as a number of craft workshops.

🏛 Millmount Museum
Millmount Square. 🅒 041 33097.
🕐 Tue–Sun. ● 10 days at
Christmas. 🎫 🖼 ♿

Monasterboice ⓳

Co Louth. 🚌 to Drogheda. 🅞 daily.

FOUNDED IN THE 5th century by an obscure disciple of St Patrick called St Buite, this monastic settlement is one of the most famous religious sites in Ireland. The ruins of the medieval monastery are enclosed within a graveyard in a lovely secluded spot to the north of Drogheda. The site includes a roofless round tower and two churches, but Monasterboice's greatest treasures are its 10th-century High Crosses, carved to help educate an illiterate populace.

Muiredach's High Cross is the finest of its kind in Ireland, and its sculpted biblical scenes are still remarkably clear. They depict the life of Christ on the west face, while the east face features mainly Old Testament scenes. These include Moses striking the rock to get water for the Israelites and David struggling with Goliath. The cross is named after an inscription on the base which reads: "A prayer for Muiredach by whom this cross was made", which, it is thought, may refer to the abbot of Monasterboice.

The 6.5-m (21-ft) West Cross, also known as the Tall Cross, is one of the largest in Ireland. The carving has not lasted as well as on Muiredach's Cross, but scenes from the Death of Christ can still be made out. The North Cross, which is the least notable of the three, features a Crucifixion illustration and a carved spiral pattern.

Round tower and West High Cross at Monasterboice

Thatched cottage in Carlingford on the mountainous Cooley Peninsula

Carlingford ②⓪

Co Louth. 🏠 650. 🚌 ℹ️ **Holy Trinity Heritage Centre** *Churchyard Rd (042 73454).* **Carlingford Adventure Centre** *Tholsel St (042 73100).*

THIS IS A PICTURESQUE fishing village, beautifully located between the mountains of the Cooley Peninsula and the waters of Carlingford Lough. The border with Northern Ireland runs right through the centre of this drowned river valley, and from the village you can look across to the Mountains of Mourne on the Ulster side. Carlingford is an interesting place to explore, with its pretty whitewashed cottages and ancient buildings clustered along medieval alleyways. The ruins of **King John's Castle**, built by the Normans to protect the entrance to the lough, still dominate the village. The **Holy Trinity Heritage Centre**, which is housed in a medieval church, traces the history of the port from Anglo-Norman times.

Carlingford is the country's oyster capital, and its oyster festival in August draws a large crowd. The lough is a popular watersports centre too, and in summer you can go on cruises around it from the village quayside.

Carlingford is well placed for hikes around the Cooley Peninsula. The **Carlingford Adventure Centre** provides information for walkers and also organizes its own tours.

ENVIRONS: A scenic route weaves around the **Cooley Peninsula**, skirting the coast and then cutting right through the mountains. The section along the north coast is the most dramatic: just 3 km (2 miles) northwest of Carlingford, in the **Slieve Foye Forest Park**, a road climbs to give a breathtaking panoramic view over the hills and lough.

The Tain Trail, which you can join at Carlingford, is a 30-km (19-mile) circuit through some of the peninsula's most rugged scenery, with cairns and other prehistoric sites scattered over the moorland. Keen hikers will be able to walk it in a day.

Dundalk ②①

Co Louth. 🏠 30,000. 🚌 🚂 ℹ️ *Jocelyn St (042 35484).* 🛍️ *Thu.*

DUNDALK ONCE marked the northernmost point of the Pale, the area controlled by the English during the Middle Ages *(see p100)*. Now, lying midway between Dublin and Belfast, it is the last major town before you reach the Northern Ireland border.

Dundalk is the gateway to the magnificent countryside of the Cooley Peninsula, but there is little worth stopping for in the town itself. However, the **County Museum**, which is housed in an 18th-century distillery, gives an insight into some of Louth's traditional industries, such as beer-making.

🏛️ **County Museum**
Jocelyn St. 🄲 *042 27056.* 🄾 *Tue–Sun.* ⬤ *25 & 26 Dec & 1 Jan.* 🅿️ 🚻

Mellifont Abbey ②②

Cullen, Co Louth. 🄲 *041 26459.* 🚌 *to Drogheda.* 🚂 *to Drogheda or Slane.* 🄾 *May–Oct: daily.* 🅿️

ON THE BANKS of the River Mattock, 10 km (6 miles) west of Drogheda, lies the first Cistercian monastery to have been built in Ireland. Mellifont was founded in 1142 on the orders of St Malachy, the Archbishop of Armagh. He was greatly influenced by St Bernard, who was behind the success of the Cistercian Order in Europe. The archbishop introduced not only Cistercian rigour to Mellifont, but also the formal style of monastic architecture used on the continent. In 1539, the abbey was closed and turned into a fortified house. William of Orange used it as his headquarters during the Battle of the Boyne in 1690. It is now a ruin, but it is still possible to

Glazed medieval tiles at Mellifont Abbey

appreciate the scale and plan of the original complex. Not much survives of the abbey church but, to the south of it, enclosed by what remains of the Romanesque cloister, is the most interesting building at Mellifont: a unique 13th-century lavabo where monks came to wash their hands in a

Ruined lavabo at Mellifont Abbey

THE BATTLE OF THE BOYNE

In 1688, the Catholic King of England, James II, was deposed from his throne, to be replaced by his Protestant daughter, Mary, and her husband, William of Orange. Determined to win back the crown, James sought the support of Irish Catholics, and challenged William at Oldbridge by the River Boyne west of Drogheda. The Battle of the Boyne took place on 12 July 1690, with James's poorly trained force of 25,000 French and Irish Catholics facing William's hardened army of 36,000 French Huguenots, Dutch, English and Scots. The Protestants triumphed and James fled to France, after a battle that signalled the beginning of total Protestant power over Ireland. It ushered in the confiscation of Catholic lands and the suppression of Catholic interests, sealing the country's fate for the next 300 years.

William of Orange leading his troops at the Battle of the Boyne, 12 July 1690

fountain before meals. Four of the building's original eight sides survive, each with a graceful Romanesque arch. On the eastern side of the cloister stands the 14th-century chapter house. It has an impressive vaulted ceiling and a floor laid with glazed medieval tiles taken from the abbey church.

The Boyne Valley ㉓

Co Meath. 🚉 to Drogheda. 🚌 to Slane or Drogheda. 🛈 Brú na Bóinne Interpretive Centre (041 24488).

KNOWN AS Brú na Bóinne, the "Palace of the Boyne", this river valley was the cradle of Irish civilization. The fertile soil supported a sophisticated society in Neolithic times. Much evidence survives, in the form of ring forts, passage graves and sacred enclosures. The most important Neolithic monuments in the valley are three passage graves: supreme among these is **Newgrange** (see pp112–13), but **Dowth** and **Knowth** are significant too. The Boyne Valley also encompasses the Hill of Slane and the Hill of Tara (see p114), both of which are major sites in Celtic mythology. The whole region is rich in prehistory, and with monuments predating

Egypt's pyramids, the Boyne Valley has been dubbed the Irish "Valley of the Kings".

Knowth and Newgrange can only be seen on a tour run by the interpretive centre near Newgrange, which also has interesting displays on the area's Stone Age heritage.

🏛 Dowth

Off N51, 3 km (2 miles) E of Newgrange. ⬤ to the public.
The passage grave at Dowth was plundered in Victorian times by souvenir hunters and has not been fully excavated since. Visitors cannot approach the tomb, but it can be seen from the road.

🏛 Knowth

1.5 km (1 mile) NW of Newgrange.
▢ as Newgrange (see pp112–13).
Knowth outdoes Newgrange in several respects, above all in the quantity of its treasures – Europe's greatest concentration of megalithic art. In addition, the site was occupied for a much longer period – from Neolithic times to about 1400.

Unusually, Knowth has two passage tombs rather than one. The tombs are closed during excavations, which have been going on since 1962. However, although just a third of the site is open, you can see into many of the 17 satellite tombs with their finely carved kerbstones.

River Boyne near the site of the Battle of the Boyne

Newgrange ㉔

THE ORIGINS of Newgrange, one of the most important passage graves in Europe, are steeped in mystery. According to Celtic lore, the legendary kings of Tara *(see p114)* were buried here, but Newgrange predates them. Built in around 3200 BC, the grave was left untouched by all invaders (though not by tomb robbers) and was eventually excavated in the 1960s. Archaeologists then discovered that on the winter solstice (21 December), rays of sun enter the tomb and light up the burial chamber – making it the oldest solar observatory in the world. Newgrange receives a flood of visitors and, if you go in summer, be prepared for long queues. The interpretative centre nearby *(see p111)* has interesting displays and also offers tours of this historic area.

Tri-spiral carving on entrance stone

Basin Stone
The chiselled stones, found in each recess, would have once contained funerary offerings and the bones of the dead.

The chamber has three recesses or side chambers: the north recess is the one struck by sunlight on the winter solstice.

Chamber Ceiling
The burial chamber's intricate corbelled ceiling, which reaches a height of 6 m (20 ft) above the floor, has survived intact. The overlapping slabs form a conical hollow, topped by a single capstone.

CONSTRUCTION OF NEWGRANGE

The tomb at Newgrange was designed by people with clearly exceptional artistic and engineering skills, who had use of neither the wheel nor metal tools. About 200,000 tonnes of loose stones were transported to build the mound, or cairn, which protects the passage grave. Larger slabs were used to make the circle around the cairn (12 out of a probable 35 stones have survived), the kerb and the tomb itself. Many of the kerbstones and the slabs lining the passage, the chamber and its recesses are decorated with zigzags, spirals and other geometric motifs. The grave's corbelled ceiling consists of smaller, unadorned slabs and has proved almost completely waterproof for the last 5,000 years.

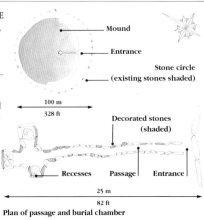

Mound
Entrance
Stone circle (existing stones shaded)

100 m
328 ft

Decorated stones (shaded)

Recesses   Passage   Entrance

25 m
82 ft
Plan of passage and burial chamber

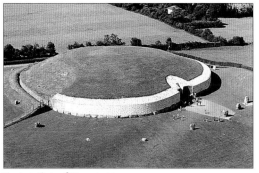

VISITORS' CHECKLIST

8 km (5 miles) E of Slane, Co
Meath. 🚉 to Drogheda. 🚌 to
Drogheda or Slane. **Brú na
Bóinne Interpretive Centre**
📞 041 24488 ⬤ May–Sep:
9am–6:30pm (Jun–mid-Sep: 7pm)
daily; Oct–Apr: 9:30am–5:30pm
(Nov–Feb: 5pm) daily; last tour: 90
mins before close. ⬤ 24–26 Dec.
📷 🚫 inside tomb. ♿ interpretive centre only. 📷 obligatory. 🍴

Restoration of Newgrange

*Located on a low ridge north of the Boyne, Newgrange
took more than 70 years to build. Between 1962
and 1975 the passage grave and mound were
restored as closely as possible to their original state.*

The standing stones in
the passage are slabs of
slate which would have
been collected locally.

Passage
*At dawn on 21
December, a beam of
sunlight shines through
the roof box (a feature
unique to Newgrange),
travels along the 19-m
(62-ft) passage and hits
the central recess in the
burial chamber.*

**The retaining
wall** around the
front of the cairn
was rebuilt using
the white quartz
and granite
stones found
scattered around
the site during
excavations.

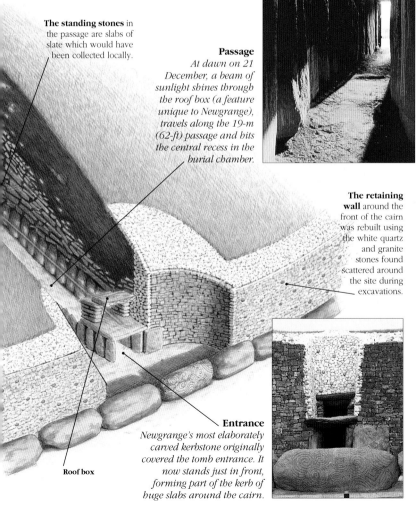

Entrance
*Newgrange's most elaborately
carved kerbstone originally
covered the tomb entrance. It
now stands just in front,
forming part of the kerb of
huge slabs around the cairn.*

Roof box

Trim Castle, set in water meadows beside the River Boyne

Slane ㉕

Co Meath. 🏘 700. 🚌

SLANE IS AN ATTRACTIVE estate village, centred on a quartet of Georgian houses. The Boyne river flows through it and skirts around the grounds of **Slane Castle**, set in glorious gardens laid out in the 18th century by the famous landscape gardener, Capability Brown. The Gothic Revival house incorporates an earlier castle built for William Burton Conyngham in 1785 that had a round ballroom with an ornate ceiling. Sadly, the castle has been closed to visitors since a bad fire in 1991.

Just to the north rises the **Hill of Slane** where, in AD 433, St Patrick is said to have lit a Paschal (Easter) fire as a challenge to the pagan High King of Tara. The event is charged with symbolism as it represents the triumph of Christianity over paganism. The local parish priest still lights a fire here every Easter.

Hill of Tara ㉖

Nr Killmessan Village, Co Meath.
📞 046 25903 (early May–Sep).
🚌 to Navan. 🕐 daily. 🎦 for Interpretive Centre. 🛒

A SITE OF mythic importance, Tara was the political and spiritual centre of Celtic Ireland and the seat of the High Kings until the 11th century. The spread of Christianity, which eroded the importance of Tara, is marked by a statue of St Patrick. Tara's symbolism was not lost on Daniel O'Connell (see p14), who chose the site for a rally in 1843, attended by over a million people.

Tours from the Interpretive Centre point out a Stone Age passage grave and Iron Age hill forts though, to the untutored eye, these earthworks look like mere hollows and grassy mounds. Clearest is the Royal Enclosure, an oval fort, in the centre of which is Cormac's House containing the "stone of destiny" (*Lialh Fail*), an ancient fertility symbol and inauguration stone of the High Kings. However, all this is secondary to the wonderful views over the Boyne Valley and the site's pervading sense of history.

Trim ㉗

Co Meath. 🏘 4,000. 🚌 ℹ Mill St (046 37111). 🛒 Fri.

TRIM IS ONE of the most pleasing Midlands market towns. A Norman stronghold on the River Boyne, it marked a boundary of the Pale (see p100). Trim runs efficient heritage and genealogy centres, including a visitors' centre next door to the tourist office.

Trim Castle was founded in 1173 by Hugh de Lacy, a Norman knight, and is one of the largest medieval castles in Ireland. It makes a spectacular backdrop so is often used as a film set, most recently seen in Mel Gibson's *Braveheart* (1995). The castle is currently closed for renovation, but visitors can peer in from the vantage point of a barbican tower that is still open. In the summer, the Nun Run, a bizarre and engrossing horse race with nuns as jockeys, takes place near the castle.

Aerial view of Iron Age forts on the Hill of Tara

Over the river is **Talbot Castle**, an Augustinian abbey converted to a manor house in the 15th century. Just north of the abbey, **St Patrick's Cathedral** incorporates part of a medieval church with a 15th-century tower and sections of the original chancel.

Butterstream Gardens, on the edge of town, are the best in the county. A luxuriant herbaceous bed is the centrepiece, but equally pleasing are the woodland, rose and white gardens. The design is enhanced by pergolas, pools and bridges.

🌢 **Butterstream Gardens**
Kildalkey Rd. 【 046 36017.
◯ Apr–Sep: daily. ♿

Mullingar ㉘

Co Westmeath. 👥 12,000. 🚌 🚆
🛈 Dublin Rd (044 48650). 🛒 Sat.

THE COUNTY TOWN of Westmeath is a prosperous market town encircled by the Royal Canal (*see p83*), which links Dublin with the River Shannon. Although Mullingar's main appeal is as a base to explore the surrounding area, pubs such as Con's and cheery Canton Casey's can make a pleasant interlude. In addition, the 20th-century cathedral features unusual mosaics of St Anne and St Patrick.

ENVIRONS: Recent restoration of the Dublin to Mullingar stretch of the Royal Canal has resulted in attractive towpaths for canalside walks, as well as good angling facilities.

The remains of the Jealous Wall at Belvedere House, near Mullingar

Lighting votive candles in Mullingar Cathedral

South of Mullingar, just off the road to Kilbeggan, stands **Belvedere House**, a romantic Palladian villa overlooking Lough Ennel. Built in 1740 by architect Richard Castle, it is decorated with Rococo plasterwork and set in wonderful gardens. However, the house and gardens are both temporarily closed for restoration work.

Shortly after the house was built, the first Earl of Belvedere accused his young wife of having an affair with his brother, and imprisoned her for 31 years in a neighbouring house. He also sued the brother and had him jailed for life. In 1755, the Earl built a Gothic folly – the Jealous Wall – in order to block the view of a more opulent mansion across the lake owned by a second brother, with whom he had also fallen out. The Jealous Wall still remains, as does an octagonal gazebo and other follies.

Charming terraces, framed by urns and yews, descend to the lake; on the other side of the house is a pretty walled garden, enclosed by an arboretum and rolling parkland.

🏛 **Belvedere House**
6.5 km (4 miles) S of Mullingar.
【 044 40861. ◯ reopening end of 1999 after restoration work. Call for details. ♿ ♿

Kilbeggan ㉙

Co Westmeath. 🏘 600. 🚌

SITUATED BETWEEN Mullingar and Tullamore, this pleasant village has a small harbour on the Grand Canal. However, the main point of interest is **Locke's Distillery**. Founded in 1757, it claims to be the oldest licensed pot still distillery in the world. Unable to compete with Scotch whisky manufacturers, the company went bankrupt in 1954, but the aroma hung in the warehouses for years and was known as "the angels' share". The distillery was reopened as a museum in 1987. The building is authentic, a solid structure that is complete with a water wheel and an indoor steam engine. A tour traces the process of Irish whiskey-making, from the mash tuns through to the vast fermentation vats and creation of wash (rough beer) to the distillation and maturation stages. At the tasting stage, workers would sample the whiskey in the can pit room. Visitors can still taste various whiskeys in the bar but, unlike the original workers at the distillery, cannot bathe in the whiskey vats.

Miniature whiskey bottles at Locke's Distillery in Kilbeggan

🏛 **Locke's Distillery**
Main St. 【 0506 32134.
◯ daily. ♿

TRAVELLERS' NEEDS

Where to Stay

WHETHER YOU ARE STAYING in exclusive luxury or modest bed-and-breakfast accommodation, one thing you can be certain of in Dublin is that you will receive a warm welcome. The Irish are renowned for their friendliness and even in big corporate hotels, where you might expect the reception to be more impersonal, the staff go out of their way to be hospitable. The choice is enormous: you can stay in an elegant, refurbished Georgian house, a comfortable bed-and-breakfast, a Victorian

Doorman at the
Conrad Hotel

town house, an old-fashioned commercial hotel or a cosy pub. Details are given here of the various types of accommodation available. The listings on pages 120–23 recommend around 50 hotels in both central Dublin and outside the city – all places of quality, ranging from basic to luxury – and should help you decide upon your choice of accommodation. Bord Fáilte (the Irish Tourist Board) and Dublin Tourism also publish comprehensive guides to recommended accommodation in the area.

**Main entrance to the fashionable
Clarence Hotel (p121)**

Hotels

AT THE TOP of the price range there are quite a few expensive, luxury hotels in the heart of Dublin. Magnificently furnished and run, they offer maximum comfort, delicious food and often have indoor facilities, such as a gym and swimming pool. As well as luxurious individual hotels there are also the modern hotel chains, such as **Jury's**, **Great Southern Hotels** and **Irish Welcome** which all offer a high standard of accommodation. However, these establishments can lack the charm and individuality of privately run hotels.

There are also numerous very moderate hotels in the centre of Dublin, providing a good standard of accommodation.

If you prefer to stay outside Dublin there are some wonderful castles and stately homes which offer the same standards as the top city hotels but which have the bonus of being set in beautiful countryside. They can often also arrange outdoor pursuits such as fishing, riding and golf.

The shamrock symbol of Bord Fáilte is displayed by hotels (and other forms of accommodation) that have been inspected and approved.

Bed-and-Breakfast Accommodation

IRELAND HAS THE reputation for the best B&Bs in Europe. Your welcome will always be friendly and the food and company excellent. Even if the house is no architectural

**The entrance to the grand Shelbourne
Hotel (see p121) on St Stephen's Green**

A typical bedroom in the
comfortable Brooks Hotel (p121)

beauty, the comfort and atmosphere will more than compensate. Not all of the bedrooms have bathrooms *en suite*. When one is available, you may possibly have to pay a little extra but, considering the generally cheap rates, the surcharge is negligible.

The Irish swear by their B&Bs and many stay in them by choice rather than paying to stay in the luxurious surroundings of some of the big hotels. The **Town and Country Homes Association** will provide details of bed-and-breakfast accommodation.

Guesthouses

MOST GUESTHOUSES are found in cities and large towns. They are usually converted family homes and have an atmosphere all of their own. Most offer a good-value evening meal and all give you a delicious full Irish breakfast *(see p126)*. Top-of-the-range guesthouses can be just as good, and sometimes even better, than hotels. You will see a much more personal side of a town or city while staying at a guesthouse. There are plenty to choose from in the Dublin area and the prices are usually extremely reasonable. The **Irish Hotel Federation** publishes a useful booklet with guesthouse listings that cover the whole of Ireland, including Dublin and its environs.

PRICES

ROOM RATES advertised are inclusive of service and tax. Hotel rates can vary by as much as 40 per cent depending on the time of year. Prices in guesthouses are influenced more by their location in relation to tourist sights and public transport.

Dublin offers a complete range of accommodation, from youth hostels through very reasonably priced bed-and-breakfasts to lavish five-star hotels such as the Merrion and the Clarence.

TIPPING

TIPPING IN DUBLIN is a matter of personal discretion but is not common practice, even at the larger hotels. Tasks performed by staff are considered part of the service. Tipping is not expected for carrying bags to your room or for serving drinks. However, it is usual to tip the waiting staff in hotel restaurants: the standard tip is around 10–15 per cent of the bill – anything in excess of that would be considered particularly generous.

The Kinlay House youth hostel in Lord Edward Street

BOOKING

IT IS WISE to reserve your accommodation during the peak season and public holidays (see p27), particularly if your visit coincides with a local festival such as the St Patrick's Day celebrations (see p24) when the city can get booked up. Bord Fáilte (see p148) can offer advice and make reservations through its accommodation service. Central reservation facilities are available at the hotel chains listed here.

Bord Fáilte accommodation sign

YOUTH HOSTELS

THERE ARE 40 youth hostels registered with **An Óige** (the Irish Youth Hostel Association), with several in the Dublin area. Accommodation is provided in dormitories

with comfortable beds and basic cooking facilities. You can only use these hostels if you are a member of An Óige or another organization affiliated to the International Youth Hostel Federation.

There are also independent hostels, and places such as universities that offer similar inexpensive accommodation in Dublin. The tourist board has listings of those that are recommended.

DISABLED TRAVELLERS

A FACT SHEET for disabled visitors is produced by Bord Fáilte and their accommodation guide indicates wheelchair accessibility. The **National Rehabilitation Board** publishes two free guides: *Accommodation for Disabled Persons* and *Dublin: A Guide for Disabled Persons*, both in conjunction with the tourist board.

DIRECTORY

CHAIN HOTELS

Irish Welcome
4 Whitefriars, Aungier St, Dublin 2.
475 7017. FAX 475 0222.

Jury's
Pembroke Rd, Ballsbridge, Dublin 4.
660 5000. FAX 660 5540.

Great Southern Hotels
6 Charlemont Terrace, Crofton Rd, Dun Laoghaire, Co Dublin.
280 8581. FAX 280 8039.

OTHER USEFUL ADDRESSES

An Óige (Irish Youth Hostel Association)
61 Mountjoy St, Dublin 7.
830 4555. FAX 830 5808.

Irish Hotel Federation
13 Northbrook Rd, Dublin 6.
497 6459. FAX 497 4613.

National Rehabilitation Board
25 Clyde Road, Ballsbridge, Dublin 4.
668 4181.

Ariel Hotel in Ballsbridge *(see p122)*

Choosing a Hotel

THESE HOTELS have been selected across a wide price range for their good value, facilities and location. The chart lists the hotels by areas, starting with central Dublin and moving on to hotels further outside the city. Many hotels have a recommended restaurant and/or bar, but for separate restaurant listings see pages 128–31. For map references, see pages 164–5.

	CREDIT CARDS	CHILDREN'S FACILITIES	PARKING FACILITIES	RESTAURANT	PUBLIC BAR
SOUTHEAST DUBLIN					
BUSWELLS Map E4. €€€ 25 Molesworth St, Dublin 2. 676 4013. FAX 676 2090. A short walk from Grafton Street, this smart hotel with its Georgian features has been family-run since the 1920s. TV 🔧 *Rooms: 65*	AE DC MC V	●	■	●	■
CONRAD HOTEL Map D5. €€€€€ Earlsfort Terrace, Dublin 2. 676 5555. FAX 676 5424. This international-style hotel, by St Stephen's Green, is geared to business people and has excellent facilities. A jolly pub with a large terrace is the only concession to traditional Dublin. TV 🔧 🍴 🔧 *Rooms: 191*	AE DC MC V	●	■	●	■
DAVENPORT Map F4. €€€€€ Merrion Square, Dublin 2. 661 6800. FAX 661 5663. The grand proportions of the Neo-Classical façade are carried through into the lobby – a vast, marble-floored atrium. Opened in 1994, it is elegant but rather like a gentleman's club. TV 🔧 🍴 🔧 *Rooms: 120*	AE DC MC V	●	■	●	
FITZWILLIAM Map E5. €€ 41 Fitzwilliam St Upper, Dublin 2. 660 0448. FAX 676 7488. A friendly, unpretentious guesthouse in an attractive Georgian street, with simple, elegant decor and comfortable bedrooms. TV *Rooms: 12*	AE DC MC V	●	■		
GEORGIAN HOUSE Map F5. €€ 18 Baggot St Lower, Dublin 2. 661 8832. FAX 661 8834. A short walk from St Stephen's Green, this small hotel is a good base for exploring Dublin. The bedrooms are large and comfortable and there's a good seafood restaurant in the basement. TV *Rooms: 47*	AE DC MC V	●	■	●	■
THE GREY DOOR HOTEL €€€ 22–23 Pembroke St Upper, Dublin 2. 676 3286. FAX 676 3287. This centrally located Georgian house has immaculately decorated, well-equipped rooms and an excellent restaurant. TV *Rooms: 7*	AE DC MC V	●		●	
HARCOURT Map D5. €€ 60 Harcourt St, Dublin 2. 478 3677. FAX 475 2013. Just off St Stephen's Green, this hotel is close to many of the city's main sights. The bedrooms are modern and well-equipped, and there is a popular bar, a restaurant for evening meals and a nightclub. TV *Rooms: 40*	AE MC V			●	■
KILRONAN HOUSE €€ 70 Adelaide Rd, Dublin 2. 475 5266. FAX 478 2841. A reasonably priced, small guesthouse in a quiet street in the centre. Charming owners and delicious breakfasts. TV *Rooms: 11*	MC V	●	■		
LEESON COURT Map E5. €€ 26 Leeson St Lower, Dublin 2. 676 3380. FAX 661 8273. Spread across two Georgian houses, this cheerfully decorated hotel has a relaxed, informal atmosphere and the service is good. St Stephen's Green is only a few minutes' walk away. TV *Rooms: 20*	AE DC MC V	●	■	●	■
LONGFIELDS Map F5. €€€ 10 Fitzwilliam St Lower, Dublin 2. 676 1367. FAX 676 1542. Two Georgian town houses have been knocked together to create this stylish hotel with an attractive sitting room and smart, pretty bedrooms. There is a very good restaurant in the basement. TV *Rooms: 28*	AE DC MC V	●		●	■
THE MERRION Map F4. €€€€€ Merrion Street Upper, Dublin 2. 603 0600. FAX 603 0700. This new top-class hotel was created from four Georgian townhouses. Its elegant interior has been kept in period style and all modern facilities make this a very luxurious hotel. 📺 🍴 🔧 TV 🍸 🔧 *Rooms: 145*	AE DC MC V	●	■	●	■

		CREDIT CARDS	CHILDREN'S FACILITIES	PARKING FACILITIES	RESTAURANT	PUBLIC BAR
Price categories for a standard double room per night, inclusive of breakfast, service charges and any additional taxes such as VAT: (£) under IR£50 (£)(£) IR£50 –£100 (£)(£)(£) IR£100 –£150 (£)(£)(£)(£) IR£150 –£200 (£)(£)(£)(£)(£) over IR£200	**CHILDREN'S FACILITIES** Cots and high chairs are available and some hotels will also provide a baby-sitting service. **PARKING FACILITIES** Parking provided by the hotel in either a private car park or a private garage close by. **RESTAURANT** The hotel has a restaurant for residents which also welcomes non-residents – usually only for evening meals. **PUBLIC BAR** The hotel has a bar that is open to non-residents as well as those staying in the hotel.					

MONT CLARE Map F4. (£)(£)(£)(£)
Merrion Square, Dublin 2. 661 6799. FAX 661 5663.
Not as grand as the nearby Davenport, but with the same club-like feel. A busy, traditional pub is on the ground floor. **Rooms: 80**

AE DC MC V — ● ▮ ● ▮

RUSSELL COURT Map D5. (£)(£)(£)
21–25 Harcourt St, Dublin 2. 478 4066. FAX 478 1576.
Jolly, welcoming hotel with young staff and a lively atmosphere in the evenings. There's a choice of bars and a more formal restaurant. Bedrooms are neat and well-equipped. **Rooms: 42**

AE DC MC V — ● ▮ ● ▮

SHELBOURNE HOTEL Map D4. (£)(£)(£)(£)(£)
Dublin 2. 676 6471. FAX 661 6006.
The Shelbourne has been the city's most distinguished hotel since it opened in the 19th century. It has every facility for the business traveller, yet manages to retain a personal atmosphere. **Rooms: 164**

AE DC MC V — ● ▮ ● ▮

STEPHEN'S HALL Map E5. (£)(£)(£)
14–17 Leeson St Lower, Dublin 2. 661 0585. FAX 661 0606.
All the rooms are suites and represent good value for families who want smart, comfortable accommodation in the centre of the city near St Stephen's Green. Cooking facilities are available. **Rooms: 37**

AE DC MC V — ● ▮

TEMPLE BAR Map D3. (£)(£)(£)
Fleet St, Temple Bar, Dublin 2. 677 3333. FAX 677 3088.
This new hotel, situated in a trendy area of Dublin, is a popular meeting place with its theme bar "Buskers" attracting a lively crowd. Bedrooms are comfortable but lack character. **Rooms: 108**

AE DC MC V — ● ● ▮

WESTBURY HOTEL Map D4. (£)(£)(£)(£)(£)
Grafton St, Dublin 2. 679 1122. FAX 679 7078.
You couldn't get much closer to the centre of things than here, only seconds from Dublin's major shopping street. It is a smart, ritzy hotel with lots of shiny floors and co-ordinated bedrooms. **Rooms: 203**

AE DC MC V — ● ▮ ● ▮

SOUTHWEST DUBLIN

AVALON HOUSE Map C4. (£)
55 Aungier St, Dublin 2. 475 0001. FAX 475 0303.
This cheap and cheerful budget accommodation is centrally located and has clean bedrooms and a self-service restaurant. **Rooms: 38**

AE MC V — ●

BLOOMS Map D3. (£)(£)
Anglesea St, Temple Bar, Dublin 2. 671 5622. FAX 671 5997.
This modern hotel is centrally situated near Trinity College, but its reception areas are slightly limited. **Rooms: 97**

AE DC MC V — ● ● ▮

BROOKS Map D4. (£)(£)(£)
59-62 Drury St, Dublin 2. 670 4000. FAX 670 4455.
A very comfortable and friendly new hotel. The decor was designed by the owners and makes the spacious rooms feel very cosy. **Rooms: 75**

AE DC MC V — ● ●

CENTRAL Map D5. (£)(£)(£)
1–5 Exchequer St, Dublin 2. 679 7302. FAX 679 7303.
As its name suggests, this hotel is centrally located. Molly Malone's on the ground floor often has live music at night, so choose your neat and functional room carefully. **Rooms: 70**

AE DC MC V — ● ● ▮

CLARENCE Map C3. (£)(£)(£)(£)
6–8 Wellington Quay, Dublin 2. 670 9000. FAX 670 7800.
The hotel is owned by the rock band U2 and has been completely refurbished. A stylish restaurant sets the standard for the rest of the hotel – one of the trendiest places to stay in town. **Rooms: 50**

AE DC MC V — ● ● ▮

Price categories for a standard double room per night, inclusive of breakfast, service charges and any additional taxes such as VAT:
(£) under IR£50
(£)(£) IR£50 –£100
(£)(£)(£) IR£100 –£150
(£)(£)(£)(£) IR£150 –£200
(£)(£)(£)(£)(£) over IR£200

CHILDREN'S FACILITIES
Cots and high chairs are available and some hotels will also provide a baby-sitting service.
PARKING FACILITIES
Parking provided by the hotel in either a private car park or a private garage close by.
RESTAURANT
The hotel has a restaurant for residents which also welcomes non-residents – usually only for evening meals.
PUBLIC BAR
The hotel has a bar that is open to non-residents as well as those staying in the hotel.

	Price	CREDIT CARDS	CHILDREN'S FACILITIES	PARKING FACILITIES	RESTAURANT	PUBLIC BAR

GRAFTON PLAZA Map D4.
Johnson's Place, Dublin 2. 475 0888. FAX 475 0908.
This neat hotel, with its Georgian façade, is tastefully decorated throughout. Only a few minutes' walk from Grafton Street, it makes an excellent city base. TV **Rooms:** 75
(£)(£)(£) — AE DC MC V — ● — ● — ●

JURY'S CHRISTCHURCH INN Map B4.
Christchurch Place, Dublin 8. 454 0000. FAX 454 0012.
The Jury's group "inns" offer spruce modern facilities. This hotel, 15 minutes from St Stephen's Green, has a good bar and restaurant, and neat, well-equipped rooms at reasonable prices. TV **Rooms:** 182
(£)(£) — AE DC MC V — ● — ● — ●

NORTH OF THE LIFFEY

GRESHAM HOTEL Map D1.
23 O'Connell St Upper, Dublin 1. 874 6881. FAX 878 7175.
One of Dublin's oldest and best known hotels. It is a popular rendezvous spot so the public areas are always busy. The bedrooms are comfortable and there is ample safe parking. TV **Rooms:** 200
(£)(£)(£) — AE DC MC V — ● — ● — ● — ●

ISAACS Map E2.
Frenchman's Lane, Store St, Dublin 1. 855 0067. FAX 836 5390.
Developed alongside an older hostel of the same name, the hotel is reasonably priced, well-run and centrally located. TV **Rooms:** 57
(£)(£) — MC V — ●

ROYAL DUBLIN Map D1.
40 O'Connell St Upper, Dublin 1. 873 3666. FAX 873 3120.
A modern hotel in one of Dublin's most famous streets, it has well-equipped rooms and is smart, though lacking in atmosphere. TV **Rooms:** 117
(£)(£) — AE DC MC V — ● — ● — ●

FURTHER AFIELD

ANGLESEA TOWN HOUSE
63 Anglesea Rd, Dublin 4. 668 3877. FAX 668 3461.
This Edwardian house is beautifully decorated and furnished. It has a lovely drawing room, very comfortable bedrooms and offers a superb breakfast – all within ten minutes' drive of the centre. TV **Rooms:** 7
(£)(£) — AE DC MC V — ● — ●

ARIEL HOUSE
52 Lansdowne Rd, Ballsbridge, Dublin 4. 668 5512. FAX 668 5845.
Near Lansdowne Road Station, this Victorian house is elegantly decorated, with comfortable bedrooms and good breakfasts. TV **Rooms:** 28
(£)(£) — MC V — ●

BERKELEY COURT HOTEL
Lansdowne Rd, Dublin 4. 660 1711. FAX 661 7238.
The very smart lobby area sets the standard for this luxury hotel, which is well located for Lansdowne Road stadium. TV **Rooms:** 198
(£)(£)(£)(£)(£) — AE DC MC V — ● — ● — ● — ●

CLARA HOUSE
Leinster Rd, Rathmines, Dublin 6. 497 5904. FAX 497 5904.
In an attractive area, ten minutes' walk from the centre, this Georgian house is a comfortable B&B with a friendly atmosphere. TV **Rooms:** 13
(£)(£) — MC V — ● — ● — ●

DOYLE TARA
Merrion Rd, Dublin 4. 269 4666. FAX 269 1027.
Conveniently situated for Dun Laoghaire, the hotel also has a number of rooms overlooking Dublin Bay. TV **Rooms:** 113
(£)(£)(£) — AE DC MC V — ● — ● — ●

GLENOGRA GUESTHOUSE
64 Merrion Rd, Ballsbridge, Dublin 4. 668 3661. FAX 668 3698.
Attractive, stylish guesthouse convenient for both Dun Laoghaire and the centre of Dublin. The bedrooms are charming and very comfortable.
TV **Rooms:** 10
(£)(£) — AE MC V — ● — ●

HIBERNIAN   £££
Eastmoreland Place, Ballsbridge, Dublin 4. 668 7666. FAX 660 2655.
Located in a quiet street but close to the centre, this impressive turn-of-the-century building has elegant, luxurious rooms. *Rooms: 41*
AE DC MC V

JURY'S HOTEL AND THE TOWERS AT JURY'S   ££££
Pembroke Rd, Ballsbridge, Dublin 4. 660 5000. FAX 660 5540.
A modern, business hotel, a short distance from the centre with excellent facilities. The Towers is an exclusive wing with de luxe bedrooms. *Rooms: 390*
AE DC MC V

MOREHAMPTON TOWNHOUSE   ££
46 Morehampton Rd, Donnybrook, Dublin 4. 660 2106. FAX 660 2566.
An attractively decorated, Victorian townhouse, ten minutes' drive from the centre, with great hospitality and delicious breakfasts. *Rooms: 7*
MC V

BEYOND DUBLIN

ARDEE *Red House*   ££
Co Louth. 041 53523. FAX 041 53523.
This attractive Georgian manor house has very comfortable rooms. Within the grounds are a swimming pool and a floodlit tennis court. *Rooms: 3*
AE MC V

CARLINGFORD *Viewpoint*   £
Omeath Rd, Co Louth. 042 73149. FAX 042 73149.
Motel-style, modern accommodation. Well-equipped bedrooms with wonderful views across Carlingford Lough. *Rooms: 10*
V

CARLINGFORD *McKevitt's Village Hotel*   ££
Market Sq, Co Louth. 042 73116. FAX 042 73144.
Popular village inn at the heart of the local scene. Rooms have real fires and a great atmosphere, bedrooms are pristine and pretty. *Rooms: 13*
AE DC MC V

DROGHEDA *Boyne Valley*   ££
Co Louth. 041 37737. FAX 041 39188.
A much extended and refurbished 18th-century manor house. Although most of the decor and furnishings are modern, the hotel preserves much of the house's traditional feel. *Rooms: 38*
AE DC MC V

DULEEK *Annesbrook*   ££
Co Meath. 041 23293. FAX 041 23024.
This 17th-century house overlooks lovely gardens. It has a welcoming atmosphere and spacious, comfortable bedrooms. *Rooms: 5*
MC V

ENNISKERRY *Enniscree Lodge*   ££
Glencree Valley, Co Wicklow. 286 3542. FAX 286 6037.
With stunning views from most of the rooms, this is a friendly place with homely, country-style furnishings. *Rooms: 10*
AE DC MC V

MULLINGAR *Greville Arms*   ££
Co Westmeath. 044 48563. FAX 044 48052.
Centrally located in Mullingar, this traditional hotel caters for both locals and tourists. Its facilities include a large bar and restaurant. *Rooms: 40*
AE DC MC V

RATHNEW *Hunter's Hotel*   ££
Co Wicklow. 0404 40106. FAX 0404 40338.
This inn on the old Dublin coaching road dates back to 1720 and is run by the fourth generation of the Hunter family. Comfortable and relaxing if a little eccentric, it's a great place to stay and the food is delicious. *Rooms: 16*
AE DC MC V

SLANE *Conyngham Arms*   ££
Co Meath. 041 24155. FAX 041 24205.
This traditional family hotel is welcoming and comfortable. It makes a good base for touring the beautiful Boyne Valley. *Rooms: 16*
DC MC V

STRAFFAN *Kildare Hotel and Country Club*   £££££
Co Kildare. 627 3333. FAX 601 7299.
Parts of this exclusive hotel building date back to the 17th century. Facilities include a championship golf course. *Rooms: 43*
AE DC MC V

WICKLOW *The Old Rectory Country House*   ££
Co Wicklow. 0404 67048. FAX 0404 69181.
A pretty house offering great comfort and good cooking. Guests can walk to the harbour and town centre. *Rooms: 8*
AE MC V

For key to symbols see back flap

RESTAURANTS, CAFÉS AND PUBS

The Bad Ass Café, Temple Bar

THE DUBLIN OF today is a modern, cosmopolitan city, something which is reflected in its vast array of restaurants. The Temple Bar area is good for modern international cuisine, and also has a large number of pubs as well as one or two Irish restaurants, if you prefer to try out traditional Irish fare. Italian, Chinese and Indian restaurants can also be found in the city. Seafood and fish is abundant in Dublin, in particular smoked salmon and oysters;

the latter is famously often consumed with Guinness. Popular for a light lunch is a serving of smoked salmon on delicious dark rye bread, with a pint of Guinness. Wherever you eat, portions are invariably generous, especially in the pubs, whose platefuls of roast meat and vegetables offer excellent value for money. A variety of takeaways, from Dublin's excellent fish and chips to pizzas and kebabs, are also widely available.

IRISH EATING PATTERNS

TRADITIONALLY, the Irish have started the day with a huge breakfast: bacon, sausages, black pudding, eggs, tomatoes and brown bread. The main meal, dinner, was served at midday, with a lighter "tea" in the early evening.

Although continental breakfasts are now available, the traditional breakfast is still included in almost all hotel and B&B rates. Most of the Irish today settle for a light lunch and save their main meal for the evening. Vestiges of the old eating patterns remain in the huge midday meals still served in pubs.

EATING OUT

ELEGANT DINING becomes considerably more affordable when you make lunch your main meal of the day. In many of the top restaurants in Dublin, the fixed-price lunch

and dinner menus offer much the same, but the bill at lunchtime will usually amount to about half the price. If you like wine to accompany your meal, the house wines are quite drinkable in most restaurants and can reduce the total cost of your meal. If you are travelling with children, look out for one of the many restaurants that offer a children's menu. Lunch in Dublin is invariably served between noon and 2:30pm, with dinner between 6:30 and 10pm, although many ethnic and city-centre restaurants stay open later. If you are staying in a bed-and-breakfast, your hosts may provide a home-cooked evening meal if given advance notice. Visa and Mastercard are the most commonly accepted credit cards in Ireland, with American Express and Diners Club also in use.

GOURMET AND ETHNIC DINING

ONCE CONSIDERABLY lacking in gourmet establishments, Dublin now offers many restaurants that rank among Europe's very best, with chefs trained in outstanding domestic and continental institutions. Increasingly it is the hotels which house some of the city's best restaurants, with award-winning cuisine. There is a choice of Irish, French, Italian, Chinese, Indian and even Russian cuisines to be found in and around Dublin, with styles ranging from traditional to regional to modern. Locations vary as widely as the cuisine, from hotel dining

rooms, town house basements and city mansions to castle hotels and tiny village cafés tucked away by the sea. In the city centre, the eating areas with the widest choice tend to be located in Temple Bar or between St Stephen's Green and Merrion Square. Outside the city, Dun Laoghaire has a good selection of restaurants and is especially worth a visit for fresh fish and seafood.

Doorman at the Khyber Tandoori

BUDGET DINING

IT IS QUITE POSSIBLE to eat well on a moderate budget in Dublin. Both in the city and outside it, there are small

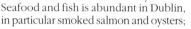
La Med restaurant, one of Temple Bar's many fashionable eating places

The Steps of Rome, off Grafton Street *(p132)*

cafés, tea rooms and family-style restaurants which offer reasonably priced meals. Sandwiches are usually made with thick, delicious slices of fresh, rather than processed, cheese or meat; salad plates feature chicken, pork, beef and the ever-popular smoked salmon; and hot meals usually come with generous helpings of vegetables, with the beloved potato often showing up in different forms, including roasted and mashed, sometimes all on one plate.

Another cheap alternative is to take picnics when you go out. Farmhouse cheeses and homegrown tomatoes make delicious sandwiches, and the beautiful countryside, fine beaches and breathtaking mountains make ideal locations for a picnic. Phoenix Park and Powerscourt both have their own picnic areas.

The cosy Old Mill restaurant in Temple Bar Square *(p129)*

PUB FOOD

IRELAND'S PUBS have moved into the food field with a vengeance. In addition to bar snacks (soup, sandwiches and so on), available from noon until late, salads and hot meals are served from midday to 2:30pm. At rock-bottom prices, hot plates all come heaped with mounds of fresh vegetables, potatoes, and good portions of local fish or meat. Particularly good value are the pub carveries that offer a choice of joints, sliced to your preference. In recent years, the international staples of spaghetti, lasagne and quiche have also appeared on pub menus, along with more Mediterranean dishes such as *bruschetta* in the trendier pubs. For a list of recommended pubs, see pages 132–3.

PUB OPENING HOURS

MANY PEOPLE come to Dublin for its endless pubs and bars and its excellent stouts and whiskeys. In the summer, pubs are open until 11:30pm. In winter they close at 11pm. They open at 10am Monday to Saturday and at noon on Sunday. Also on Sunday, the more traditional pubs observe "holy hour", closing their doors between 2pm and 4pm. If you are already inside you can stay and continue to drink, but no-one can enter between those hours. Late bars tend to stay open until 1am or 2am, the nightclubs even later.

FISH AND CHIPS AND OTHER FAST FOODS

THE IRISH, from peasant to parliamentarian, love their "chippers", immortalized in Roddy Doyle's novel *The Van*, and any good pub night will often end with a visit to the nearest fish-and-chip shop. At virtually any time of day, however, if you pass by Leo Burdock's in Dublin, there will be a long queue for this international institution *(see p132)*. With Ireland's long coastline, wherever you choose, the fish will usually be the freshest catch of the day – plaice, cod, haddock, whiting or ray (a delicacy). As an alternative to fish and chips, there are numerous good pasta and pizza restaurants around the city, including the Steps of Rome and Milano, which also does takeaways. In addition Dublin has become home to the ubiquitous burger chains, including McDonald's, as well as other form of fast food outlets such as KFC.

Picnickers enjoying the sunshine outside at Dublin Zoo *(p79)*

VEGETARIAN FOOD

AS WITH MOST western European cities, there is plenty of scope for vegetarians to eat well in Dublin. Although much traditional Irish food is meat-based, most restaurants will have vegetarian dishes on the menu, particularly in the modern international and Italian restaurants, but there are also some excellent exclusively vegetarian restaurants in the city. If you happen to go somewhere to eat and realize that there is no vegetarian option, most restaurants will be more than happy to make something up for you, such as a salad or a vegetable stir fry.

What to Eat in Dublin

IRELAND'S RICH PASTURELAND, unpolluted rivers and extensive coastline provide tender lamb, beef and pork, an array of fish and seafood and fresh fruit and vegetables. From hearty rural fare that makes the most of the ingredients available, Irish cooking has evolved into the gourmet cuisine created by internationally trained chefs. Often you will find the best of both worlds, with Irish stew or ham and cabbage on the same menu as more exotic dishes. The ideal end to a meal is an Irish coffee – coffee, cream and whiskey.

Irish coffee

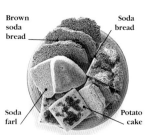

Bread, invariably baked daily, comes in a variety of different guises. Traditional soda bread may be brown or white.

Brown soda bread — Soda bread — Soda farl — Potato cake

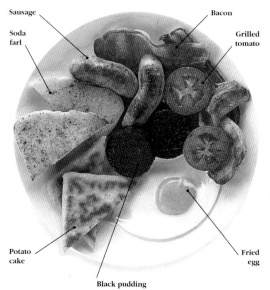

Sausage — Bacon — Grilled tomato — Soda farl — Potato cake — Fried egg — Black pudding

A traditional Irish breakfast consists of home-baked soda farls (soft bread cakes leavened with soda and butter-milk) and potato cakes (bread made from mashed potato, butter and flour), as well as the basic ingredients of a fry-up. Known as a "fry", this is a perfect way to set yourself up for the day. Without the soda farls and potato cakes, meals like this are consumed with relish at any time of day.

Mushroom soup makes a wholesome starter or snack. It is normally made with freshly picked local mushrooms and a generous amount of cream.

Smoked salmon, available all over Ireland and very popular, is generally served as simply as possible – enabling you to enjoy the full flavour of the fish.

Mussel soup is a substantial dish made with fresh local mussels in a creamy fish stock fla-voured with vegetables and herbs. Try it with brown soda bread.

Fresh oysters, here served on a bed of seaweed and cracked ice, make a light but delicious lunch – especially when accom-panied by a glass of Guinness.

Dublin coddle, a traditional Saturday night supper dish, consists of chopped sausages and ham or bacon cooked in stock with potatoes and onions.

Irish stew, originally a peasant dish, is a thick casserole made with lamb or mutton, onions, and parsley, topped with potatoes.

Fresh salmon is often poached in fish stock or wine and herbs. Galway salmon is particularly sought after for its fine taste.

Lamb cutlets are usually served with mint sauce or jelly. Lamb from Kerry and Wicklow is renowned for its tenderness.

Mashed potato

Roast potatoes

Vegetables are served in generous portions, usually as an accompaniment to the main course. It is not uncommon to be given potatoes in a number of different forms – roast, boiled, mashed, baked or chipped – together with whichever vegetables happen to be fresh and in season.

Broccoli

Boiled potatoes

Carrots

Baked ham, coated with cloves and brown sugar, is commonly served with boiled cabbage in butter and eaten at Christmas or on other festive occasions.

Strawberries and cream are the archetypal summer dessert. They are sometimes sweetened with honey rather than sugar.

Porter cake, a classic Irish cake made with dried fruit, is most famous for the inclusion of stout, usually in the form of Guinness.

Apple tart, or "cake" as the Irish often call it, is eaten all year round but is traditionally associated with Hallowe'en.

Brown scone

Fruit scone

CHEESES

For centuries, cheese has been made in farms and monasteries throughout Ireland. Cheese-making has expanded in the last 25 years and Ireland now produces cheeses with a worldwide reputation, from semi-soft ones such as Cashel Blue and St Killian, which is similar to Camembert, to Gouda-like Carrigaline and smoked Durrus.

St Killian

Carrigaline

Cashel Blue

Durrus

Tea-time favourites include sponges, fruit cakes and scones with or without fruit. Barm brack, a doughy, fruity bread, is traditionally eaten at Hallowe'en and on All Saints Day, when a ring is hidden in the cake. According to tradition, the finder of the ring will marry by the following Easter.

Plain scone

Barm brack

Choosing a Restaurant

THIS CHART LISTS restaurants, selected for their good value, exceptional food and/or interesting location. The chart highlights some of the factors which may influence your choice. The restaurants are listed by areas, starting with Southeast Dublin. For Dublin map references, see the Street Finder map on pages 164–5.

	CREDIT CARDS	OPEN LUNCH TIME	OPEN LATE	FIXED-PRICE MENU	GOOD WINE LIST
SOUTHEAST DUBLIN					
ANTE ROOM Map F5. 20 Baggot St Lower, Dublin 2. (661 8832. Lobster, oysters and clams are served fresh from their seawater tanks in this cosy basement restaurant in the Georgian House Hotel. 🏃 ⓔⓔⓔⓔ	AE DC MC V	●			▪
BEWLEY'S ORIENTAL CAFÉ Map D4. 78–79 Grafton St, Dublin 2. (677 6761. This Dublin institution is open from breakfast time onwards. Its breads, pastries and home-made soups are superb. 🔥🏃💱 V ⓔⓔ	AE DC MC V	●	▪		▪
THE COMMONS Map D5. Newman House, St Stephen's Green South, Dublin 2. (478 0530. Specially commissioned paintings by Irish artists share the honours in this tasteful restaurant with gourmet specialities. On sunny days, aperitifs can be taken in the pretty courtyard. 🔥💱 V ⓔⓔⓔⓔ	AE DC MC V	●	▪	●	▪
DOBBIN'S WINE BISTRO Map F5. 15 Stephen's Lane, Mount St Upper, Dublin 2. (676 4679. An intimate, friendly bistro with an innovative monthly menu and one of Dublin's best wine lists. 💱 V ⓔⓔⓔⓔ	AE DC MC V	●	▪	●	▪
EAMONN O'REILLY'S ONE PICO RESTAURANT ⓔⓔ 1 Upper Camden Street, Dublin 2. (478 0307. This award-winning restaurant offers the unusual combination of Irish food with Mediterranean and Californian cuisine. V	AE DC MC V	●	▪	●	▪
L'ECRIVAIN Map F5. 109 Baggot St Lower, Dublin 2. (661 1919. In the heart of Georgian Dublin, French classics here have an Irish touch, with such dishes on the menu as breast of guinea fowl with a black pudding mousse. 💱 V ⓔⓔⓔⓔ	AE DC MC V	●	▪	●	▪
GOTHAM CAFÉ Map D4. 8 Anne St South, Dublin 2. (679 5266. The American-style menu at this bright, friendly café includes "Bowery", "Upper East Side" and "Central Park" gourmet pizzas. 🔥🏃💱 V ⓔⓔⓔ	MC V	●	▪		▪
THE GREY DOOR ⓔⓔⓔⓔ Grey Door Hotel, 23 Pembroke St Upper, Dublin 2. (676 3286. Award-winning Russian-Scandinavian cuisine in elegant surroundings. Specialities include blini with caviar, borshch and gravlax. 💱 V	AE DC MC V	●	▪		▪
KILKENNY SHOP RESTAURANT Map E4. The Kilkenny Shop, 6–10 Nassau St, Dublin 2. (677 7066. A busy restaurant, overlooking Trinity College playing fields, offering traditional Irish cooking and an extensive cheeseboard. 🏃💱 V ⓔⓔ	AE DC MC V	●			▪
LLOYDS Map D4. 20 Upper Merrion Street, Dublin 2. (662 7240. This basement brasserie is minimalist in style and serves excellent modern European food. The unusual breads are a speciality. V ⓔⓔⓔ	AE DC MC V	●	▪		▪
THE MARRAKESH Map D4. 28 Anne St South, Dublin 2. (660 5539. Authentic cooking in a delightfully replicated Moroccan setting. Excellent soups, tagines and couscous. V ⓔⓔⓔ	DC MC V		▪	●	▪
PIER 32 ⓔⓔⓔ 22–23 Pembroke St Upper, Dublin 2. (676 1494. The regularly changing menu includes seafood and regional dishes. Try hare and champ (mashed potatoes, spring onions and butter). 💱 V	MC V	●	▪		▪

	Credit Cards	Open Lunch Time	Open Late	Fixed-Price Menu	Good Wine List

Average prices for a three-course meal for one, half a bottle of house wine and unavoidable charges such as service and cover:
£ under IR£10
££ IR£10–15
£££ IR£15–25
££££ IR£25–50

OPEN LUNCH TIME
Many restaurants open only in the evening, but those in large towns and attached to pubs often open at lunch time.
OPEN LATE
Restaurant remains open with the full menu available after 10pm.
FIXED-PRICE MENU
A good-value fixed-price menu on offer at lunch, dinner or both, usually with three courses.
GOOD WINE LIST
Denotes a wide range of good wines, or a more specialized selection of wines.

RAJDOOT TANDOORI Map D4. £££ 26–28 Clarendon St, Dublin 2. 679 4274. This North Indian restaurant serves mildly spiced curries and, from the clay oven, tandoori barbecued beef, chicken and lamb.	AE DC MC V	●	■	◐	■
SANDBANK SEAFOOD BAR Map D4. £££ Westbury Hotel, Grafton St, Dublin 2. 679 1122. There is a delightful buzz about this pub and restaurant full of maritime memorabilia. The fresh oysters washed down with Guinness are particularly good.	AE DC MC V	●	■	◐	■
LA STAMPA Map D4. ££££ 35 Dawson St, Dublin 2. 677 8611. This up-market Italian restaurant in the heart of Dublin is noted for its sumptuous, highly ornate Georgian decor. Service is efficient and there is a lively atmosphere. Book at weekends.	AE DC MC V	●	■	◐	■

SOUTHWEST DUBLIN

AURIGA Map D3. £££ 2 Temple Bar Square, Dublin 2. 671 8228. International cuisine is served here in a modern but comfortable setting. This second-floor restaurant has an excellent view across Temple Bar Square.	AE MC V	●	■		■
ELEPHANT AND CASTLE Map D3. £££ 18 Temple Bar, Dublin 2. 679 3121. This boisterous American-style restaurant serves up-market fast food from tortillas to hamburgers. It is popular for brunch on Sunday.	AE DC MC V	●	■		
LEO BURDOCK'S Map C4. £ 2 Werburgh St, Dublin 8. 454 0306. Dublin's oldest fish-and-chip takeaway attracts a mix of patrons. The fish is fresh, and the chips made from top-grade Irish potatoes.		●	■		
LORD EDWARD Map B4. ££££ 23 Christchurch Place, Dublin 8. 454 2420. Dublin's oldest seafood restaurant serves lunch in the ground-floor pub and evening meals in the upstairs restaurant. Service is courteous.	AE DC MC V	●	■	◐	■
LA MED Map D3. £££ 22 East Essex Street, Temple Bar, Dublin 2. 670 7358. This bright and airy restaurant serves a range of Mediterranean dishes as its name suggests, and has a lively atmosphere. It is also a venue for live jazz some evenings.	AE MC V	●	■		■
THE OLD MILL Map D3. £££ 14 Temple Bar, Merchants' Arch, Dublin 2. 671 9262. This cosy French restaurant with its low, beamed ceilings has a romantic atmosphere. The menu is changed daily.	MC V	●	■		■

NORTH OF THE LIFFEY

CHAPTER ONE RESTAURANT Map C1. ££££ Below Dublin Writers' Museum, Parnell Square, Dublin 1. 873 2266. The decor features pictures of Irish writers. Deep-fried Parmesan and sage gnocchi are on the menu.	AE DC MC V	●	■	◐	■
CONWAY'S PUB AND RESTAURANT Map D1. £ 70 Parnell St, Dublin 1. 873 2474. Decor in this pub reflects its 1745 origin, and its patrons include Dubliners and actors from the Gate Theatre as well as visitors. The menu features unexpected items, such as tiger prawns in filo pastry.		●	■	◐	

For key to symbols see back flap

Average prices for a three-course meal for one, half a bottle of house wine and unavoidable charges such as service and cover: ⓔ under IR£10 ⓔⓔ IR£10–15 ⓔⓔⓔ IR£15–25 ⓔⓔⓔⓔ IR£25–50	**OPEN LUNCH TIME** Many restaurants open only in the evening, but those in large towns and attached to pubs often open at lunch time. **OPEN LATE** Restaurant remains open with the full menu available after 10pm. **FIXED-PRICE MENU** A good-value fixed-price menu on offer at lunch, dinner or both, usually with three courses. **GOOD WINE LIST** Denotes a wide range of good wines, or a more specialized selection of wines.	CREDIT CARDS	OPEN LUNCH TIME	OPEN LATE	FIXED-PRICE MENU	GOOD WINE LIST

FLANAGAN'S RESTAURANT Map D2.   ⓔⓔ
61 O'Connell St Upper, Dublin 1. (873 1388.
Popular Flanagan's is great value for money with an extensive menu ranging from burgers and salads to vegetarian and pasta choices. ⚇ ⚡ V
MC V · Open Lunch Time ● · Open Late · Fixed-Price Menu ● · Good Wine List

THE ITALIAN CONNECTION Map D2.   ⓔ
95 Talbot Street, Dublin 1. (878 7125.
A friendly, relaxed atmosphere makes dining at this restaurant a pleasure. The menu offers a range of classic Italian dishes. ⚇ ⚡ V
AE DC MC V · Open Lunch Time ● · Open Late · Good Wine List

SHERIES RESTAURANT Map D2.   ⓔⓔ
3 Lower Abbey Street, Dublin 1. (874 7237.
Serving both traditional Irish dishes and modern European food, Sheries is open from breakfast time onwards but closes at 8pm. V
AE DC MC V · Good Wine List

101 TALBOT Map E2.   ⓔⓔ
100–102 Talbot St, Dublin 1. (874 5011.
Vegetarians have a wide choice in this restaurant near the Abbey Theatre. Try the broccoli, fennel, courgette and blue cheese strudel. ⚇ ⚡ V
AE DC MC V · Open Lunch Time ● · Open Late · Good Wine List

FURTHER AFIELD

ABBEY TAVERN   ⓔⓔⓔ
Abbey St, Howth. (839 0307.
A 16th-century tavern complete with original stone walls, gas lights and open turf fires, overlooking Howth Harbour and specializing in seafood. Its Irish music sessions are an institution. Book ahead. ⚡ V
AE DC MC V · Open Lunch Time ● · Fixed-Price Menu ● · Good Wine List

ADRIAN'S RESTAURANT   ⓔⓔ
Abbey Street, Howth. (839 1696.
Specialities include freshly caught fish and seafood, simply cooked and attractively presented at reasonable prices. ♿ V
AE DC MC V · Open Lunch Time ● · Open Late · Good Wine List

BON APPETIT   ⓔⓔⓔⓔ
9 St James Terrace, Malahide. (845 0314.
A superb range of seafood, meat dishes and game, when in season, are offered here. The wine list is extensive and the staff helpful. V
AE V · Open Lunch Time ● · Open Late · Fixed-Price Menu ● · Good Wine List

CHARTERS   ⓔⓔⓔⓔ
5 St James Terrace, Malahide. (845 0833.
This charming restaurant offers fine French cuisine in a cosy, old world setting. The seafood dishes are particularly good. ♿
AE DC MC V · Open Lunch Time ● · Open Late · Good Wine List

CONSERVATORY RESTAURANT   ⓔⓔⓔ
Berkeley Court Hotel, Lansdowne Rd, Ballsbridge, Dublin 4. (660 1711.
In this bright, conservatory-style room in one of the city's most luxurious hotels, meals from the extensive menu are excellent value for money. Very popular with Dubliners. ♿ ⚇ ⚡ V
AE DC MC V · Open Lunch Time ● · Open Late · Fixed-Price Menu ● · Good Wine List

LE COQ HARDI   ⓔⓔⓔⓔ
35 Pembroke Rd, Ballsbridge, Dublin 4. (668 9070.
French classical cuisine uses the best Irish ingredients in this lovely restaurant, winner of countless awards. Book ahead for dinner. V
AE DC MC V · Open Lunch Time ● · Open Late · Fixed-Price Menu ● · Good Wine List

EASTERN TANDOORI   ⓔⓔⓔ
1 New St, Malahide. (845 4154.
Decor and cuisine are authentically Indian in this restaurant located by the marina. Flavours to suit all tastes are served. V
AE DC MC V · Open Late · Fixed-Price Menu ● · Good Wine List

KING SITRIC FISH RESTAURANT   ⓔⓔⓔⓔ
East Pier, Howth. (832 5235.
Howth crab and lobster star on the menu in this elegant restaurant. In summer, a seafood bar serves lunch. Reserve for dinner. ♿ ⚡
AE DC MC V · Open Lunch Time ● · Open Late · Fixed-Price Menu ● · Good Wine List

RESTAURANT NA MARA £££ | AE DC MC V
1 Harbour Rd, Dun Laoghaire. (280 6767.
This delightful restaurant, overlooking the harbour, serves the best just-caught seafood in the area. Non-fish dishes are also available. The modern menu is complemented by the elegant setting. 🏧 🏮 🎇 **V**

ROLY'S BISTRO ££££ | AE DC MC V
7 Ballsbridge Terrace, Ballsbridge, Dublin 4. (668 2611.
Lively bistro with Irish cuisine, including seasonal delights such as venison pie with juniper berries and wood mushrooms. Book ahead. 🏧 🎇 **V**

BEYOND DUBLIN

ARDEE *The Gables* £££ | MC V
Dundalk Rd. (041 53789.
The accent here is definitely French, using the freshest local ingredients available. Choose from classics like snails with garlic butter. 🏧 🎇 **V**

CARLINGFORD *Jordan's Town House Restaurant* £££ | AE MC V
Newry St. (042 73223.
A renovated 19th-century warehouse overlooking the harbour is the setting for culinary gems with organically grown local ingredients. 🎇 **V**

CARLOW *The Beams Restaurant* £££ | MC V
59 Dublin St. (0503 31824.
A family-run restaurant with beamed ceilings and an old wall oven. Dishes include wild Atlantic salmon with white wine sauce, plus a huge choice of Irish cheeses. 🎇 **V**

CARRICKMACROSS *Nuremore Hotel* ££££ | AE DC MC V
Carrickmacross. (042 61438.
This beautiful restaurant has an imaginative menu, including French and Irish cuisine, served in a tranquil setting. 🏧 🏮 🎇 **V**

DUNDALK *Quaglino's Restaurant* £££ | AE DC MC V
88 Clanbrassil St. (042 38567.
This bright, town-centre restaurant features superb Continental dishes, which the menu lists in no fewer than four languages. 🏮 🎇 **V**

GOREY *Marlfield House* ££££ | MC V
Courtown Rd. (055 21124.
This Regency mansion houses one of the Southeast's premier dining rooms. Only organically grown vegetables are used. 🏧 🎇 **V**

KILDARE *Silken Thomas* £££ | AE MC V
The Square. (0455 22232.
Located near the Norman castle keep in the town centre, this restaurant includes beef stroganoff and Gaelic steak on its menu. 🏧 🏮 🎇 **V**

MULLINGAR *Crookedwood House* £££ | AE DC MC V
Crookedwood. (044 72165.
This 200-year-old restaurant changes its menu with the seasons. A summer speciality is River Moy salmon with hollandaise sauce. 🏮 🎇 **V**

NAAS *Manor Inn* ££ | AE DC MC V
Main St. (045 897471.
A haunt of punters en route to and from the nearby Curragh racecourse. Fish, steaks, pasta and grills feature on the menu. 🏧 🏮 **V**

RATHNEW *Hunter's Hotel* £££ | AE DC MC V
Rathnew. (0404 40106.
Cheerful hotel dining room attracting patrons from Dublin and nearby, with its friendly ambience and superb meat and fish dishes. 🏧 🏮

TULLAMORE *Moorhill Country House* £££ | AE DC MC V
Clara Rd. (0506 21395.
Stone walls, oak beams and open fires welcome you to this traditional but imaginative restaurant in renovated stables. 🏧 🏮 🎇 **V**

WICKLOW *The Old Rectory Country House and Restaurant* ££££ | AE MC V
Co Wicklow. (0404 67048.
The pretty dining room is the setting for gourmet meals centred around pure wholefoods, organically grown vegetables and edible flowers, local meats and seafood. Book in advance. 🏮 🎇 **V**

For key to symbols see back flap

Pubs, Bars and Cafés

D UBLIN'S PUBS are a slice of living history, famous as the haunts of literary figures, politicans and rock stars alike. Today, as well as the memorabilia on the walls, it is the singing, dancing, talk and laughter that make a pub tour of Dublin a necessity *(see p142)*.

There are nearly 1,000 pubs inside the city limits. Some excel in entertainment, others the quality of their Guinness and their pub food, but there are also many modern bars to match the best in Europe.

In recent years Dublin has become very cosmopolitan and, as well as the pubs, there is a wide range of cafés offering quick and inexpensive food. The ones listed here are good for those on a busy sightseeing schedule.

TRADITIONAL PUBS

E ACH DUBLIN PUB has its own character and, while many of them are rather touristy, they retain a trademark clientèle: **Doheny & Nesbitt** and the **Horseshoe Bar** attract politicians, journalists and lawyers while **Neary's** pulls in a theatrical crowd. Others have a strong literary connection; Brendan Behan drank at **McDaid's** while **Davy Byrne's** was featured in Joyce's *Ulysses*. Some of the best and most ornate interiors include the **Brazen Head**, the **Stag's Head**, the **Long Hall** and **Kehoe's** with its great snugs. **Mulligan's**, founded in 1782, claims to have the best Guinness. If you fancy something different, **Porter House** in Parliament Street brews its own, including an excellent oyster stout.

MUSIC PUBS

D UBLIN'S MOST FAMOUS traditional music sessions take place at **Slattery's**. Another good place is **O'Donoghue's**. The **International Bar** focuses on singers and comedians while **Whelan's** has a proper venue room next door that has a wonderfully eclectic range of acts for an average IR£5 cover.

MODERN BARS

R ECENTLY, a number of continental-style bars have cropped up which cater to a young and fashionable crowd. **Hogan's**, the **Globe** and **Thomas Reed's** are all on the edge of Temple Bar. The main bar at the **Clarence Hotel** does great cocktails. Inventive drinks are also on the menu at the trendy **Chocolate Bar**.

PUB FOOD

M ANY OF DUBLIN'S grand old pubs offer tasty and good value pub lunches. Just off Grafton Street are **O'Neill's** and the very traditional **Old Stand**. In Temple Bar, **Oliver St John Gogarty** is probably the best option. Also excellent for food is **Rasher's Geraghty**, located in old vaults along Wicklow Street.

MUSEUM AND SHOP CAFÉS

M ANY OF DUBLIN'S tourist attractions offer good quality cafés and snack bars. One of the best is at the **National Gallery**: it serves mainly Mediterranean food and is operated by the Fitzer's chain. Food at the **National Museum** has more of a traditional Irish choice while the **Irish Film Centre** offers an eclectic range. Food at **Habitat** is highly-rated if a little more expensive than the others and, for a unique place to eat, try the upstairs café at the **Winding Stair Bookshop**.

BREAKFAST

M OST HOTELS AND B&Bs serve reasonable breakfasts, an essential start to a full day's sightseeing. A particular favourite of Dubliners is **Café Java**, while the great **Billboard Café** stays open 24 hours a day from Thursday at 7:30am to Sunday at 8pm and serves breakfast throughout. **Bewley's Oriental Café** and **Café Kylemore** also make a good breakfast.

COFFEE AND CAKES

I N AN ATTRACTIVE setting among the stalls at Powerscourt Townhouse, **Chompy's** offers generous portions of cheesecake and other gateaux. The **Espresso Bar** is a swish and stylish Italian coffee bar that serves a great Java.

PIZZA AND PASTA

I RISH-ITALIAN CAFÉS and restaurants offer some of the best value meals in the city. Two very popular ones, the family-oriented **Little Caesar's Palace** and the tiny **Steps of Rome**, lie off Grafton Street. Temple Bar's **Bad Ass Café** has a youthful feel and serves pizza, pasta and salads. This is where Sinead O'Connor worked before making it in music. **Milano**, currently with two branches in the city, is a branch of the popular British chain Pizza Express.

TRADITIONAL FOOD

O NE OF THE MOST famous meeting points in the city is the original **Bewley's Oriental Café** on Grafton Street. However, these days some prefer the simple fare at **Café Kylemore** which is run by a major city bakery. For good honest fish and chips try the venerable **Leo Burdock's**.

VEGETARIAN

P ERHAPS THE BEST vegetarian place in the city is **Marks Bros** but nowadays it is only open in the evening. However, another long-running café, **Cornucopia**, is also open for breakfast and lunch. **Blazing Salads II** is a fun place to eat in the Powerscourt Townhouse while the **Well Fed Café** offers an alternative feel. The **Alamo Café** is the pick of the city's Mexican restaurants and offers lots of choice for vegetarians but also serves meat dishes.

DIRECTORY

TRADITIONAL PUBS

The Brazen Head
20 Bridge St Lower.
Map A3.
[679 5186.

Davy Byrne's
21 Duke St.
Map D4.
[677 5217.

Doheny & Nesbitt
5 Lower Baggot St.
Map F5.
[676 2945.

Horsehoe Bar
Shelbourne Hotel,
27 St Stephen's Green.
Map E4.
[676 6471.

Kehoe's
9 Anne St South.
Map D4.
[677 8312.

The Long Hall
51 South Great George's
St. **Map** C4.
[475 1590.

McDaid's
3 Harry St.
Map D4.
[679 4395.

Mulligan's
8 Poolbeg St.
Map E3.
[677 5582.

Neary's
1 Chatham St.
Map D4.
[677 8596.

Porter House
Parliament St.
Map C3.
[679 8850

Stag's Head
1 Dame Court, off Dame St.
Map C3.
[679 3701.

MUSIC BARS

International Bar
23 Wicklow St.
Map D3.
[677 9250.

O'Donoghue's
15 Merrion Row.
Map C5.
[660 7194.

Slattery's
29 Capel St.
Map C2.
[872 7971.

Whelan's
25 Wexford St.
Map C5.
[478 0766.

MODERN BARS

Chocolate Bar
Harcourt St, at Hatch St
Lower.
Map D5.
[478 0166.

Clarence Hotel
Essex St East entrance.
Map C3.
[670 9000.

The Globe
11 South Great George's St.
Map C4.
[671 1220.

Hogan's
35 South Great George's St.
Map C4.
[677 5904.

Thomas Reed
1 Parliament St.
Map C3.
[670 7220.

PUB FOOD

The Old Stand
37 Exchequer St.
Map D3.
[677 7220.

**Oliver St John
Gogarty**
57 Fleet St.
Map D3.
[671 1822.

O'Neill's
2 Suffolk St.
Map D3.
[679 3671.

**Rasher's
O'Geraghty**
6–8 Wicklow St.
Map D3.
[670 4220.

MUSEUM AND SHOP CAFÉS

Habitat
St Stephen's Green
(nr Grafton St).
Map D4.
[677 1433.

Irish Film Centre
6 Eustace St.
Map C3.
[677 8788.

National Gallery
Merrion Square West.
Map E4.
[661 5133.

National Museum
Kildare St.
Map E4.
[677 7444.

**Winding Stair
Bookshop & Café**
40 Ormond Quay Lower.
Map C3.
[873 3292.

BREAKFAST

Billboard Café
43 Lower Camden St.
Map C5.
[475 5047.

Café Java
5 Anne St South.
Map D4.
[670 7239.
145 Leeson St.
Map E5.
[660 0675.

COFFEE AND CAKES

Chompy's
Powerscourt Townhouse,
South William St.
Map D4.
[679 4552.

Espresso Bar
Westbury Mall, off
Grafton St.
Map D4.
[670 7056.

PIZZA AND PASTA

Bad Ass Café
9 Crown Alley.
Map D3.
[671 2596.

**Little Caesar's
Palace**
1–3 Balfe St. **Map** D4.
[670 4534.

Milano
38 Dawson St.
Map D4.
[670 7744.
19 Essex St East.
Map C3.
[670 3384.

Steps of Rome
Unit 1, Chatham Court,
Chatham St.
Map D4.
[670 5630.

TRADITIONAL FOOD

**Bewley's Oriental
Café**
78 Grafton St.
Map D4.
[677 6761.

Café Kylemore
O'Connell St, at North
Earl St. **Map** D2.
[878 0496.

Leo Burdock's
2 Werburgh St.
Map C4.
[454 0306.

VEGETARIAN

Alamo Café
22 Temple Bar.
Map C3.
[677 6546.

Blazing Salads II
Powerscourt Townhouse,
South William St.
Map D4.
[671 9552.

Cornucopia
19 Wicklow St.
Map D3.
[677 7583.

Marks Bros
7 South Great George's St.
Map C4.
[677 1085.

Well Fed Café
The Resource Centre,
6 Crows St.
Map C3.
[677 2234.

SHOPPING IN DUBLIN

DUBLIN IS A paradise for shoppers, with its wide streets, indoor markets, craft stores and out-of-town shopping centres. Popular buys include chunky Aran sweaters, Waterford crystal, Irish linen, hand-loomed tweed from Donegal and tasty farmhouse cheeses. The thriving crafts industry is based on traditional products with an innovative twist. Typical of contemporary Irish crafts are good design, quality craftsmanship and a range spanning

Pottery from DESIGNyard

Celtic brooches and bone china, knitwear and designer fashion, carved bogwood and books of Irish poetry. Kitsch souvenirs also abound, from leprechauns and shamrock emblems to Guinness tankards and garish religious memorabilia. Irish whiskeys and liqueurs are always popular and very reasonable to buy in Dublin.

In the directory on page 137, a map reference is given for each address that features on the Dublin Street Finder map on pages 164–5.

Johnson's Court alley behind Grafton Street in southwest Dublin

WHERE TO SHOP

THERE ARE two major shopping quarters in Dublin: the north side of the Liffey, centred on O'Connell and Henry Streets, and the more salubrious south side, around Grafton and Nassau Streets. The Temple Bar area contains a number of trendy craft shops. The two main markets are Mother Redcap's indoor flea market in Christchurch at weekends, and the fruit and vegetable market which is set up in Moore Street from Monday to Saturday.

WHEN TO SHOP

MOST SHOPS are open from Monday to Saturday, 9am to 5:30 or 6pm. Shops open late on Thursday nights. Shops are closed at Easter and Christmas and on St Patrick's Day but are open on most other public holidays.

HOW TO PAY

MAJOR CREDIT cards such as VISA and MasterCard are accepted in most large stores, but smaller shops may prefer cash. Traveller's cheques are accepted in major stores with a passport as identification. Eurocheques are generally no longer acceptable.

SALES TAX AND REFUNDS

MOST PURCHASES are subject to VAT (sales tax) at 21 per cent, a sum included in the sales price. However, visitors from outside the European Union (EU) can reclaim VAT prior to departure. If you are shipping goods overseas, refunds can be claimed at the point of purchase. If taking your goods with you, look for the CashBack logo in shops, fill in the special voucher, then visit the CashBack offices at Dublin airport.

SHOPPING CENTRES

DUBLIN HAS several large shopping centres – some in the city centre and some outside. The **Dun Laoghaire Shopping Centre** is on several floors and has a huge range of clothes shops, bookshops and electronics shops. In central Dublin is the **St Stephen's Green Shopping Centre**, the **Jervis Shopping Centre** and the **Ilac Centre**, all offering the comfort of covered shopping. A more unusual centre is the **Powerscourt Townhouse** (see p58), more of an indoor market than a shopping centre, selling various Irish crafts.

BOOKS

BOOKSHOPS ABOUND in Dublin. **Eason and Son**, on O'Connell Street, is the biggest bookseller in the city with a wide range of Irish literature and national and

The Ha'penny Bridge Galleries on Bachelors Walk

Brown Thomas department store on Grafton Street

international newpapers. For antiquarian books, **Fred Hanna Ltd** on Nassau Street has an excellent selection.

Foreign-language books are available in Dublin – try **International Books** for the best range. **Hodges Figgis** specializes in Irish literature and academic publications. They also have a coffee shop in the store. One of the best for general books is the **Dublin Bookshop** on Grafton Street (part of the Dubray Books chain). On two floors, they have an extensive Irish section and a good range of tourist guides as well as general fiction and children's books. **Waterstone's** and **Hughes & Hughes** are also both good general booksellers.

MUSIC

TRADITIONAL MUSICAL instruments are made in many regions of Ireland, but Dublin has a history of specializing in hand-made harps. Several shops sell musical instruments, such as hand-crafted bodhráns (traditional goatskin hand-held drums) and uilleann pipes (bagpipes). **Waltons** sells traditional instruments and sheet music, while **Claddagh Records** is a specialist folk shop, selling Irish folk and ethnic music. For a standard range of pop and classical music there are two branches of the **HMV** music store in Dublin.

ANTIQUES

DUBLIN HAS its own antiques centre, in the form of Francis Street in the south west of the city. **Lantern Antiques** specializes in old pub fittings such as mirrors and old advertisements. For rugs and carpets try **Forsyth's Antiques**. For 20th-century decorative arts visit **Odeon**. **The Ha'Penny Bridge Galleries** sell everything from furniture through to cast iron and marble. **Courtville Antiques** in the Powerscourt Townhouse has a beautiful collection of antique jewellery, silver, paintings and objets d'art. On Grafton Street, **McCormack** is particularly good for antique jewellery and watches.

Sign outside Eason and Son

CRAFTS

THE **Crafts Council of Ireland** in Dublin recommends good outlets for Irish crafts, and the tourist offices

Bodhráns of perfect pitch for sale in Dublin

provide lists of local workshops, where you can often watch the production process. Many craft shops, such as **The Kilkenny Shop**, sell different crafts including tiles, rugs, metalwork, leatherwork and woodwork. For contemporary crafts, visit **DESIGNyard** in Temple Bar *(see p56)*.

JEWELLERY

IN ITS GOLDEN AGE, Celtic metalwork was the pride of Ireland. Many contemporary craftspeople are still inspired by traditional designs on Celtic chalices and ornaments. Silver and gold jewellery is made all over Ireland in many designs and widely available in Dublin. The Claddagh ring is the most famous of all – the lovers' symbol of two hands cradling a heart with a crown. In the Powerscourt Townhouse, shops have handmade and antique jewellery on display and gold- and silversmiths can be seen at work. **McDowell** jewellers specialize in handcrafted gold and silver Irish jewellery.

CHINA, CRYSTAL AND GLASSWARE

IRELAND'S MOST FAMOUS make of crystalware is Waterford Crystal. Still made today in the town of Waterford, south of Dublin, this beautiful crystal and glassware is known all over the world for its outstanding quality.

Dublin Crystal, in Blackrock, south of the city, makes and sells on the premises fine quality hand-cut crystal.

There are many producers of fine china in Ireland. Royal Tara China in Galway is Ireland's leading fine bone china manufacturer, with designs incorporating Celtic themes. The best place to buy china and glassware is in department stores, such as Clery's and Brown Thomas.

LINEN

DAMASK LINEN was brought to Armagh in Northern Ireland by Huguenot refugees fleeing French persecution. Linen is widely available all over Ireland today, and fine Irish linen can be bought at many outlets in Dublin, including the **Brown Thomas** department store, which has an excellent linen shop. Another good supplier is **Murphy, Sheehy and Co**, who are located behind the Powercourt Townhouse. As well as being famous for fine quality Irish linen, they also sell tweeds.

Sign for the linen department at Brown Thomas store

KNITWEAR AND TWEED

ARAN SWEATERS are sold all over Ireland, but originate in County Galway and the Aran Islands themselves, off the west coast of Ireland. One of Dublin's best buys, these oiled, off-white sweaters used to be handed down through generations of Aran fishermen. Legend has it that each family used its own motifs so that, if a fisherman were lost at sea and his body unidentifiable, his family could recognize him by his sweater. Warm and rain-resistant clothes are generally of good quality, from waxed jackets and duffel coats to sheepskin jackets. **Exclusively Irish** offer an excellent selection of quality Irish clothing. Knitwear is sold everywhere in Dublin.

Good buys include embroidered waistcoats and handwoven scarves. **The Sweater Shop** has woollens and tweeds at reasonable prices.

Donegal tweed is noted for its texture and subtle colours (originally produced by local plant and mineral dyes). Tweed caps, scarves, ties, jackets and suits are sold in outlets such as **Kevin & Howlin** in Dublin. For menswear specialists, try **Kennedy & McSharry**. Outside Dublin, the **Avoca Handweavers** in Bray are worth a visit.

FASHION

INSPIRED BY a predominantly young population, Ireland is fast acquiring a name for fashion. Conservatively cut tweed and linen suits continue to be models of classic good taste, while younger designers are increasingly experimental, using bold lines and mixing traditional fabrics.

A-Wear is an Irish chain store that has a branch in Dublin. In the Design Centre in Powerscourt Townhouse Shopping Centre are clothes by the best Irish designers including John Rocha, Paul Costelloe, Louise Kennedy, Quin and Donnelly and Mariad Whisker. The department stores **Brown Thomas** and **Clery's** have an excellent selection of men's, women's and children's clothing. Shoe and clothing sizes are identical to British fittings.

Fresh cheeses in Meetinghouse Square

FOOD AND DRINK

SMOKED SALMON, home-cured bacon, farmhouse cheeses, preserves, soda bread and handmade chocolates make perfect last-minute gifts. **Butlers Irish Hand-made Chocolates** are particularly delicious. Several shops will package and send Irish salmon overseas.

Bewley's teas and coffees are sold in **Bewley's Oriental Café** and Bewley shops all over Ireland. Guinness travels less well and is best drunk in Ireland. Irish whiskey is hard to beat as a gift or souvenir. Apart from the cheaper Power and Paddy brands, the big names are Bushmills and Jameson. Rich Irish liqueurs to enjoy include Irish Mist and Bailey's Irish Cream.

Fresh fruit stall off O'Connell Street

DIRECTORY

SHOPPING CENTRES

Dun Laoghaire Shopping Centre
Marine Road,
Dun Laoghaire.
(280 2981.

Ilac Centre
Henry Street,
Dublin 1. **Map** D2.

Jervis Shopping Centre
Mary Street,
Dublin 1.
Map C2.
(878 1323.

Powerscourt Townhouse Shopping Centre
South William Street,
Dublin 2. **Map** D4.
(679 4144.

St Stephen's Green Shopping Centre
St Stephen's Green West,
Dublin 2.
Map D4.
(475 7816.

BOOKS

Dublin Bookshop
24 Grafton Street,
Dublin 2.
Map D4.
(677 5568.

Eason and Son
80 Abbey Street Middle,
Dublin 1. **Map** D2.
(873 3811.

Fred Hanna Ltd
27–29 Nassau Street,
Dublin 2. **Map** E4.
(677 1255.

Hodges Figgis
56–58 Dawson Street,
Dublin 2.
Map D4.
(677 4754.

Hughes & Hughes
St Stephen's Green
Shopping Centre,
Dublin 2,
Map D4.
(478 3060.
Also at
Dublin Airport.
(844 4900.

International Books
18 Frederick Street South,
Dublin 2.
Map E4.
(679 9375.

Waterstone's
7 Dawson Street,
Dublin 2.
Map D4.
(679 1415.
Also at
Jervis Shopping Centre.
Map C2.
(878 1311.

MUSIC

Claddagh Records
2 Cecilia Street,
Temple Bar, Dublin 2.
Map C3.
(677 0262.

HMV
18 Henry Street,
Dublin 1.
Map D2.
(873 2899.
Also at
Grafton Street,
Dublin 2.
Map D4.
(679 5334.

Waltons
2–5 Frederick Street
North, Dublin 1.
(874 7805.

JEWELLERY

McDowell
3 Upper O'Connell Street,
Dublin 1.
Map D2.
(874 4961.

ANTIQUES

Courtville Antiques
Powerscourt Townhouse
Shopping Centre,
Dublin 2.
Map D4.
(679 4042.

Forsyth's Antiques
89 Francis Street,
Dublin 8.
Map B4.
(473 2148.

The Ha'Penny Bridge Galleries
15 Bachelors Walk,
Dublin 1.
Map D3.
(872 3950.

Lantern Antiques
56 Francis Street,
Dublin 8. **Map** B4.
(453 4593.

McCormack
51 Grafton Street,
Dublin 2. **Map** D4.
(677 3737.

Odeon
89–70 Francis Street,
Dublin 8. **Map** B4.
(473 2384.

CRAFTS

Crafts Council of Ireland
Powerscourt Townhouse
Shopping Centre,
William Street South,
Dublin 2. **Map** D4.
(679 7368.

DESIGNyard
12 East Essex Street,
Temple Bar,
Dublin 2. **Map** C3.
(677 8453.

The Kilkenny Shop
6 Nassau Street,
Dublin 2. **Map** E4.
(677 7066.

CERAMICS, CHINA AND CRYSTAL

Dublin Crystal
Brookfield Terrace
(off Carysfort Avenue),
Blackrock, Co Dublin.
(288 7932.

LINENS

Brown Thomas Linen Shop
Grafton Street,
Dublin 2. **Map** D4.
(677 0316.

Murphy, Sheehy and Co
14 Castle Market (off
South William Street),
Dublin 2. **Map** D4.
(677 0316.

KNITWEAR AND TWEED

Avoca Handweavers
Kilmacanogue, Bray,
Co Wicklow.
(286 7466.

Exclusively Irish
14–15 O'Connell Street
Upper, Dublin 1. **Map** D2.
(874 6064.

Kennedy and McSharry
39 Nassau Street,
Dublin 2. **Map** D3.
(677 8770.

Kevin and Howlin
31 Nassau Street,
Dublin 2. **Map** D3.
(677 0257.

The Sweater Shop
9 Wicklow Street,
Dublin 2. **Map** D3.
(671 3270.

FASHION

A-Wear
26 Grafton Street,
Dublin 2.
Map D4.
(671 7200.

Brown Thomas
88–95 Grafton Street,
Dublin 2.
Map D4.
(679 5666.

Clery's
18–27 O'Connell
Street Lower,
Dublin 1.
Map D2.
(878 6000.

FOOD AND DRINK

Bewley's Oriental Café
78 Grafton Street,
Dublin 2.
Map D4.
(677 6761.

Butlers Irish Handmade Chocolates
51 Grafton Street,
Dublin 2.
Map D4.
(677 6761.

What to Buy in Dublin

St Brigid's cross

THE MANY GIFT and craft shops scattered throughout Dublin make it easy to find Irish specialities to suit all budgets. The best buys include linen, tweeds and lead crystal. Local crafts make unique souvenirs, from delicate hand-made silver jewellery and hand-thrown ceramics to traditional musical instruments. Religious artifacts are also widely available. Irish food and drink, especially whiskey, are evocative reminders of your trip.

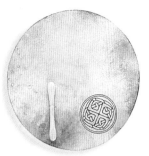

Traditional hand-held drum (*bodhrán*) and beater

Connemara marble "worry stone"

Traditional Claddagh ring

Enamel brooch

Modern jewellery and metalwork draw on a long and varied tradition. Craftspeople continue to base their designs on sources such as the Book of Kells (see p38) and Celtic myths. Local plants and wildlife are also an inspiration. Claddagh rings – traditional betrothal rings – originated in County Galway but are widely available in Dublin.

Fuchsia earring from Dingle

Celtic-design enamel brooch

Celtic-design silver pendant

Donegal tweed jacket and waistcoat

Tweed jacket and skirt

Clothing made in Ireland is usually of excellent quality. Tweed-making still flourishes in Donegal where tweed can be bought ready-made as clothing or hats or as lengths of cloth. Knitwear is widely available throughout Dublin in department stores and local craft shops. The many hand-knitted items on sale, including Aran jumpers, are not cheap but should give years of wear.

Tweed cap

Tweed fisherman's hat

Aran jumper

Irish linen is world-famous and the range unparalleled. There is a huge choice of table and bed linen, including extravagant bedspreads and crisp, formal tablecloths. On a smaller scale, tiny, intricately embroidered handkerchiefs make lovely gifts as do linen table napkins. Tea towels printed with colourful designs are widely available. You can also buy linen goods trimmed with fine lace, which is still handmade in many parts of the country.

Set of linen placemats and napkins

Fine linen handkerchiefs

Nicholas
Mosse
plate

Belleek
teapot

Nicholas
Mosse
cup

Irish ceramics come in traditional and modern designs. You can buy anything from a full dinner service by established factories, such as Royal Tara China or the Belleek Pottery, to a one-off contemporary piece from a local potter's studio.

·IRISH·
PROVERBS

ILLUSTRATED BY
KAREN BAILEY

Book of Irish Proverbs

Irish crystal, hand-blown and hand-cut, can be ordered or bought in many shops in Dublin. Pieces from the principal manufacturers, such as Waterford Crystal, Tyrone Crystal and Jerpoint Glass, from glasses and decanters to elaborate chandeliers, are widely sold.

Books and stationery are often beautifully illustrated. Museums and bookshops stock a wide range.

**Celtic-design
cards**

**Waterford crystal tumbler
and decanter**

Food and drink will keep the distinctive tastes of Dublin fresh long after you arrive home. Whiskey connoisseurs should visit the Old Jameson Distillery (see p73) to sample their choice of whiskeys. The Guinness Hop Store (see p80) is a must for aficionados of the dark stout. Good regional food can be found all over the Dublin area.

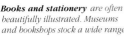

**Jameson
whiskey**   **Bushmills
whiskey**   **Fruit cake made
with Guinness**   **Jar of Irish
marmalade**   **Packet of dried
seaweed**

ENTERTAINMENT IN DUBLIN

ALTHOUGH DUBLIN is well served by theatres, cinemas, night-clubs and rock venues, what sets the city apart from other European capitals is its pubs. Lively banter, impromptu music sessions and great Guinness are the essential ingredients for an enjoyable night in any one of dozens of lively, atmospheric hostelries in Dublin.

One of the most popular entertainment districts is the Temple Bar area. Along this narrow network of cobbled streets you can find

Traditional Irish dancer

everything from traditional music in grand old pubs to the latest dance tracks in a post-industrial setting. The variety of venues makes the centre south of the Liffey the place to be at night, although the north side does boast the two most illustrious theatres, the largest cinemas and the 7,000-seater Point Theatre, a converted 19th-century rail terminal beside the docks. It is now the venue for all major rock concerts and stage musicals as well as some classical music performances.

Street entertainer in central Dublin

Colourful façade of the Olympia Theatre on Dame Street

ENTERTAINMENT LISTINGS

THE MAIN LISTINGS magazine, *In Dublin*, comes out every two weeks and is readily available from all newsagents. *Hot Press*, a national bimonthly newspaper that covers both rock and traditional music, has comprehensive listings for Dublin. The *Dublin Event Guide* is a free sheet available from pubs, cafés, restaurants and record shops. Like *In Dublin*, it is published every two weeks, and is particularly strong on information about the city's music and nightclubs.

The listings magazine, *In Dublin*, published every other week

BOOKING TICKETS

TICKETS FOR many events are available on the night, but it is usually safer to book in advance. The principal venues accept payment over the telephone by all the major credit cards. The **Ticket Shop** accepts phone bookings by credit card for many of the major shows and events in

and around Dublin, while the main branches of **HMV** sell tickets over the counter for theatre shows and rock gigs.

THEATRE

ALTHOUGH DUBLIN has only a limited number of theatres, there is almost always something worth seeing and the productions are of a very high standard. Most of Dublin's theatres are closed on Sunday.

The most famous venue is Ireland's national theatre, the **Abbey** *(see p68)*, which concentrates on major new Irish productions as well as revivals of works by Irish playwrights such as Brendan Behan, Sean O'Casey, JM Synge and WB Yeats. The smaller Peacock Theatre downstairs covers more experimental works.

Also on the north side is the **Gate Theatre** *(see p70)*, founded in 1929 and noted for its interpretations of well-known international plays. The main venue south of the Liffey, the **Gaiety Theatre**, stages a mainstream mix of plays, emphasizing the work of Irish playwrights. Some of the best fringe theatre and modern dance in Dublin can be seen at the **Project Arts Centre** in Temple Bar and the **City Arts Centre**, which sometimes has midnight performances. **Andrews Lane Theatre** provides a forum for up-and-coming new writers and directors. The **Olympia Theatre** on Dame Street has the feel of a Victorian music hall. Specializing in comedy and popular

Buskers playing near Grafton Street in Southeast Dublin

drama, the Olympia also occasionally attracts some of the top performers to stage rock and Irish music concerts in the theatre's intimate setting.

Every October the **Dublin Theatre Festival** takes over all the venues in the city with a mix of mainstream, fringe, Irish and international plays.

CLASSICAL MUSIC, OPERA AND DANCE

DUBLIN MAY not have the range of classical concerts of other European capitals, but it has a great venue in the **National Concert Hall**. In the 1980s, this 19th-century exhibition hall was completely redesigned and acoustically adapted, and is where the National Symphony Orchestra plays most Friday evenings. The National Concert Hall's programme also includes jazz, dance, opera, chamber music, and some traditional music.

The **Hugh Lane Municipal Gallery of Modern Art** *(see p71)* has regular Sunday lunchtime concerts. Other classical venues include the **Royal Hospital Kilmainham** *(see p82)* and the main hall and showground of the **Royal Dublin Society (RDS)**. International opera is staged in the **Point Theatre**. The DGOS (Dublin Grand Opera Society) performs every April and November at the Gaiety Theatre on King Street South.

TRADITIONAL MUSIC AND DANCE

TO MANY IRISH PEOPLE the standard of music in a pub is just as important as the quality of the Guinness. Central

Dublin has a host of pubs reverberating to the sound of bodhráns, fiddles and uilleann pipes. One of the most famous is **O'Donoghue's**, where the legendary Dubliners started out in the early 1960s. The long-established **Slattery's** and the **Auld Dubliner** are also renowned venues for local and foreign bands. Established acts play venues such as **Mother Redcap's Tavern**, which is a fun place occupying a spacious old factory and appealing to all ages. **Jury's Hotel** and the **Castle Inn** stage nightly Irish cabaret featuring dancing, singing and lively, toe-tapping music.

The Laughter Lounge

ROCK, JAZZ, BLUES AND COUNTRY

DUBLIN HAS HAD a thriving rock scene ever since local band Thin Lizzy made it big in the early 1970s. U2's international success acted as a further catalyst for local bands, and there's a gig

somewhere in the city on most nights. **Whelan's** and the **Baggot Inn** feature the best new Irish bands nightly. The likeable **International Bar** caters mostly for acoustic acts and singer-songwriters, while **Break for the Border** is a popular nightclub featuring a variety of live bands. All the big names play at either the Point Theatre or, in summer, local sports stadia.

An annual highlight for jazz and blues fans is the **Temple Bar Blues Festival** in July. Country music also enjoys a big following in Ireland, and **Bad Bob's Backstage Bar** is a lively country music venue, usually with lots of dancing.

HOTEL BARS

THE PUBS of Dublin have started to overflow and, as a result, a new breed of bar has taken off. The hotel bars are the city's sophisticated watering holes, appealing to those who wish to escape the "craic" of the more traditional pubs. One such haven is the **Inn on the Green**, located in the Fitzwilliam Hotel. The decor is Nineties metal and the atmosphere is cool. At the Merrion Hotel, you can hide from the hubbub of the city in the **Cellar Bar**. Trendy media types hang out at the mellow **Octagon Bar** at The Clarence but, if it's glamour you seek, head for a shot of whiskey in **The Horseshoe Bar** at the famous Shelbourne Hotel.

Crowds enjoying the Temple Bar Blues Festival

Comedian at The Ha'Penny Bridge Inn on Wellington Quay

NIGHTCLUBS

UNTIL A CLUSTER of new dance venues opened in the early 1990s, Dublin's club-life was fairly unremarkable. Nowadays the **POD** (Place of Dance) attracts visiting stars taking time out from their film or video shoots in the city. Another trendy venue is the **Kitchen**, downstairs in the (U2-owned) Clarence Hotel, which has a wide range of music and a great atmosphere. Once every fortnight, the club puts on *Quadraphonic*, an evening of drum 'n' bass. **Ri-Rá** (Irish for uproar) is a venue at the cutting edge of dance music, while **Lillie's Bordello** caters for a more mainstream dance sound.

For a small venue, head for **The Da Club**, which offers not only live music and DJs, but also stand-up comedy routines in the Ultra Lounge every other Thursday. **The Laughter Lounge** is a top comedy venue, attracting big names. Every Tuesday night is comedy night at **The Ha'Penny Bridge Inn**. **The River Club** is theoretically

only open to members but, if you adhere to the smart-casual dress code, you may be admitted. Most clubs close at 2am but there are some which stay open until 5am.

PUB CRAWLS AND TOURS

THERE ARE numerous pub crawls in Dublin, most of which cover the character pubs and those with a long and colourful history. The **Dublin Literary Pub Crawl** is perhaps the most famous of these, featuring pubs once frequented by Ireland's most famous authors and play-wrights. The two-and-a-half-hour tours that start in The Duke pub, on Duke Street, are by far the most entertaining way to get a real feel for the city's booze-fuelled literary heritage.

A handful of tours around the city offer an insight into Dublin's dark and spooky history. **Walk Makabre** visits scenes of murder and intrigue in the city. Alternatively if you prefer to be driven around, The **Dublin Ghost Bus Tour** offers on-board entertainment as well as lessons in bodysnatching and the story behind Stoker's *Dracula*.

If tracing Dublin's musical heritage is of more interest, join the **Rock Trail**. This takes you to the sites where bands such as U2 and Thin Lizzy first found fame. The **Baggot Inn** is where rock 'n' roll band Moving Hearts were seen performing in their early days. The **Musical Pub Crawl** is another tour that traces the history of Irish music, with musicians performing from pub to pub. The **Historical Walking Tour** of Dublin takes in many of the significant locations of the city's colourful past.

Record shop and ticket office in Crown Alley, Temple Bar

CINEMA

DUBLIN'S CINEMAS have had a boost thanks to the success of Dublin-based films such as *My Left Foot* (1989), *The Commitments* (1991) and *Michael Collins* (1996) and a subsequent growth in the country's movie production industry. The **Irish Film Centre** *(see p56)* opened its doors in 1992 and was a most welcome addition to the city's entertainment scene. Housed in an original 17th-century building in Temple Bar, the centre shows mostly independent and foreign films, along with a programme of lectures, seminars and masterclasses. It boasts two screens, a bar, a restaurant and an archive of old film material. Two other cinemas whose repertoire is mostly art house are the **Screen**, near Trinity College, and the **Light House**, which is north of the river. The large first-run cinemas, such as the multiplex **Virgin Cinemas**, are all located on the north side. These usually offer tickets at reduced prices for their afternoon screenings and show late-night movies at the weekend. The **Dublin Film Festival**, which is held over ten days between late February and early March, shows a selection of international and Irish releases, from high- to low-budget films.

'Mr Screen' cinema sign

The National Concert Hall on Earlsfort Terrace

DIRECTORY

BOOKING TICKETS

HMV
18 Henry St. **Map** D2.
【 *873 2899.*
65 Grafton St. **Map** D4.
【 *677 5930.*

Ticket Shop
2nd Floor, Grafton House,
70 Grafton St. **Map** D4.
【 *456 9569.*

THEATRE

Abbey Theatre
Abbey St Lower. **Map** E2.
【 *878 7222.*

Andrews Lane Theatre
9–11 St Andrew's Lane.
Map D3.
【 *679 5720.*

City Arts Centre
23–25 Moss St. **Map** E2.
【 *677 0643.*

Dublin Theatre Festival
47 Nassau St. **Map** D3.
【 *677 8439.*

Gaiety Theatre
King St South. **Map** D4.
【 *677 1717.*

Gate Theatre
Cavendish Row. **Map** D1.
【 *874 4368.*

Olympia Theatre
Dame St. **Map** C3.
【 *677 7744.*

Project Arts Centre
The Mint, Henry Place.
Map D2.
【 *671 2321.*

Riverbank Theatre
Merchant's Quay. **Map** B3.
【 *677 3370.*

CLASSICAL MUSIC, OPERA AND DANCE

Hugh Lane Municipal Gallery of Modern Art
Charlemont House, Parnell
Sq North. **Map** C1.
【 *874 1903.*

Irish Museum of Modern Art
Kilmainham, Dublin 8.
【 *612 9900.*

National Concert Hall
Earlsfort Terrace. **Map** D5.
【 *475 1666.*

Point Theatre
East Link Bridge, North
Wall Quay. **Map** F2.
【 *836 3633.*

Royal Dublin Society (RDS)
Ballsbridge.
【 *668 0866.*

TRADITIONAL MUSIC AND DANCE

Auld Dubliner
24–25 Temple Bar.
Map D3.
【 *677 0527.*

Castle Inn
5–7 Lord Edward St.
Map C3.
【 *475 1122.*

Jury's Hotel
Pembroke Rd, Ballsbridge.
【 *660 5000.*

Mother Redcap's Tavern
Back Lane, Christchurch.
Map B4.
【 *453 8306.*

O'Donoghue's
15 Merrion Row. **Map** E5.
【 *660 7194.*

Slattery's
129 Capel St. **Map** C2.
【 *872 7971.*

ROCK, JAZZ, BLUES AND COUNTRY

Bad Bob's Backstage Bar
35 East Essex St, Temple
Bar. **Map** C3.
【 *677 5482.*

Baggot Inn
143 Baggot St Lower.
Map E5.
【 *676 1430.*

Break for the Border
Grafton Plaza Hotel,
Lower Stephen St.
Map D4.
【 *478 0300.*

International Bar
23 Wicklow St. **Map** D3.
【 *677 9250.*

Temple Bar Blues Festival
Temple Bar Information
Centre, 18 Eustace St.
Map C3.
【 *671 5717.*

Whelan's
25 Wexford St. **Map** C5.
【 *478 0766.*

NIGHTCLUBS

The Da Club
Lower Stephen St.
Map D4.
【 *670 3137.*

The Ha'Penny Bridge Inn
Wellington Quay. **Map** C3.
【 *677 0616.*

Kitchen
6–8 Wellington Quay.
Map C3.
【 *677 6635.*

Lillie's Bordello
Adam Court, off Grafton St.
Map D4.
【 *679 9204.*

Murphy's Laughter Lounge
4–6 Eden Quay. **Map** D2.
【 *874 4611.*

POD
Harcourt St. **Map** D5.
【 *478 0166.*

Ri-Rá
11 South Great George's St.
Map C3.
【 *677 4835.*

River Club
Merchants' Arch, off Aston
Quay. **Map** D3.
【 *677 2382.*

PUB CRAWLS AND TOURS

Dublin Ghost Bus Tour
【 *873 4222.*

Dublin Literary Pub Crawl
【 *670 5602.*

Historical Walking Tour
【 *878 0227.*

Musical Pub Crawl
【 *478 0193.*

Rock Trail
【 *679 5077/670 8949.*

Walk Makabre
【 *605 7769.*

HOTEL BARS

Cellar Bar
Merrion Hotel,
24 Merrion Street Upper.
Map E5.
【 *603 0600.*

The Horseshoe Bar
The Shelbourne Hotel,
27 St Stephen's Green
North. **Map** E4.
【 *676 6471.*

Inn on the Green
Fitzwilliam Hotel,
12 St Stephen's Green
West. **Map** D4.
【 *478 7000.*

Octagon Bar
The Clarence,
6–8 Wellington Quay.
Map C3.
【 *670 9000.*

CINEMA

Dublin Film Festival
1 Suffolk St. **Map** D3.
【 *679 2937.*

Irish Film Centre
6 Eustace St, Temple Bar.
Map C3.
【 *679 5744.*

Light House
106 Middle Abbey St.
Map D2.
【 *873 0438.*

Screen
D'Olier St. **Map** D3.
【 *671 4988.*

Virgin Cinemas
Parnell St. **Map** C2.
【 *872 8444.*

Outdoor Activities

THE CITY OF DUBLIN is only minutes away from open countryside, and Ireland has many activities to tempt all lovers of the outdoors. The beautiful Wicklow Mountains are within easy reach for scenic walks, and the coastline from Dublin Bay to Dun Laoghaire offers a range of sports including sailing, fishing and windsurfing. There are plenty of opportunities to go horse riding and cycling in the Dublin area. Entire holidays can be based around outdoor activities. In addition to the contacts on page 145, Bord Fáilte and Dublin Tourism *(see pp148–9)* have information on all sports and recreational activities in and around the city.

Backpackers walking in the Dublin area

The beautiful gardens of Powerscourt House *(see pp106–7)*

WALKING

WALKING IN IRELAND puts you in the very midst of some glorious countryside. The network of waymarked trails takes you to some of the loveliest areas, inaccessible by car. Information on long-distance walks is available from Bord Fáilte. Routes include the Wicklow Way which leads from the south of Dublin into the heart of the beautiful Wicklow Mountains *(see p105)*. All the walks may be split into shorter sections for less experienced walkers or those short of time.

Hill walking, rock climbing and mountaineering holidays are also available in Ireland. For more specialized information, contact the **Association for Adventure Sports**. When out walking or climbing always make sure that you go well-equipped for the notoriously changeable Irish weather.

HORSE RIDING AND PONY TREKKING

MANY RIDING CENTRES, both residential and non-residential, offer trail riding and trekking along woodland trails, deserted beaches, country lanes and mountain routes. **Equestrian Holidays Ireland** organizes holidays for riders of various abilities. There are two types of trail riding – post-to-post and based. Post-to-post trails follow a series of routes with accommodation in a different place each night. Based trail rides follow different routes in one area and you stay at the same place for the whole holiday. Lessons are available at many riding centres for beginners to more advanced riders. Bord Fáilte publish details of riding centres and courses.

Horseriding in Phoenix Park

Fishing in the canal at Robertstown, County Kildare

FISHING

THE CLAIM that Ireland is a paradise for anglers is no exaggeration. Coarse, game and sea fishing all enjoy widespread popularity. Coastal rivers yield the famous Irish salmon, and, among other game fish, sea trout and brown trout also offer a real challenge.

Flounder, whiting, mullet, bass and coalfish tempt the sea angler; deep-sea excursions chase abundant supplies of dogfish, shark, skate and ling. You can organize sea-angling trips from many places.

Maps and information on fishing locations are provided by the **Central Fisheries Board** and the **Irish Federation of Sea Anglers**.

CYCLING

CYCLING is very popular both in central Dublin and in the countryside. **Dublin Bike Tours** offer guided cycling tours of the city centre that take advantage of quiet backstreets. They also offer a Dublin at Dawn tour – one of the best times to admire the city's architecture. Alternatively, you can enjoy the quiet roads of the countryside. The paths along Dublin Bay offer fun routes and the Wicklow Mountains are more of a challenge. If you bring your own bike, you can transport it fairly cheaply by train or bus. If not, try the **Raleigh Rent-a-Bike** dealers, or the **Bike Store** in Dublin.

WATER SPORTS

WITH A COASTLINE of over 4,800 km (3,000 miles), it is small wonder that water sports are among Ireland's favourite recreational activities. Surfing, windsurfing, water-skiing, scuba diving and canoeing are the most popular, and there are facilities for all of these along the Dublin coast and in Dublin Bay itself.

The **Irish Windsurfing Association** will put you in touch with your nearest clubs, of which there are plenty in the Dublin area. There is a similar organization controlling the water-skiing clubs, called the Irish Water-Ski Federation, which is also based in Dublin.

There is a wide range of diving conditions off the coast of Ireland and the **Irish Underwater Council** will give you details of courses and their facilities.

Dun Laoghaire harbour at dusk

CRUISING AND SAILING

A TRANQUIL CRUISING holiday is an ideal alternative to the stress and strain of driving, and Ireland's many rivers and lakes offer a huge variety of conditions for those who want a waterborne holiday. Stopping over at waterside towns and villages puts you in touch with the Irish on their home ground. Hiring a boat and drifting down the Grand Canal (see p83) from Dublin to the Shannon gives a unique view of the countryside.

Another popular sailing area is the scenic Howth peninsula, and the harbour of Dun Laoghaire southeast of Dublin, where you will find sailing schools offering tuition at all levels. For details of these schools, contact the **Irish Sailing Association**.

SPORTS FOR THE DISABLED

SPORTS ENTHUSIASTS with a disability can obtain details of facilities for the disabled from the **Irish Wheelchair Association**. Central and local tourist boards, and many of the organizations listed in the directory under each sport, will be able to offer facilities for disabled visitors. To be sure of this, it is advisable to call the venue first to check what is available.

Cycling in the Irish countryside

DIRECTORY

WALKING

Association for Adventure Sports
House of Sport,
Longmile Road,
Dublin 12.
(450 9845.

HORSE RIDING AND PONY TREKKING

Association of Irish Riding Establishments
11 Moore Park
Newbridge,
Co. Kildare.
(045 431584.

Equestrian Holidays Ireland
1 Sandyford Office Park,
Foxrock, Dublin 18.
(295 8928.

FISHING

Central Fisheries Board
Balnagowan House,
Mobhi Boreen,
Glasnevin, Dublin 9.
(837 9206.

Irish Federation of Sea Anglers
Mr Hugh O'Rorke,
67 Windsor Drive,
Monkstown,
Co Dublin.
(280 6901.

CYCLING

Bike Store
58 Lower Gardiner Street,
Dublin 1.
(872 5399.

Dublin Bike Tours
(679 0899.

Raleigh Rent-a-Bike
PO Box 3520, Raleigh
House, Kylemore Road,
Dublin 10.
(626 1333.

WATER SPORTS

Irish Underwater Council
78a Patrick Street, Dun
Laoghaire, Co Dublin.
(284 4601.

Irish Windsurfing Association
Haydock, Westminster
Road, Blackrock, Dublin.
(289 5636.

CRUISING AND SAILING

Irish Sailing Association
3 Park Road,
Dun Laoghaire,
Co. Dublin.
(280 0239.

SPORTS FOR THE DISABLED

Irish Wheelchair Association
Aras Chuchulain,
Blackheath Drive,
Clontarf, Dublin 3.
(833 8241.

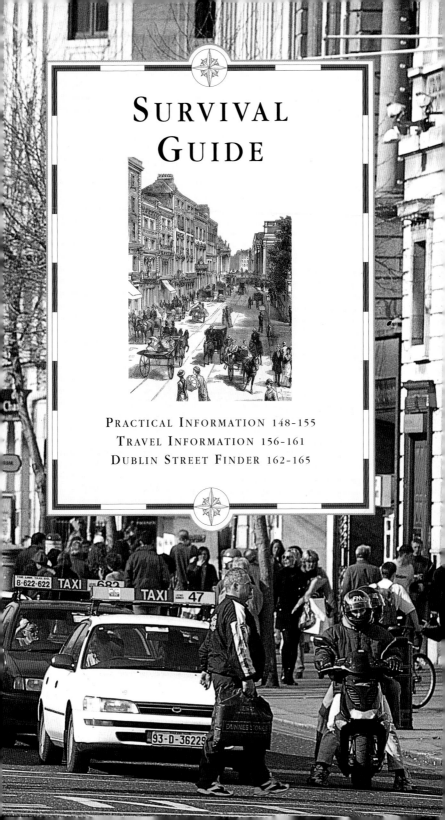

SURVIVAL
GUIDE

PRACTICAL INFORMATION

I N THE PAST FEW YEARS, Dublin has enjoyed a new lease of life and has become a vibrant young city. The renovation of the Temple Bar area, combined with the numerous museums, galleries and shops, attracts visitors in their thousands all year round. The best time to visit the city is probably in late spring, before the peak summer season. Dublin is generally a safe place, but it does have a wide mixture of areas. You can very quickly find yourself out of a tourist area and in a less desirable part of town. It is wise to avoid the rougher areas to the north of the Liffey, away from O'Connell Street, especially at night. Transport around the city is good and taxis are readily available in the town centre. Dublin Tourism has geared itself up to the increasing demands of the tourist and their office, in a converted church, is well organized with helpful and friendly staff.

Bord Fáilte logo

Sign to Ardgillan Demesne

VISAS

V ISITORS FROM the EU, US, Canada, Australia and New Zealand require a valid passport but not a visa for entry into Ireland. All others, including those wanting to study or work, should check with their local embassy first. UK nationals do not strictly need a passport to enter Ireland but should take it with them for identification.

TOURIST INFORMATION

I N ADDITION TO the Irish Tourist Board (Bord Fáilte), Dublin also has its own tourist organization, **Dublin Tourism**. The main office is in a converted church in Suffolk Street. As well as providing free local information, the tourist offices sell maps and guide books and can arrange car rental and reserve accommodation. The Tourist Board, in conjunction with Dublin Tourism, runs a telephone service known as **The Ireland Info and Reservations Service**. Museums and libraries also often stock a selection of useful tourist literature.

If you pick up a list of accommodation, note that not every hotel and guesthouse will be included – these lists recommend only those approved by the Tourist Board.

ADMISSION CHARGES

S OME OF DUBLIN'S major sights have an admission fee but many are free. For each place of interest in this guide, we specify whether or not there is a charge. Entrance fees are usually between IR£1 and IR£5 with discounts for students and the elderly. The **Office of Public Works** (OPW) maintains parks, museums, monuments and inland waterways and issues a Heritage Card which allows unlimited access to all its sites for a year.

Heritage card giving access to historic sites

Students at Trinity College, Dublin

STUDENT INFORMATION

S TUDENTS WITH a valid ISIC card (International Student Identity Card) benefit from numerous travel discounts as well as reduced admission to museums and concerts. Buy a Travelsave stamp from any branch of **USIT** and affix it to your ISIC card to get a 50 per cent discount on Irish Rail and Irish Ferries. A Travelsave stamp will also entitle you to discounts on Bus Éireann routes and special rates on commuter tickets (Sep–Jun only) in Dublin. ISIC cards can be obtained easily from any branch of USIT in Dublin. USIT will also supply non-students under 26 with an EYC (European Youth Card) for discounts in restaurants, shops and theatres.

DUTY-FREE GOODS

A DULTS TRAVELLING between the Republic of Ireland and other countries, including the British Isles (but not Northern Ireland), can buy duty-free goods at the airport, on the plane or on the ferry. Current allowances include a litre of spirits, 50 grams of perfume and 200 cigarettes. EU regulations allow travellers within the European Union 55 litres of beer, 45 litres of wine and 800 cigarettes. Note that duty free allowances are likely to end in mid-1999.

A selection of daily newspapers

RELIGIOUS SERVICES

FOR MOST PEOPLE in Ireland churchgoing is a way of life. The Republic is 95 per cent Roman Catholic. Tourist offices, hotels and B&Bs keep lists of church service times.

IRISH TIME

THE WHOLE of Ireland is in the same time zone as Great Britain; five hours ahead of New York and Toronto, one hour behind Germany and France, and ten hours behind Sydney. Clocks go forward one hour for summer time.

NEWSPAPERS AND MAGAZINES

THE REPUBLIC of Ireland has six national daily papers and five Sunday papers. Quality dailies include the *Irish Independent*, the *Irish Press*, the *Cork Examiner* and *The Irish Times*. The broadsheets are useful for information on theatre and concerts. Ireland's daily tabloid is the *Star*.

British tabloids are on sale throughout Dublin. Broadsheets such as *The Times* are also available and cost less than the quality Irish press. Local papers give details of what is on where, and when.

OPENING TIMES

FEW PLACES are open on a Sunday morning, and some museums are shut on Monday. Opening hours are generally between 10am and 5pm. It is always worth ringing before you visit anywhere.

METRICATION

THIS HAS been taking place over several years now. Although most road signs are now shown in kilometres, speed limits are still displayed in miles. Fuel is sold in litres but beer is still sold in pints.

RADIO AND TELEVISION

IRELAND HAS TWO TV channels, RTE 1 and Network 2. There are three national radio stations, including an Irish-language service, and many local ones. The five British television channels can also be picked up in most parts of Ireland. Cable and satellite TV is quite common and is offered by most hotels.

FACILITIES FOR THE DISABLED

MOST SIGHTS in Ireland have access for wheelchairs. However it is always worth phoning to check details. The Access Department of the **National Rehabilitation Board** provides helpful information on amenities.

DIRECTORY

THE IRELAND INFO AND RESERVATIONS SERVICE

In Ireland
- 1850 230 330 (info).
- 1800 668 66866 (reservations).

In the UK
- 0171 493 3201 (info).
- 00800 668 66866 (res.).

In the United States
- 1800 223 6470 (info).
- 1800 SHAMROCK (info).
- 1800 668 66866 (res.).

EMBASSIES AND CONSULATES

Australia
Fitzwilton House, Wilton Terrace, Dublin 2.
- 676 1517.

Canada
65–68 St Stephen's Green, Dublin 2.
- 478 1988.

UK
31-33 Merrion Road, Dublin 4.
- 676 2464.

United States
24 Elgin Road, Ballsbridge, Dublin 4.
- 668 7122.

USEFUL ADDRESSES

Dublin Tourism Centre
Suffolk Street, Dublin 2.
www.visit.ie/Dublin

Office of Public Works
51 St Stephen's Green, Dublin 2.
- 661 3111 ext 2386.

National Rehabilitation Board
25 Clyde Road, Ballsbridge, Dublin 4.
- 668 4181.

USIT
19/21 Aston Quay, Dublin 2.
- 677 8117.

LANGUAGE

The Republic of Ireland is officially bilingual – almost all road signs have names in English and Irish. English is spoken everywhere except for a few parts of the far west, an area known as the Gaeltachts, but now and then you may find signs only in Irish. On the right are some of the words you are most likely to come across when travelling around the Republic.

Sign using old form of Gaelic

USEFUL WORDS

an banc – **bank**
an lár – **town centre**
an trá – **beach**
ar aghaidh – **go**
bád – **boat**
bealach amach – **exit**
bealach isteach – **entrance**
dúnta – **closed**
fáilte – **welcome**
fir – **men**
gardai – **police**
leithreas – **toilet**
mná – **women**
oifig an poist – **post office**
oscailte – **open**
óstán – **hotel**
siopa – **shop**
stop/stad – **stop**
ticéad – **ticket**
traein – **train**

Personal Security and Health

Aの rarity, in recent years bag-snatching, pickpocketing and car break-ins have become more and more prevalent on the streets of Dublin. Levels of crime are still low by international standards, but Dublin is a modern city with most of the accompanying problems, and visitors should not allow the fabled Irish friendliness to lull them into complacency. Tourist offices and hoteliers will gladly point out the areas to be avoided, but anyone who takes simple precautions should enjoy a trouble-free stay.

Police motorcyclist patrolling the busy Dublin streets

Garda station situated on Pearse Street, near the centre of Dublin

PERSONAL SECURITY

THE POLICE in Dublin and the rest of the Republic, should you ever need them, are called the **Gardaí**. Until recently, street crime was very rare in Dublin but, because of poverty and a degree of heroin addiction in certain areas of the city, it is now on a steady increase. However, if you use common sense when wandering around, there should be little cause for concern: avoid the backstreets or poorly lit areas at night; don't draw attention to yourself by wearing flashy jewellery; sit near the driver on buses; use a bag that can be held securely; be alert in crowded places.

You may be approached in the street by people asking for money. This rarely develops into a troublesome situation, but it is still best to avoid eye contact and leave the scene as quickly as possible. In general, safety in the city is about being alert to your surroundings. If you feel uncomfortable anywhere, especially at night, walk away confidently and head for well-lit, populated areas.

Light outside Garda station

PERSONAL PROPERTY

BEFORE YOU leave home, make sure your possessions are insured, as it can be expensive and difficult to do so in Ireland. Travel insurance for the UK will not cover you in the Republic, so ensure your policy is adequate.

As pickpocketing and petty theft can be a problem in Dublin, it is best not to carry your passport, air tickets or large amounts of cash around with you, or even leave them in your room. Most hotels have a safe and it makes sense to take advantage of this facility. Visitors carrying large amounts of money around should use traveller's cheques rather than cash (see p152–3). When sitting in pubs and restaurants, keep your bag on your lap, if possible, and don't leave your wallet lying on the table. A money belt that can be worn under clothing is a good investment, as is a shoulder bag that can be carried across the chest with the opening facing inwards. When withdrawing money from cash machines, put the notes away as quickly as possible; don't stand around counting them.

Also, if there is a cash machine inside the bank, use that one in preference to one in the street.

If travelling by car, ensure that all valuables are out of sight and the car is locked, even when leaving it for just a few minutes. When you arrive at a hotel, ask the receptionist about secure parking in the area and, on trips out of Dublin to other towns, use guarded parking areas rather than street parking.

LOST PROPERTY

REPORT ALL LOST or stolen items at once to the police. To make an insurance claim, you will need to get a copy of the police report. Most rail and bus stations in Dublin and the surrounding towns operate a lost property service.

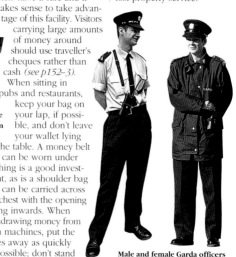
Male and female Garda officers in ordinary uniform

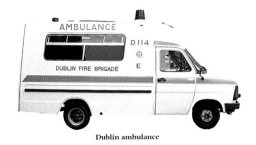

Dublin ambulance

Dublin fire engine

Garda patrol car

Pharmacy in the city showing old-fashioned snake and goblet symbol

In some of the smaller towns in outlying areas, however, you may discover that a pharmacist is opposed to contraception and does not sell condoms.

MEDICAL TREATMENT

RESIDENTS OF COUNTRIES in the European Union can claim free medical treatment in the Republic of Ireland by getting form E111 before setting out. In the event of illness, to avoid having to pay for any treatment or prescribed medicines, you will need to show your E111 and a form of identification, such as a driver's licence or passport. Also, be sure to let the doctor know that you want treatment under the EU's social security regulations. Travellers from outside the EU should either have their own accident and health insurance or be willing to pay for any treatment received.

In a medical emergency, either call an ambulance (by dialling 999 or 112) or head for the 24-hour accident and emergency department at **Beaumont Hospital**. For emergency dental needs, a central option is the **Grafton Street Dental Practice**.

PHARMACIES

A WIDE RANGE of medical supplies is available over the counter at pharmacies. However, many medicines are available only with a prescription from a local doctor. If you are likely to require specialized

drugs during your stay, take your own supplies or ask your doctor to write a letter specifying the generic name of the medicine you require. Always obtain a receipt for insurance claims. For after-hours medical requirements, try **O'Connell's**, a chain of pharmacies with extended opening hours.

Until recently, condoms were not freely available in Dublin or the rest of the Republic but are now fairly easy to obtain.

Pharmacy in the fashionable Temple Bar area

Banking and Currency

BANKS IN DUBLIN generally provide a very good service and, along with most of the post offices, will exchange traveller's cheques, often without charging commission. There are various different banks, but all of them will change currency and many have a cash machine which can be used during non-banking hours, although a fee will be charged if you do not have an account with the bank in question or an associated bank. Outside the city in small towns and villages you may find that the banks do not always have cash machines and the opening hours may vary slightly from those in the city centre. Traveller's cheques are by far the safest way to carry money around but credit cards are the most convenient and are widely accepted.

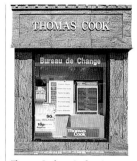

Thomas Cook on Grafton Street in central Dublin

Drawing money from an Allied Irish Bank cash dispenser

USING BANKS

THE FIVE RETAIL BANKS in the Republic of Ireland are the Bank of Ireland, the Allied Irish Bank (AIB), the Ulster Bank, the National Irish Bank and the TSB Bank.

The usual banking hours in Dublin are Monday to Wednesday and Friday from 10am to 4pm and Thursday 10am to 5pm. In rural areas banks often stay open late on market day instead. Some of the smaller branches further out of the city centre may shut at lunch time. Branches of the TSB Bank remain open at lunch time and till 7pm on Thursdays and up to 5pm on other weekdays. All the banks are closed on public holidays (*see p27*). Banks in Dublin and most other towns are provided with 24-hour automated teller machines (ATMs), or cash dispensers, so if you happen to discover the bank is closed, it isn't necessarily a major catastrophe. Most of the banks are VISA/Delta affiliated so if you have a card bearing the VISA or the Cirrus logo, you should be able to withdraw cash at these machines. Once you have put your card in, you will be usually given a choice of languages in which to conduct the withdrawal.

Allied Irish Bank logo

National Irish Bank logo

CREDIT CARDS

THROUGHOUT DUBLIN you can pay by credit card in nearly all hotels, petrol (gas) stations, large shops and supermarkets. The hotels (*see pp120–23*) and restaurants (*see pp128–31*) listings indicate which establishments accept which credit cards. VISA and MasterCard are the most widely accepted credit cards. Fewer businesses are also prepared to accept American Express and Diners Club cards. In more rural areas you may not always be able to use your credit card so be sure to carry cash or traveller's cheques with you as an alternative.

TRAVELLER'S CHEQUES

TRAVELLER'S CHEQUES are the safest way to carry around large amounts of money. These are best changed at one of the main banks but, failing this, many shops and restaurants accept them in place of cash although there is usually a small charge to do this. Hotel receptions will also often change them.

Traveller's cheques can be bought before setting out at American Express, Thomas Cook or at your own bank at home. In Ireland, traveller's cheques can be purchased at banks or from *bureaux de change*, which can be found in Dublin and other large towns and at the airport.

Façade of the Bank of Ireland on College Green in central Dublin

EUROCHEQUES

Eurocheques are now being phased out by most banks and so it is not a good idea to rely on them in Ireland. It is better to take a mixture of traveller's cheques and cash with you and to take any credit or debit cards you may have as these can be used (with a PIN number) in ATMs to withdraw local currency.

BUREAUX DE CHANGE

In addition to the banks, there are some private *bureaux de change* in Dublin. As with most other exchange facilities, *bureaux de change* open later than banks. However, it's worth checking their rates before undertaking any transactions. Some department stores also offer *bureaux de change* facilities.

BUREAUX DE CHANGE

American Express
116 Grafton Street, Dublin 2.
☎ 677 2874.

Thomas Cook
51 Grafton Street, Dublin 2.
☎ 677 7422
118 Grafton Street, Dublin 2.
☎ 677 0476.

CURRENCY IN THE REPUBLIC OF IRELAND

The unit of currency in the Republic is the punt (IR£), often called the Irish pound. It is divided into 100 pence (p). Though there are no restrictions on bringing currency into the Republic, you cannot take more than IR£150 in banknotes out. However, you can take out the same amount of foreign currency as you bring in, up to IR£1,200.

Banknotes
The Republic's banknotes are issued in denominations of IR£50, IR£20, IR£10 and IR£5. They increase in size according to value and depict famous figures from the country's past.

IR£50 note

IR£20 note

IR£10 note

IR£5 note

Coins
The Republic of Ireland issues the following coins: IR£1, 50p, 20p, 10p, 5p, 2p and 1p. Although the denominations are the same as those used in the United Kingdom, the appearance of the coins is very different.

IR£1 coin

50 pence

20 pence

10 pence

5 pence

2 pence

1 penny

Telephones and Mail Services

Telecom Eireann logo

THE REPUBLIC'S national telephone company, Telecom Eireann, once ran all the telephone services in the country, but changes in the law have meant that other companies can now provide public phones on the streets of Dublin. TE's service includes up-to-date coin, card and credit card telephones that provide a modern and efficient service. Although it is improving all the time, the mail service in the Republic is still quite slow – allow three to four days when sending a letter to Great Britain and at least six days for the United States.

The modern St Andrews Post Office, in central Dublin

A typical post office in rural Ireland

MAILING A LETTER

MAIN POST OFFICES in Dublin are usually open from 9am to 5:30pm during the week and from 9am to 1pm on Saturdays. Some smaller post offices do not open on Saturdays and close for lunch on weekdays. The General Post Office on Anne Street South is well placed for tourist sights and is open at lunchtime on weekdays. Standard-value stamps can also be bought from selected newsagents around the city.

Dublin and the rest of the Republic of Ireland do not have a first- and second-class mail system, and sending a postcard anywhere in the world costs the same as sending a letter (weighing less than 25g). The rate to Great Britain is the same as that within Ireland, but letters to the rest of Europe cost slightly more.

All air-mail letters (including ones heading for Great Britain) should carry a blue *Priority Aerphost* sticker. These are available without charge at all post offices.

MAILBOXES AND POSTE RESTANTE

MAILBOXES in the city and in the rest of the Republic are green. In Dublin, some have two slots, marked *Dublin Only* and *All Other Places*. Many of the Republic's mailboxes are quite historic. Some even carry Queen Victoria's monogram on the front, a relic from the days of British rule. Even the smallest towns have a mailbox, and the mail is collected regularly: anything from once to four times daily.

The easiest way to receive mail in Dublin is to have it sent to your hotel. Otherwise, a Poste Restante service is available at major post offices. In the city centre the General Post Office on O'Connell Street *(see p69)* is the most convenient, with longer opening hours than any other post office.

Irish Post logo

List of the daily collection times

Monogram of Queen Victoria

30p stamp

32p stamp

45p stamp

Standard mailbox

Rural mailbox

Using Dublin's Telephones

THE MAJORITY of the city's phone booths are still controlled by Telecom Eireann. The wording around the top of each phone booth indicates whether it is a coin, phonecard or credit card phone. For those intending to spend more than IR£4 on calls during their stay, it can be cheaper to use phonecards as they offer reasonable discounts. Also, there are now more card phones in Dublin than coin phones. TE phonecards are available from newsagents, post offices, supermarkets and other retail outlets. Another company, ITG, also provides coin and credit card phones. Calls on ITG phones cost the same as those on TE phones.

Telecom Eireann phone boxes

USING A TE COIN PHONE

1 Lift the receiver and wait for the dial tone.

2 Insert any of the coins below. The illuminated display shows the minimum amount required.

3 Dial the number and wait to be connected.

4 The display indicates how much money you have put in and the credit left. A rapid bleeping noise means your money has run out. Insert more coins.

5 If you want to make a further call and you have money left in credit, do not replace the receiver, press the follow-on-call button.

6 When you have finished speaking, replace the receiver and collect your change. Only wholly unused coins are refunded.

USING A TE CARD PHONE

1 Lift the receiver and wait for the dial tone.

3 The display shows how many units are left. The minimum charge is one unit (20p).

4 Dial the number and wait until you are connected.

5 When your phonecard runs out you will hear a rapid bleeping noise. To continue, press the "change card" button and the old card will come out. Remove it and insert a new card.

6 If you want to make a further call and you have money left in credit, do not replace the receiver, press the follow-on-call button.

2 Insert a TE Callcard in the direction of the arrow on the card.

7 To adjust the volume in your earpiece, press the button with the upward-pointing arrow to increase it, and the button with the downward-pointing arrow to decrease it.

TE phonecards come in 10, 20, 50 and 100 units. A unit is worth 20p.

MAKING A PHONE CALL FROM DUBLIN

Cheap rate calls within the Republic and to the UK are from 6pm to 8am weekdays and all day at weekends. Off-peak times for international calls vary from country to country, but are generally as above.
- If you are making a call within the Dublin area, dial the seven-digit Dublin number.
- If you are calling from outside the Dublin area, dial 01 plus the seven-digit number.
- To call the UK: dial 0044, the area code (minus the leading 0), then the number.
- To call Northern Ireland: dial 08, then the area code, followed by the number.

- To call other countries: dial 00, followed by the country code (for example, 1 for the US, 61 for Australia), the area code (minus the leading 0), then the number.
- For directory enquiries: call 1190 for numbers in the Republic and Northern Ireland, 1197 for numbers in Great Britain and 1198 for numbers in other countries.
- For assistance in making a call: dial 10 for numbers within Ireland and Britain, 114 for international calls.
- To send a telemessage: dial 196.
- For emergencies: dial 999.

TRAVEL INFORMATION

**Aer Lingus
Airbus in flight**

AS DUBLIN BECOMES an increasingly popular tourist destination, the city becomes even easier to get to, with extremely frequent flights from the UK and good connections from elsewhere in the world. Ferry services are an alternative method of travel from the UK, docking at Dun Laoghaire or Dublin harbour itself. From both the airport and the harbours it is a short ride by car or bus into the city centre. If you are planning to stay in the city centre, it is not necessary to rent a car – most of the sights are within easy walking distance of one another and the roads in the city centre can become very congested, particularly O'Connell Street. Should your feet require a rest, the bus services are frequent and taxis are invariably in fairly plentiful supply.

The modern exterior of Dublin International Airport

FLYING TO DUBLIN

FLIGHTS from most of the major cities in Europe arrive at **Dublin Airport**, which is the Republic of Ireland's busiest airport. Regular services to Dublin depart from all five of the London airports (Heathrow, City, Gatwick, Luton and Stansted) and from 15 other cities in Britain, such as Leeds and Manchester, as well as the Isle of Man and the Channel Islands.

The major airline operating scheduled flights between Britain and Dublin is Ireland's national airline **Aer Lingus**, although since deregulation the rival firm, **Ryanair**, has grown fast as a result of its policy of cheap fares. From the United States, Aer Lingus and **Delta Air Lines** fly direct to Dublin Airport. However there are no direct flights to Dublin from Australia and New Zealand, so popular connecting points used by travellers include London, Moscow and Amsterdam.

AIR FARES

AIRLINES OFFER a host of options on air fares to Ireland from Britain. Usually, the amount you pay is determined by how flexible you are prepared to be and how far in advance you book your flight. The best bargains tend to be on flights for which the dates are not changeable. Flights from the United States can double in price in the summer and around Christmas when the fares are most expensive. Mid-week flights are often cheaper than weekend ones. The cheapest place to fly from in the UK is usually London – in recent years, the air fares from Stansted and Luton to Dublin Airport have been particularly low as these airports are

Arrivals ← ✈
↑ **Shops** **Siopaí** 🖼
↑ **Bar** 🚻 **Beár**
↑ **Snacks** ✗ **Sólaistí**

**Airport sign in
English and Gaelic**

the London airports furthest from the centre. Ticket prices from the UK are generally fairly consistant throughout the year except at Christmas and during the summer when there are comparatively few discounted fares available. During these periods, due to the increased demand by visiting friends and relatives – usually referred to by airline companies as "VFR" – seats are taken well in advance so it is advisable to book as early as possible if you are intending to travel at these times. Many airlines offer discounts to those under 25, while USIT *(see p148)* and Campus Travel often have cheaper rates for students and the under-26s.

GETTING TO AND FROM THE AIRPORT

AN EXPRESS bus service runs between Dublin Airport and the city's main rail and bus stations about every 20 minutes, from early morning to midnight. The journey takes half an hour and tickets are purchased on board. Alternatively, the number 41 Dublin bus runs from the airport to Eden Quay next to O'Connell Bridge in the city centre. There is a taxi stand outside the airport and car rental companies inside. If you are flying from Dublin and wish to leave your car there or are collecting someone, there are both long- and short-stay parking facilities.

The frequent-running Airlink bus

Irish Ferries ship loading up in the harbour

FERRIES TO DUBLIN AND DUN LAOGHAIRE

THERE IS A GOOD CHOICE OF ferry services from Wales to Ireland. **Irish Ferries**, the country's largest shipping company, is the sole operator on the Holyhead-Dublin route and has two crossings a day. Unlike the service to Dun Laoghaire, there is no high-speed service – only the conventional ferry, which takes about 3½ hours. Bear in mind that Irish Ferries does not operate on Christmas Day and St Stephen's Day (26 Dec).

The service from Holyhead to the Dublin suburb of Dun Laoghaire – traditionally the busiest port in Ireland – is operated by **Stena Line**. This route is served by conventional ferries and the Stena HSS (High-speed Sea Service) introduced into service in September 1995. As the world's largest fast ferry, the HSS has the same passenger and vehicle capacity as the conventional ferries but its jet-engine propulsion gives it twice the speed.

Directions for ferry passengers

Vehicle loading and unloading times on the Stena HSS are also shorter than on other ferries – the loading time for cars is about 20 minutes as opposed to a minimum of 30 minutes with most other ferries. Passengers requiring special assistance at ports or on board the ship should contact the company they are booked with at least 24 hours before the departure time. Like most other ferry companies, Irish Ferries and Stena Sealink take bicycles free of charge, but this should be mentioned when you make a reservation.

In 1998 a new Super SeaCat service between Liverpool and Dublin was introduced that operates a twice daily service. Run by the **Isle of Man Steam Packet Company** the service takes four hours. There is also a service from the Isle of Man, which takes two hours, forty-five minutes.

PORT CONNECTIONS

ALL IRELAND'S PORTS have adequate bus and train connections. At Dublin Port, available buses (with an extra fare) take ferry passengers into the city centre. From Dun Laoghaire, DART trains run into Dublin every 10 to 15 minutes calling at Pearse Street, Tara Street and Connolly Stations. These depart from the railway station near the main passenger concourse. Buses also run from Dun Laoghaire to Eden Quay and Fleet Street in the city centre every 10 to 15 minutes. At all ports, taxis are readily available to meet arriving passengers.

Stena Sea Lynx leaving Dun Laoghaire harbour

Getting Around Dublin

Dublin Bus logo

DUBLIN IS A fairly easy city to get around. The centre is relatively compact, so most of the sights are within walking distance of one another, and much of it, particularly south of the Liffey, is pedestrianized. If you are travelling into the city centre there is an excellent bus service and the local DART railway runs an efficient service to three city centre stations. Alternatively, if you prefer to be driven around, taxis are in plentiful supply but are fairly expensive.

Parliament Street viewed from City Hall

Passengers boarding a Dublin Bus near Trinity College

GETTING AROUND BY BUS

DUBLIN BUS runs all the bus services in central Dublin and the Greater Dublin area (which includes parts of Wicklow, Kildare and Meath), while city buses in towns further afield in the Republic are operated by **Bus Éireann**. Bus stops for **Dublin Bus** are green, and the numbers on them indicate which buses stop there. Buses in the city centre run approximately every 10–20 minutes from about 6am until 11:30pm, but do allow plenty of time if you have an appointment as they can run late. There is also a night bus service called Nitelink, which

departs every hour from midnight to 3am three nights a week. If you are using the bus two or three times in a day, it is worth getting a one-day pass, costing around IR£3. There are also four-day, weekly or monthly passes.

The national bus company in the Republic of Ireland is Bus Éireann, who operate a country-wide network of buses serving all the cities and most of the towns. In Dublin, the main bus station is the Busáras on Store Street, a short walk from O'Connell Street.

There are also numerous private bus companies which either compete with the national network or provide services on routes not covered by Bus Éireann. Local tourist offices should be able to point out the most reliable firms.

Bus times (and stops) in villages and the more remote places are often best found by asking the locals. Local bus services in cities and large towns throughout the Republic are generally well-run and reasonably priced. All Bus Éireann routes and times can be found in their timetable, which costs about 50p and is available at all main bus stations.

DART SERVICE

THE CONVENIENT local electric rail service in Dublin known as the **DART** (Dublin Area Rapid Transit) serves 25 stations between Howth, County Dublin and Bray, County Wicklow, with several stops in Dublin city centre. A Dublin Explorer ticket allows four consecutive days' travel on DART trains and also covers Dublin Bus services and local suburban rail services. A Rambler ticket offers the same but just for one day and costs around IR£5. Family tickets for two adults and up to four children under the age of 16 are very good value. Tickets can be purchased at any of the DART stations. Bicycles can be taken on

Dart service sign

the trains if there is room, but there is a small charge. There are presently major works going on along the DART line, including station refurbishment and extensions to the line. There are plans to extend the line northwards to Malahide and southwards to Greystones.

The DART is very crowded at peak times during the week – in the mornings the rush hour is between 7am and 9am and in the evenings it is busy between 5pm and 7pm so it is advisable to avoid travelling at these times.

Logo on Bus Éireann local and express buses

TAXIS IN DUBLIN

IN DUBLIN, cruising taxis are around but the best places to find cabs are at taxi stands at rail or bus stations or hotels. Prices are based on metered mileage and the minimum charge is around IR£2. There are a whole range of taxi companies in the city, such as **City Cabs**. If you want any information about taxis, the **Irish Taxi Federation** is happy to supply details and information about taxi companies.

Taxis lined up outside the arrivals building at Dublin Airport

FARES AND TICKETS

IN THE REPUBLIC, long-distance buses are about half the price of the equivalent rail journey. If you are making the return trip on the same day, ask for a day-return ticket, which is much cheaper than the normal return fare. Also, between Tuesday and Thursday you can buy a "period" return ticket for the price of a single journey. Under 16s pay half the adult fare. Students with a Travel-save stamp *(see p148)* get a 30 per cent reduction. For those intending to do a lot of travelling it is cheaper to buy a "Rambler" ticket. This allows unlimited bus travel throughout the Republic for a certain number of days in a set period, for example, 15 days' travel out of 30 consecutive days.

BUS TOURS

BUS ÉIREANN and some local companies run half- and one-day excursions in Dublin. Dublin Bus (Bus Átha Cliath) runs the Dublin City Tour, which leaves from O'Connell Street Upper and takes in the city's most famous sights, including St Stephen's Green, the Bank of Ireland and the Parliament as well as some more obscure sights, such as Oscar Wilde's home. The witty commentary alone makes the tour well worth doing.

DRIVING

IF YOU DO NOT take your own car, there are plenty of car rental firms to choose from. Car rental can be expensive in peak season and the best rates are often obtained by booking in advance. Broker companies, such as **Holiday Autos**, use the major rental companies and will shop around to get the best deal. Car rental usually includes unlimited mileage plus passenger indemnity insurance and

The distinctively marked Dublin City Tour bus

cover for third party, fire and theft, but not vehicle damage.

To rent a car, you must show a full driver's licence, which you have held for two years without violations. Cars are usually rented only to those aged between 23 and 70, but some companies may make exceptions. For a list of suggested car rental companies in Dublin see p161.

PARKING

DUBLIN HAS either parking meters or (fairly expensive) car parks. Parking on the street is allowed, though a single yellow line along the edge of the road means there are some restrictions (there should be a sign nearby with permitted parking times). Double yellow lines indicate no parking at any time.

Disc parking – a version of "pay and display" – also operates in Dublin. Discs can be bought from local newsagents, petrol (gas) stations, tourist offices and many small shops.

A busy Hertz car rental desk at Dublin Airport

Travelling Outside Dublin

O NE OF THE BEST WAYS to see the magnificent scenery in the countryside around Dublin is by car. The roads are often empty and make driving a real pleasure. One of the quickest ways to get to more distant destinations is by train. Ireland's national rail network is fast and efficient and also provides an ideal way to see the country's dramatic landscape. Alternatively, you can enjoy the countryside at your own leisurely pace by touring around by bicycle, although a certain degree of fitness is advisable if you are going to tackle the beautiful Wicklow Mountains.

Rural petrol pump

Purchasing a rail ticket at a station ticket office

TRAIN SERVICES IN IRELAND

T HE TWO MAIN rail stations in Dublin are Connolly, for trains to the north, northwest and Rosslare, and Heuston, which serves the west, midlands and southwest. These two stations are connected by the No. 90 bus service which runs every 10 to 15 minutes and takes a quarter of an hour – traffic permitting. Irish Rail operates a satisfactory service out of Dublin to most of the large cities and towns. Going by rail is probably the fastest and most convenient way of travelling to other

major places. All trains have standard and super-standard (first-class) compartments. Bicycles can be taken on trains but for this there is a supplement of around IR£6.

TICKETS AND FARES

T HROUGHOUT IRELAND, train tickets are generally quite expensive, but there are lots of good value incentive or concessionary passes. Most of these include bus travel, so you can get virtually anywhere in Ireland on one ticket.

The most comprehensive ticket available is the Emerald Card, which can be used on all Irish Rail, Dublin Bus and Bus Éireann services. For around IR£100 the Emerald Card gives eight days' unlimited travel in a 30-day period. An eight-day Irish Explorer ticket is slightly cheaper and is valid on all Irish Rail and Bus Éireann transport. The Irish Rover ticket is good value for money. It is valid on all Irish Rail journeys for five days within a 15-day

period. Students can buy a Travelsave Stamp *(see p148)* to affix to their ISIC cards. For those under 26, Faircards give 50 per cent off all Irish Rail single journeys. Older travellers can get InterRail Plus 26 cards costing slightly more.

DRIVING YOUR OWN CAR

I F YOU INTEND to use your own car, check your insurance to find out how well you are covered. To prevent a comprehensive policy being downgraded to third-party cover, ask your insurance company for a Green Card. Carry your insurance certificate, Green Card, proof of ownership of the car and, importantly, your driver's licence. If your licence was issued in the UK, bring your passport with you for identification.

Yield (give way) road sign in Gaelic

Membership of a reputable breakdown service is advisable unless you are undaunted by the prospect of breaking down in remote countryside. Non-members can join up for the duration of their holiday only. Depending on the type of cover you have, breakdown organizations may offer only limited services in Ireland so check before you travel.

If you are renting a car, make sure the insurance cover meets your needs. You will need to show your driver's licence – if you are a US citizen you will need an International Driving Permit, available from the **AAA**.

Platform of Heuston Station in Dublin

RULES OF THE ROAD

EVEN FOR THOSE unused to driving on the left, driving in Ireland is unlikely to pose any great problems. For many visitors, the most difficult aspect of Ireland's roads is getting accustomed to passing other vehicles on the right and giving way to traffic on the right at roundabouts. The wearing of safety belts is compulsory for drivers and for all front-seat passengers; where they are fitted, rear safety belts must also be worn. All children must have a suitable restraint system. Motorcyclists and their passengers are obliged by law to wear crash helmets.

View of Dun Laoghaire from the road around Killiney Hill *(p89)*

Junction ahead   **Unprotected quay or river ahead**

Dangerous bends ahead   **Children or school ahead**

ROAD SIGNS

MOST ROAD SIGNS in Ireland are in both Gaelic and English. Most are also now in kilometres although some signs may still appear in miles. The sign "Yield" is the same as the UK "Give Way". Brown signs with white lettering indicate places of historic or cultural interest.

BUYING FUEL

UNLEADED FUEL and diesel fuel are available just about everywhere in Ireland. Although prices vary, fuel is relatively cheap by European standards. Almost all the petrol (gas) stations accept VISA and MasterCard, though check before filling up, particularly in rural areas.

SPEED LIMITS

THE MAXIMUM speed limits in Ireland, which are shown in miles, are more or less the same as those in Britain:
• 30 mph (50 km/h) in built-up areas.
• 60 mph (95 km/h) outside built-up areas.
• 70 mph (110 km/h) on highways.
On certain roads, which are marked, the speed limits are 40 mph (65 km/h) or 50 mph (80 km/h). Where there is no indication, the speed limit is 60 mph (95 km/h). Vehicles towing caravans (trailers) must not exceed 55 mph (90 km/h) on any road.

CYCLING

THE QUIET ROADS of Ireland help to make touring by bicycle a real joy. The **Raleigh Rent-a-Bike** network of cycle dealers operates a reasonably priced rental plan throughout Ireland. Also local shops, such as **Rent-a-Bike** in Dublin, rent cycles to tourists. You can often rent a bike in one

Road signs in the Republic in Gaelic and English

town and drop it off at another for a small charge. Many dealers can also provide safety helmets, but bring your own waterproof clothing to help cope with the weather.

Street Finder Index

KEY TO THE STREET FINDER

▦ Major sight	🚖 Taxi rank	⊠ Post office
▦ Place of interest	🅿 Main car park	▦ Railway line
▦ Railway station	ℹ Tourist information office	One-way street
🚇 DART station	✚ Hospital with casualty unit	▦ Pedestrian street
🚌 Main bus stop	🚓 Police station	0 metres 200
🚍 Coach station	✝ Church	0 yards 200 1:11,500

KEY TO ABBREVIATIONS USED IN THE STREET FINDER

Ave	Avenue	E	East	Pde	Parade	Sth	South
Br	Bridge	La	Lane	Pl	Place	Tce	Terrace
Cl	Close	Lr	Lower	Rd	Road	Up	Upper
Ct	Court	Nth	North	St	Street/Saint	W	West

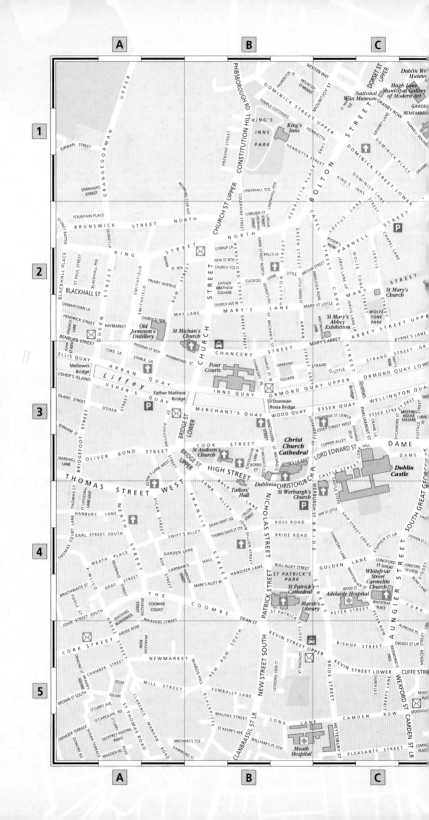

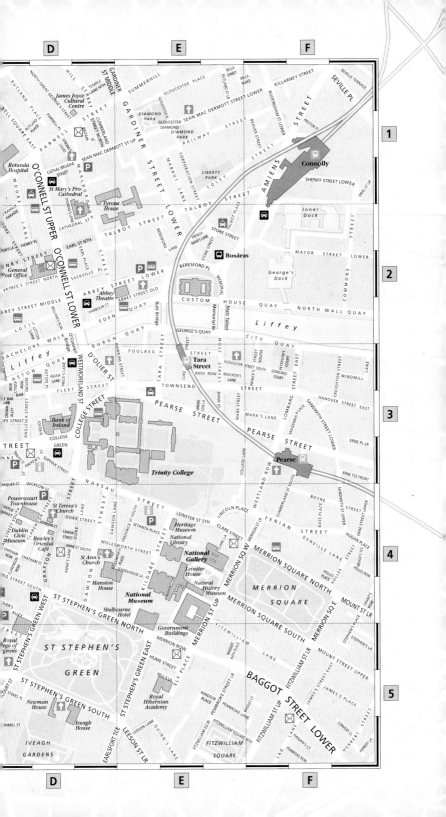

General Index

Acknowledgments

DORLING KINDERSLEY would like to thank the following people whose contributions and assistance have made the preparation of this book possible.

MAIN CONTRIBUTOR
TIM PERRY, from Dungannon, County Tyrone, writes on travel and popular music for various publishers in North America and the British Isles. He was also a contributor to the *Eyewitness Travel Guide to Ireland*.

EDITORIAL ASSISTANCE
Sophie Warne.

INDEXER
Hilary Bird.

PROOFREADER
Stewart Wild.

ADDITIONAL PICTURE RESEARCH
Monica Allende, Brigitte Arora, Anna Grapes.

ADDITIONAL ILLUSTRATIONS
Joy Fitzsimmons.

SPECIAL ASSISTANCE
Particular thanks go to Niall Kennedy at Dublin Tourism for his invaluable help throughout this project.

Thanks also to everyone at the National Museum, especially Dr Felicity Devlin, Damien Debarra and Aoife O'Shea, to Adrian le Harivel at the National Gallery, to Telecom Eireann and the General Post Office.

PHOTOGRAPHY PERMISSIONS
THE PUBLISHER would like to thank all those who gave permission to photo- graph at various cathedrals, churches, museums, restaurants, hotels, shops, galleries and other sights that are too numerous to list individually.

PICTURE CREDITS
tl = top left; tc = top centre; tr = top right; cla = centre left above; ca = centre above; cra = centre right above; cl = centre left; c = centre; cr = centre right; clb = centre left below; cb = centre below; crb = centre right below; bl = bottom left; bc = bottom centre; br = bottom right.

The Publisher would like to thank the following individuals, companies and picture libraries for permission to reproduce their photographs:

AER LINGUS/AIRBUS INDUSTRIE: 156t.

AKG London: 12cb, 20c.

BORD FAILTE/IRISH TOURIST BOARD: 112tr, 112tl; Brian Lynch 17t, 27clb.

CENTRAL BANK OF IRELAND: 153.

CHESTER BEATTY LIBRARY, DUBLIN: 55t.

BRUCE COLEMAN LTD: George McCarthy 104tl.

COLLECTIONS: Image Ireland 24t, 83b; Slide File 28crb;

CORBIS UK LTD: Bettmann/Reuters 17b; Hulton-Deutsch Collection 21t, 21crb; Library of Congress 20bl; National Gallery, London 20t.

MARY EVANS PICTURE LIBRARY: 7c, 11c, 13c, 15tr, 29c, 55cl, 68b, 117c, 146c.

GUINNESS IRELAND LTD: 80bc, 80br, 81bl, 81tl, 81tr, 81br.

HULTON GETTY: 16bc, 36bl, 91t.

THE IRISH ANTIQUE DEALERS FAIR: Louis O'Sullivan 26cr.

THE IRISH PICTURE LIBRARY: 13t.

IRISH TIMES: 106br.

JAROLD COLOUR PUBLICATIONS: 36bc.

TIMOTHY KOVAR: 56b, 141b.

MANSELL/TIME INC: 63bl.

HUGH MCKNIGHT PHOTOGRAPHY: 83t.

JOHN MURPHY: 96cb.

JOHN MURRAY: 27c, 78c.

NATIONAL CONCERT HALL, DUBLIN: Frank Fennell 142b.

NATIONAL GALLERY OF IRELAND, DUBLIN: 59tr, 71b, 82cr, 100b; *For the Road,* JB Yeats 46cl; *The Houseless Wanderer,* JH Foley 46tl; *Pierrot,* Juan Gris 46tr; *Judith with the Head of Holofernes,* Andrea Mantegna 47crb; *The Castle of Bentheim,* Jacob van Ruisdael 47c; *The Sick Call,* Matthew James Lawless 47b; *The Taking of Christ,* Caravaggio 47tr; *Convent Garden, Brittany,* c. 1913, William John Leech, ADAGP, Paris and DACS, London 1998 48ca; *A View of Powerscourt Waterfall,* George Barret the Elder 48bl; A *Group of Cavalry in the Snow,* Ernest Meissonier 49tl; *Virgin and Child Hodigitria,* Constantinople 49cra; *Guards at the Door of a Tomb,* Jean-Léon Gérôme 49cla; *Peasant Wedding,* Peter Bruegel the Younger 49br; *Portrait of James Joyce,* Jacques Emile Blanche/ADAGP, Paris and DACS, London 1998 70bl.

NATIONAL MUSEUM OF IRELAND, DUBLIN: 19tl, 33crb, 42tr, 42cl, 42b, 43c, 43tr, 43bc, 43crb, 84clb, 85tl, 85cra, 85bl.

NATIONAL LIBRARY OF IRELAND: 6/7, 10, 103t, 111t.

NORTON ASSOCIATES: 52clb.

OFFICE OF PUBLIC WORKS, IRELAND: 112cl, 113cr, 113t, 114b.

POWERSCOURT ESTATE: 107tl.

RETROGRAPH ARCHIVE LTD: Martin Ranicar-Breese 44c.

REX FEATURES: 20b.

SLIDE FILE: 16br, 17cl, 24crb, 24bl, 25ca, 26cl, 26b, 27b, 60tl, 97c, 104cl, 104b, 110t, 114t, 140t.

TELECOM EIRANN: 155br, 155cr.

TRINITY COLLEGE, DUBLIN:, 37cr, 38c, 38b, 38crb, 38cra; *The Marriage of Princess Aoite and the Earl of Pembroke,* Daniel Maclise 12t.

TRIP ART DIRECTORS: 102c.

Jacket: all commissioned photography except © Trinity College: front bl.

TITLES PUBLISHED TO DATE

THE GUIDES THAT SHOW YOU WHAT OTHERS ONLY TELL YOU

COUNTRY GUIDES

AUSTRALIA • FRANCE • GREAT BRITAIN • GREECE:
ATHENS & THE MAINLAND • THE GREEK ISLANDS
IRELAND • ITALY • PORTUGAL
SPAIN • THAILAND

REGIONAL GUIDES

CALIFORNIA • FLORENCE & TUSCANY
FLORIDA • HAWAII • LOIRE VALLEY
NAPLES WITH POMPEII & THE AMALFI COAST
PROVENCE & THE COTE D'AZUR • SARDINIA
SEVILLE & ANDALUSIA • VENICE & THE VENETO

CITY GUIDES

AMSTERDAM • ISTANBUL • LISBON • LONDON
MOSCOW • NEW YORK • PARIS • PRAGUE
ROME • SAN FRANCISCO • ST PETERSBURG
SYDNEY • VIENNA • WARSAW

TO BE PUBLISHED IN SPRING 1999
MADRID • BUDAPEST • DUBLIN

Dublin Transport Map

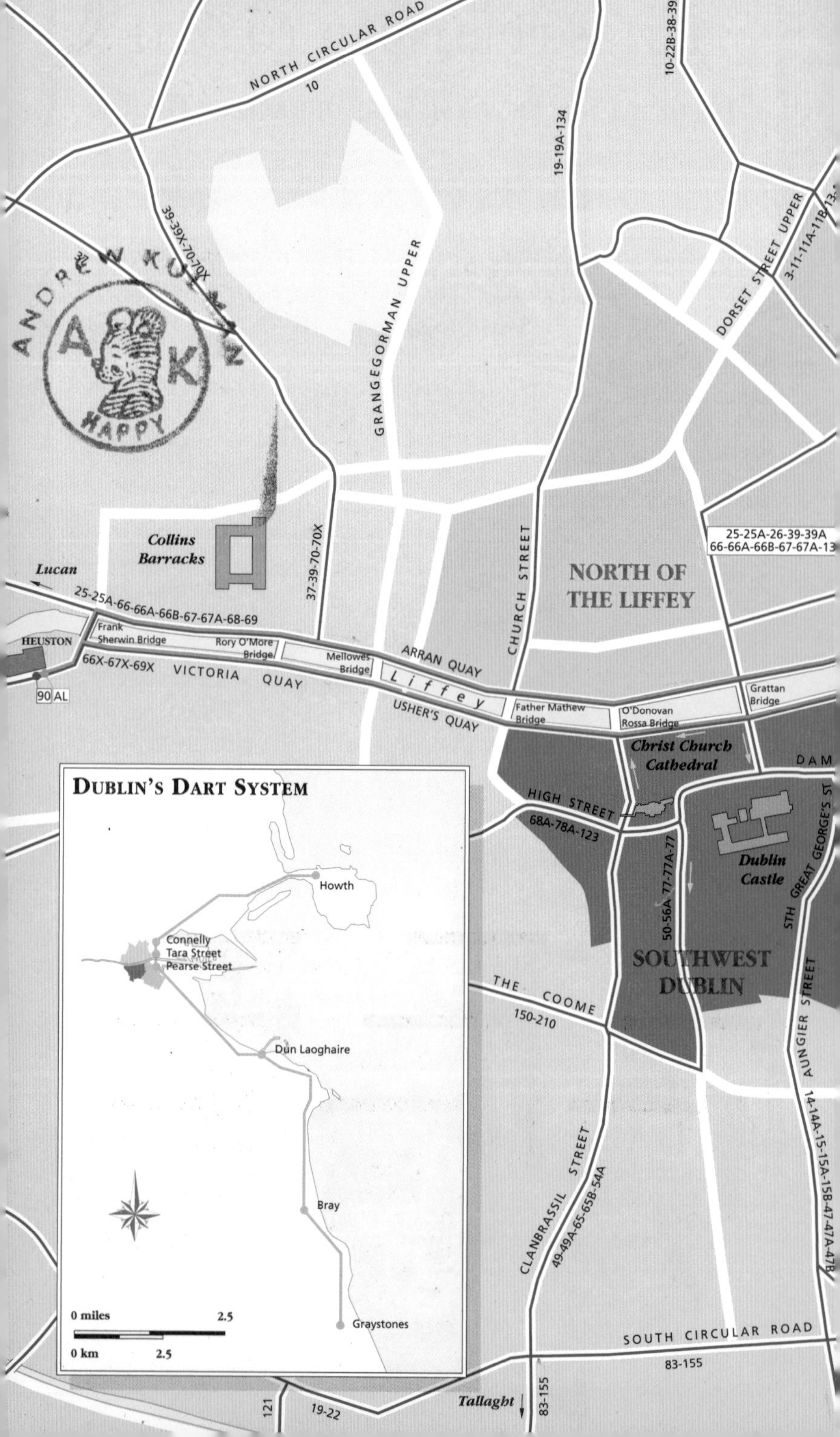

NORTH CIRCULAR ROAD
10

39-39X-70-70X

ANDREW KUEZ
A K
HAPPY

GRANGEGORMAN UPPER

37-39-70-70X

10-22B-38-39X-120

19-19A-134

DORSET STREET UPPER

3-11-11A-11B-13

Collins Barracks

CHURCH STREET

25-25A-26-39-39A
66-66A-66B-67-67A-13

NORTH OF THE LIFFEY

Lucan

25-25A-66-66A-66B-67-67A-68-69

HEUSTON

Frank Sherwin Bridge | Rory O'More Bridge | Mellowes Bridge | ARRAN QUAY

66X-67X-69X VICTORIA QUAY

90 AL

Liffey

USHER'S QUAY Father Mathew Bridge O'Donovan Rossa Bridge

Grattan Bridge

DAM

Christ Church Cathedral

HIGH STREET

68A-78A-123

50-56A 77-77A-77

Dublin Castle

5TH GREAT GEORGE'S ST

DUBLIN'S DART SYSTEM

Howth

Connelly
Tara Street
Pearse Street

Dun Laoghaire

Bray

Graystones

0 miles   2.5

0 km   2.5

THE COOME

150-210

SOUTHWEST DUBLIN

AUNGIER STREET

14-14A-15-15A-15B-47-47A-47B

CLANBRASSIL STREET

49-49A-65-65B-54A

121

19-22

Tallaght ↓

83-155

SOUTH CIRCULAR ROAD

83-155